C1/u MA

HC
240
.EUR
1977

£13-40

20-7-77

D1429243

302077241Q

European Economic Issues

John S. Marsh
Wolfgang Hager
Fabio Basagni
François Sauzey
Miriam Camps

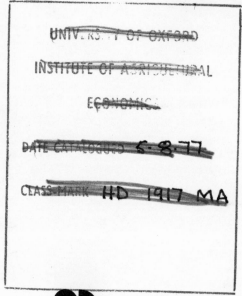

Published for the Atlantic Institute
For International Affairs

The Praeger Special Studies program—
utilizing the most modern and efficient book
production techniques and a selective
worldwide distribution network—makes
available to the academic, government, and
business communities significant, timely
research in U.S. and international economic, social, and political development.

European Economic Issues

Agriculture, Economic Security, Industrial Democracy, the OECD

Atlantic Institute Studies—III

Praeger Publishers   New York   London

PRAEGER SPECIAL STUDIES IN INTERNATIONAL ECONOMICS AND DEVELOPMENT

Library of Congress Cataloging in Publication Data
Main entry under title:

European economic issues.

   (Atlantic Institute studies ; 3) (Praeger special
studies in international economics and development)
   1. Europe—Economic conditions—1945-
2. Organization for Economic Cooperation and
Development. I. Marsh, John Stanley. II. Series:
Atlantic Institute for International Affairs.
Atlantic Institute Studies ; 3.
HC240.E836   330.9'4'055   76-30359
ISBN 0-275-24410-5

A slightly modified version of "Europe's Economic
Security," by Wolfgang Hager has been published under
the title "Westeuropas wirtschaftliche Sicherheit,
Arbeitspapier zur internationalen Politik," by the
Research Institute of the German Society for Foreign
Affairs (Europa Union Verlag GmbH Bonn).

PRAEGER PUBLISHERS
200 Park Avenue, New York, N.Y. 10017, U.S.A.

Published in the United States of America in 1977
by Praeger Publishers, Inc.

FOREWORD
John W. Tuthill

The apparently ever-increasing interdependence of both the highly industrialised developed and the developing (Third World) nations is proclaimed by all who write or speak on the subject of international relations. It is also widely accepted that this interdependence complicates the task of those concerned with domestic problems within individual nations. While recognition of the true nature of a problem is the essential first step in dealing with it, further steps must be taken.

Governments have not yet learned to take adequately into account the effects of their domestic actions on the economies and welfare of their neighbours nor of the reverse. In fact, during periods of large unemployment, high rates of inflation and related domestic troubles, governments have concentrated on domestic issues and have seemed to ignore both the constraints and the implicit responsibilities created by global economic interdependence. The Atlantic Papers reproduced in this volume are concerned with three important substantive issues—agricultural and trade policies and labour-management relations—where domestic and foreign policies are intertwined. The fourth paper deals with the efforts of the Organisation of Economic Co-operation and Development (OECD) to improve co-ordination within the "First World" countries and between such countries and those of the Third World. While the initial emphasis in most of these papers is on the problems within Europe, the discussion moves on to include the other developed countries and the developing countries as well.

The first paper, written by Mr. John Marsh of the University of Reading, brings up to date a 1971 Institute report produced by a panel of experts on the subject of "A Future for European Agriculture". Working with the same group of experts, Mr. Marsh re-examined the earlier proposals in the light of the changes in the international economic scene since 1971. Mr. Marsh recognises that the European Common Agricultural Policy (CAP) by itself is inadequate to deal with the problem of low farm incomes. An increase by the Community of agricultural prices further aggravates income inequalities within both the agricultural sector and the general economy. Low income farmers benefit very little from higher prices while the larger and generally richer farmers gain substantially. Increased burdens are imposed on consumers—rich and poor alike—thereby creating a further distortion of income in the economies of countries, many of which are already characterized by deep maldistribution.

While the CAP was a major constructive element in the early years of the development of the Community, Mr. Marsh states "in recent years, agricultural policy has tended to exemplify disunity rather than convergence among members". He points out that the very high rates of inflation within certain European countries, together with wide fluctuations of exchange rates, have tended to restore national restriction and have required compensatory payments.

Mr. Marsh makes several proposals for gradually removing border taxes and subsidies which, he feels, would allow for the maintenance of the unity of the European agricultural market even in the altogether likely event of future substantial changes in exchange rates.

The Institute has sponsored the paper by Mr. Marsh not only for the relevance of the analysis and specific recommendations, but also as evidence of the Institute's continuing interest in the problem of the role of agriculture in relations between our various nations, both industrialised and developing. Once more, as the trade negotiations get underway in Geneva, there will be much discussion of external agricultural trade. It is generally recognised that one can only talk sensibly about international agricultural policy if one starts with national domestic agricultural policies. An understanding by the countries outside of the European Community of what is happening within the Community (as explained by Mr. Marsh) can make a contribution to removing long-standing bottlenecks in these forthcoming negotiations.

The second paper in this series is by Wolfgang Hager. This paper was jointly sponsored by the Forschungsinstitut der Deutschen Gesellschaft für Auswärtige Politik in Bonn and the Atlantic Institute for International Affairs.

Mr. Hager makes a number of unorthodox proposals. Recognising the large and increasing degree of dependence of most European economies on exports, he stresses the dangers of this situation.

This very substantial dependence upon a highly variable element (exports) complicates efforts within individual European countries to manage their internal economies. Each country in fact makes its estimates of growth, employment, investment, and so on on the basis of various assumptions about world economic conditions and world trade. Yet this major determining factor is largely out of the control of these governments. He feels that the European countries are simply postponing necessary adjustments to changing international economic relationships through their frequent attempts to maintain exports through credits and other subsidies. Mr. Hager favours increased emphasis upon expansion of internal markets—with one exception. This concerns exports to developing countries which, he feels, are entitled, in some cases, to subsidies. He justifies this position largely in terms of "global welfare objectives".

On behalf of both the Forschungsinstitut der Deutschen Gesellschaft für Auswärtige Politik and the Atlantic Institute, he is continuing to examine various policy options in a world in which trading relations are changing considerably and in which most European governments are engaged in domestic planning while attempting to reduce risks produced by factors outside of their own national control.

In the third paper of this series, which includes a forward-looking commentary by Professor Benjamin C. Roberts of the London School of Economics, the emphasis is once more put upon the European experiences, this time in labour participation in the decision making processes of individual industrial concerns. Especially Germany and, to a lesser extent, the Netherlands and Sweden, have now had experience in this area. France and the United Kingdom have established Commissions to examine the issue of labour participation on company boards and the European Commission itself (as set forth in the paper by Commissioner Finn Olav Gundelach) has made specific proposals in this regard.

Surely this is one of the major elements of concern in the democratic countries. If our societies are to remain stable in a social sense and to grow in an economic sense, it is absolutely essential that workers are convinced that they have a stake and an essential role to play in productive, profitable, and thereby employment-creating, enterprises. Some think that this can be achieved by the unions through the practice of collective bargaining. Others feel that collective bargaining should be supplemented by more explicit labour participation in a wide range of management decisions. This participation can be at various levels within a firm. Most of the proposals discussed in this paper draw heavily on the German experience of *Mitbestimmung*, involving direct employee participation on the supervisory boards. However, other experiences may also be relevant outside of the national context in which they were developed and transferable from one to another as Professor Roberts aptly suggests.

This paper again represents simply the first step in the work of the Institute. Together with the Trilateral Commission, the Institute is proceeding with a project financed by the German Marshall Fund, entitled "The Changing Relationship of Labour and Industry to Each Other and to Government and Society". Professor Roberts will be the project director and will be joined in this capacity by two additional 'rapporteurs'—Professor George Lodge of the Harvard Business School and by Professor Sueaki Okamoto of Hosei University, Tokyo. The Trilateral Commission and the Institute plan to conduct a series of seminars at which papers will be prepared on various aspects of this issue which is so central to satisfactory social and economic development in our countries. An Institute book and a Triangle Paper will be produced by mid-1978.

The last of the papers in this volume was written by Mrs. Miriam Camps as part of a project co-sponsored by the Council on Foreign Relations, New York and this Institute. Mrs. Camps has concentrated, in this paper, on the relationship between the OECD member countries, namely the northern industrialised market-economy countries. Mrs. Camps has analysed what has been achieved to date in collaboration at the OECD. She makes proposals designed to reinforce that collaboration in the light of the perplexing problems that flow out of interdependence. These include the problems of agriculture (as analysed by Mr. Marsh), of trade (as analysed by Mr. Hager) and a variety of other significant relationships which require strengthening of the consultative processes of the OECD countries.

Progress in this respect has been made over recent years but obviously much needs to be done if governments and parliaments are adequately to take into account the international repercussions of, and constraints on, domestic decisions. As in the case of Mr. Hager, there are some who believe that European countries should explicitly turn their attention increasingly away from the current dependence upon foreign markets to a greater emphasis upon domestic markets and presumably a more even distribution of income within individual countries. This raises the question as to whether it is possible to maintain adequate rates of growth without a continuing expansion of external trade. This, in turn, involves the basic question as to whether a redistribution of income will be possible within any country, or within any group of countries, unless it occurs at a time of expanding economies. Expanding economies and further inequalities of income distribution would of course be a sure route towards social unrest and disaster. On the other hand, a mere improved distribution without adequate growth could be expected to lead to stagnation and also to social unrest.

This is basically the policy dilemma facing the democratic governments and underlying all the topics raised in these papers. Central to this, workers must be convinced that they have a real and personal stake in the profitability of enterprises and thus, in an increase in investments, and thus the maintenance of old and the creation of new jobs.

The Atlantic Institute for International Affairs, in collaboration with the institutions mentioned above, will continue to work on this range of problems. It is hoped that these continuing studies will shed some light on the issues which must be faced and thus help policy makers both in governments and in the private sector.

CONTENTS

EMPLOYEE PARTICIPATION AND COMPANY REFORM

edited by Fabio Basagni and François Sauzey

"FIRST WORLD" RELATIONSHIPS:
The Role of the OECD

Miriam Camps

LIST OF TABLES

EUROPEAN AGRICULTURE IN AN UNCERTAIN WORLD

EUROPE'S ECONOMIC SECURITY

European Economic Issues

European Agriculture in an Uncertain World

JOHN S. MARSH

Rapporteur for a panel of experts

D. Bergmann
Lord Kaldor
H.-B. Krohn
M. Rossi-Doria
J.-A. Schnittker
C. Thomsen
P. Uri
H. Wilbrandt

Preface

In 1970, the Atlantic Institute convened a small group of economists and experts to reconsider the European agricultural policy. The purpose was to bring about a better balance between products, between producers, between member countries. The most original proposal was that, if some prices had to be adjusted downward to avoid mounting surpluses, compensation should be paid in a way which would raise the smaller farmers' income and encourage a shift to deficit productions. After the violent movement of prices in the world which brought wheat from one half to twice the level of the Community, it was worthwhile examining how far the proposals of the 1970 report remained justified and whether they needed an updating or adjustment.

If anything, the sudden shortages and upswing in prices have demonstrated the wastefulness of export dumping which missed the opportunity of buoyant markets and left the main producers without stocks while millions were starving. The emphasis on stockpiling in the 1970 report proves more fundamental than ever.

There is now a tendency in certain quarters to consider that in the face of such sudden shortages the schemes to facilitate a reduction of agricultural employment were ill-advised, that in the face of export restrictions by some major producers increased self-sufficiency alone can improve the security of supply. All to the contrary, the more pressing the needs in the world, the more urgent a rational utilization of land and manpower to achieve low-cost production. And stability can better be assured in a broader framework than the Community alone. A choice between freer trade and a stabilization of markets is a false issue: freer trade in agricultural products can be pursued only among countries which join forces in stabilization schemes. The Community has the bargaining power to carry with it in these attempts the main producing and consuming countries. If it fails, increased self-sufficiency is only second-best.

These views are in line with the positions taken in the 1971 report. If we went wrong, it was in the implicit assumption that world prices would remain permanently below Community prices. The adjustments and compensations which we had suggested for that case may still be used to cope with shorter-term fluctuations.

The same group has discussed the ideas included in this new report. They are not based on long-term forecasts which have all proven wrong, including

3

its own, but on the obvious necessity to reduce the instability of supply and prices and to avoid the extreme disruption between world and domestic markets. The report offers a detailed scheme for international or Community-wide buffer stocks which, contrary to export restitutions, could be financed through bank credit instead of taxation: this in turn would ease the debate on burden-sharing among Community countries and release more resources for structural reform and regional development. It suggests a particular scheme for commodities that are hard or costly to store, like meat: in time of surplus, they should be sold at a discount in favour of the less privileged citizens. It offers a combination of Community and national action to support the income of the farmers and more adjustable price policies to that effect. It provides for a gradual elimination of the barriers to agricultural trade inside the Community combined with transitional arrangements in case of new exchange rate changes. The purpose would be a return to the play of comparative advantage and to a normal contribution of agriculture to the restoration of equilibrium in the balances of payments.

This joint proposal by some of the best experts may facilitate the solution of British problems in the Community, and the planned revision of agricultural policy, as well as the forthcoming GATT negotiations.

The group held its first meeting on June 29-30, 1974, on the basis of a preliminary paper produced by John Marsh, and its second session on January 10-11, 1975, supported by a very extensive document from the same rapporteur, which provided all the materials for a brainstorming exercise. The present text is the outcome of that discussion which sharpened the issues and the proposals. The group as a whole has contributed its full share to the thinking. It was not requested to approve the detailed expression of ideas which was left to be agreed between the rapporteur and the signatory of this preface.

Pierre Uri

4

Panel of Experts

DENIS BERGMANN,
Directeur de Recherches, Institut National de la Recherche Agronomique, Paris.

LORD KALDOR,
Professor, Cambridge University.

HANS-BRODER KROHN,
Former Deputy Director General of Agriculture, presently Director General of Development and Cooperation, the Commission of European Communities, Brussels.

JOHN S. MARSH,
University of Reading, *rapporteur*.

MANLIO ROSSI-DORIA,
Professor, University of Naples, and President of the Agricultural Committee, Senate of the Italian Republic.

JOHN A. SCHNITTKER,
Former Under-Secretary of Agriculture, presently economic consultant, Washington D.C.

CARL THOMSEN,
The Royal Veterinary and Agricultural University, Copenhagen.

PIERRE URI,
Counsellor for Studies, Atlantic Institute for International Affairs, Professor Paris IX, Member of the French Economic and Social Council.

HANS WILBRANDT,
Director, Institute für ausländische Landwirtschaft an der Georg-August Universität, Göttingen.

Professor Rossi-Doria was represented by his colleague Professor Di Stefano at the first meeting, and was unable to attend the second one. Mr. Schnittker missed the first session, and Dr. Krohn the second. All of them have received the successive documents and the final text.

5

The Changing International Environment of European Agricultural Policy

In 1970 the Common Agricultural Policy (CAP) appeared to have reached an untenable position. The cost of the policy to the Community's budget had risen at a rapid rate since the mid-1960s. The cost of food to the consumer was forced up by farm prices which were far above the level at which competitive supplies were available from the world market. Despite these high prices, many of the Community's farmers lived in poverty. Surplus production of wheat, dairy products and sugar not only burdened the Community's budget, it also further disrupted world agricultural markets.

As things then stood, there seemed little prospect of improvement. The Commission of the European Communities had made proposals for a structural reform programme which would in the 1970s ensure that some five million people left agriculture and some five million hectares of land would be taken out of farming. Such a programme, it was believed, would contribute to the reduction of surpluses, the improvement of farming and the raising of farmers' incomes. No parallel suggestions were made for changing the level at which farm prices were set. Any substantial reduction in nominal prices was ruled out by political considerations and its effect on farmers' incomes. Price increases for many of the most important products were similarly ruled out by the need to avoid costly surpluses. Without adjustments, in particular reductions in prices, the prospect of success in the structural reform programme seemed remote. There was a danger that considerable expenditure on improving the productivity of farm resources would lead to growing surplus and an ever-increasing burden in maintaining the guaranteed prices fixed under the CAP.

As a contribution to the reformation of the CAP, an Atlantic Institute study group suggested three innovations, relating to prices, farm incomes and the reform of the world market. In order to bring Community prices closer to the levels then prevailing in the main producing countries, a stage-by-stage reduction in CAP prices for products in surplus, notably wheat and sugar beet, was recommended. Such a change in price would eventually eliminate surpluses but it would immediately reduce the incomes of producers. To counteract the effect of this, especially on the smaller and less flexible farmer, the group proposed a system of income compensation. In essence this would have made payments to farmers related to four elements: the average yield of the product in the Community, the amount each farm produced in the years preceding the decision to reduce prices, lifetime of the operator and the size of farms. Compensation paid in this way would create no incentive to increase output. Each

6

farmer would have to make that decision in the light of expected costs and prices which would be lower than in the past. By giving compensation on the basis of average yields and making the proportion of production eligible for compensation less for large than small farms, the proposed scheme would tend to raise the incomes of some of the poorer of the Community's farmers. By continuing to pay compensation for price reductions, even if the farmer decided to produce some other commodity, the system ensured that production would be induced to respond to the new pattern of prices.

The reform of the world market could, it was suggested, be brought about by the elimination of dumping and the establishment of international buffer stocks. The Community could unilaterally impose anti-dumping duties on exports from countries whose home market prices were raised by protective devices. To make a buffer stock policy work would require international co-operation but the Community could promote such agreements, stressing the necessity of linking freer trade in agricultural goods with an assurance of market stability. Within such a reformed world market, freed from dumping and more stable than in the past, the Community could gradually reduce its agricultural price level until the margin of protection accorded to agriculture was in proportion to that received by industry. At price levels of this order, variable import levies would do no more than stabilise Community prices against residual short-run fluctuations in international prices and freight rates.

The proposals made by the study group were founded on three principles. First, that prices within the Community should be brought nearer to those in world markets. This would promote a more economic use of resources within Europe and avoid the necessity of dumping high cost agricultural production on the world market. Second, the compensation for this adjustment in prices should be paid to those affected in a way which would not encourage excessive resources to remain in agricultural or, even more, in surplus production. Third, given suitable conditions of stability in world markets the Community should aim at a policy of freer trade in agricultural goods.

Since 1970 important changes have occurred both within the Community and in world agricultural trade. It is therefore necessary to consider how far the suggestions made in the original study remain valid, how far they now need to be modified or supplemented.

The years since 1970 have been relatively prosperous in the industrialised countries of the world. Up to 1974 incomes grew in Europe, North America and Japan. However, this expansion has been associated with a very sharp rise in commodity prices and increased rates of inflation in almost all countries. Food prices rose more sharply than commodity prices in general, and remained high for longer. By 1975, commodity prices had fallen from peak levels and the prices of many agricultural goods dropped. The end of the boom in world markets did not end inflationary pressures in the industrialised countries. Faced by a reduction in the purchasing power of money, workers sought higher wages. In turn, these added to production costs and precipitated further price increases.

The boom in world agricultural prices was not foreseen by the study group which prepared the Atlantic Institute report of 1970. In common with most informed opinion at the time, the group anticipated that world prices would remain below the level then prevailing within the Community. Its proposals thus assumed that a closer relationship between CAP prices and world prices would involve a reduction in the prices received by Community farmers.

It does not follow that the suggestions made in 1970 have been proved to be of little value. In fact, as will be argued in this paper, recent events have demonstrated more than ever the urgency of improving the working of world markets and of reforming agricultural policy within the Community. More stable international prices and an effective device for safeguarding the real incomes of farmers are a pre-condition of progress.

The effects of higher world prices upon the operation of the Common Agricultural Policy are profound. In 1971 expenditures on guaranteeing the price of cereals were 703.5 m.u.a. [1] and on sugar 199.6 m.u.a. By 1974, world prices for cereals and sugar were above Community prices, and export levies had been imposed on cereals, so that, for a time at least, expenditure in support of the prices of these commodities was not needed.

The change in prices also affected the relative costs and benefits of the CAP for different member countries. When world prices are below CAP prices, import levies raise the cost of food to importing countries and maintain the receipts of agricultural exporters within the Community. In the more recent situation, importing countries within the Community have had access to supplies from other members at prices below those which prevailed in world markets. As a result, at least, it can be claimed that in this period agricultural exporters have subsidised agricultural importers. Similarly, when world prices exceed EEC prices farmers may be said to have supported the real incomes of consumers, since had goods been freely exported from the Community, food prices would have been higher. Higher world prices have not meant greater profits for all farmers. For cereal growers incomes have risen, but for livestock farmers the higher price of feed has tended to narrow margins. When as has happened at some stages the price of cattle, pig meat, broilers or eggs has fallen, the livestock producer may have been unable to sell at a profit. For the Community of Six, cereals accounted for about 12% of Gross Agricultural Output in 1971, livestock production for 57%. In the new member countries the proportion of agricultural output derived from livestock was even larger. The period of high cereal prices has not been therefore one of continuous prosperity for most of Europe's farmers. This experience illustrates again the fallacy of treating agriculture as if it were an industry selling a single product. As the 1970 report made clear, high cereal prices benefit only some farmers; for most, especially the smaller and poorer they raise costs.

Although high world prices have diminished the cost of the CAP price guarantees and have meant that the policy has been of unexpected benefit to

1. m.u.a.=million units of account.

8

consumers and to net importing countries, it has stiffened resistance within the community to further price rises. Official prices have risen each year. Despite some disagreement among members an interim increase in prices was made in September 1974 and a further increase was agreed in March 1975. However, these price increases have lagged behind the rate of inflation in all member countries except Germany. Resistance to further price increases is strengthened by the desire to avoid adding to inflationary pressures. Farmers' confidence in the CAP has been weakened because in a period when many costs have risen rapidly the prices of their output have not kept pace.

In the light of the changes outlined, the proposals made by the Atlantic Institute study group in 1970 now need to be supplemented. Those proposals were directed to aiding more effectively the poorer members of the agricultural population whilst relating prices more purposefully to the volume of output required from Community agriculture. Today there are still too many poor farmers. In real as distinct from monetary terms their position may have deteriorated as a result of rising costs and less rapidly rising prices. Thus a mechanism for income support is still needed. In the 1960s it was the effect of low world prices which threatened to disrupt the Community's agriculture. More recently the damage caused to the economy as a whole by upward fluctuations in price has been more pressing. The 1940 report emphasized the need for greater stability in world markets. Given a more orderly world market, a more flexible price policy within the Community could be used to relate agricultural production to the opportunities for international trade.

Experience has vindicated this approach. By dumping on the world market instead of stockpiling, the Community has added to the forces which destabilize agricultural trade, depressed prices, discouraged production in low cost countries, and made it unattractive for them to hold stocks. Thus when a series of poor harvests resulted in a sudden increase in the demand for imports, stocks fell to very low levels and prices rose sharply. The Community paid twice: first to subsidise exports to a depressed world market, and second to buy imports at much higher prices when world markets were buoyant. There was a human price too. The shortages of supplies which the protective policies of the Community and other countries helped to bring about meant that food was not available to meet the needs of the hungry in low-income countries when their own crops failed. For many, 1974 will be remembered as a year of famine, starvation and death.

The sharp swings in world market prices experienced since 1970 indicate the fragile nature of any policy which is based upon expectation of a particular price level. The only certainty is that prices will fluctuate. What is needed is a policy which can operate in any market conditions, which stands ready to face shortages caused by the inevitable but unpredictable periods of drought and harvest failure and can prevent periods of surplus from disrupting the working of agricultural markets.

Agricultural Policy in the Community since 1970

Agricultural policy within the Community since 1970 has been influenced by the accession of new members, by the disruptive effects of variations in exchange rates, by the introduction of new measures relating to structural policy, by the internal development of trade structures and prices, and by the implications of the boom in world agricultural prices.

Enlargement

Denmark, Ireland and the United Kingdom became members of the EEC on 1st January 1973. The problems facing Britain were expected to be especially severe since she needed to adjust to higher agricultural prices. It was agreed that this adaptation should be made gradually through a five-year period to 1978. In practice, increased world prices forced much more violent changes in Britain than had been anticipated. The CAP tended to have a moderating influence helping to hold UK food prices at levels lower than they would otherwise have reached.

In 1974 a Labour government took office in Britain committed to "re-negotiation of the terms of entry." This process has been completed in 1975 and there is to be a referendum within the UK concerning Britain's continued membership in the Community. Agricultural policy figures in this debate both because it affects the British contribution to the Community's budget and because there is concern that food prices should not be maintained at levels far in excess of those at which adequate supplies might be purchased from the world market.

Quite apart from the details of discussions between Britain and other members of the Community, the fact of enlargement has changed the balance of interests represented in the CAP. Two of the new members, Ireland and Denmark, have significant agricultural export surpluses. The U.K. is a large importer and has close trading links not only with Community countries but with a large number of third world countries. Within Europe, too, changes have occurred which change the balance of interest in the CAP. Employment in agriculture has fallen from 22.7% of the civilian labour force of the Six in 1958 to 11.5% in 1972. Agricultural output, which made up more than 10% of gross domestic production in 1958, contributed only 5.8% in 1972. In political terms farming continues to be important and in some places the farm vote may be crucial to electoral success.

In total, however the relative importance of industrial and urban needs has increased and in the longer term, at least, this is likely to require a new balance within the CAP between producers and consumers.

Exchange Rate Variation

The operation of the Common Agricultural Policy has been greatly complicated by the proliferation of border taxes and subsidies. Two types of payments must be distinguished. During the transitional period official prices in Britain are to rise step by step until they reach full Community levels in 1978. To enable trade between the rest of the Community and the UK to take place, a subsidy equal to the price differential is placed on agricultural goods moving from other countries to Britain and a tax of equal value on goods moving in the reverse direction. These payments are known as "accessionary compensatory amounts," or ACAs, and will disappear by the end of the transitional period.

The second type of payment arises because the rates of exchange of member country currencies change. Official prices are fixed in units of account and payments are made in each country in its own currency. Should that currency be devalued, prices specified in units of accounts should rise in terms of the local currency. If they do not it would pay traders whose currency had depreciated to sell, into intervention if necessary, in other member countries. Similarly, a country whose currency rises in value should reduce its prices to farmers if it is to avoid a speculative inflow of agricultural commodities which would be sold to its own intervention agency. Governments are, however, reluctant to put up food prices in devaluing countries or reduce prices to farmers in countries where the currency has appreciated. To avoid this, subsidies have been paid on imports into devaluing countries and taxes placed on their imports. For revaluing countries the taxes are on imports and the subsidies on exports. These payments, known as "monetary compensatory amounts," or MCAs, are made from or to the Community's funds.

One effect to these adjustments has been to erect a complex set of taxes and subsidies at the frontiers of Community countries. Another has been to destroy the common market in agricultural goods in the sense that prices received by farmers are determined not only by the CAP but also by exchange rate policies in member states. Should such MCAs continue for long they would also frustrate the operation of comparative advantage within the Community, tending to freeze the location of agricultural production in its present form.

The Development of the CAP

Despite this breakup of the market, the Common Agricultural Policy has made encouraging progress since 1970. The Council of Ministers agreed on the main feature of a revised structural policy in 1971. By April 1972 three directives had been approved, on farm modernization, the provision of retirement aids and vocational guidance.

Perhaps the most important innovation was the recognition, at Community level, that development aid should be confined to farms which seemed likely to yield an income similar to that earned by workers in other occupations in the same region. Implicitly this accepted the contention that solutions to the acute problems of low income on many farms which were not eligible for structural aid would have to depend on action taken outside the area of agricultural prices and costs.

The first of the 1972 directives concerned the modernization of farm land. This provides that farmers who submit approved development plans demonstrating that within a period of six years the farm can achieve, for one or two labour units, an earned income comparable to that in other local employment, may receive aids. Assistance is given only to those whose main business is farming and who possess adequate professional ability. Further exclusions prevent grants to aid the purchase of land, or pigs, poultry or calves for the meat market. Where grants are given for pigs the businesses which receive support must produce at least 33% of their pigfeed requirements.

The second directive concerned the use of farmland. Encouragement is provided to give up farming. Farmers who are aged between 55 and 65 years and who retire may receive an annual allowance (900 u.a. [1] for married, 600 u.a. for single farmers), or a lump sum payment. In addition, a further payment may be made from a member state's own resources, in relation to the effective area of agricultural land released. At least 85% of the farmland released by people who benefit from the incentives to give up farming must be transferred to farms capable of expansion or else permanently withdrawn from agricultural use. The transfer of land released to new uses may be by sale to official agencies established by member governments with a view to structural improvement or by long-term lease for a period of at least twelve years.

The third of the 1972 structural directives provided that vocational guidance and training should be given to help people working in agriculture assess their own prospects in or out of the industry and to assist those who choose to leave to re-train for new jobs. Special socio-economic advisers must be appointed and contributions are to be made from Community sources to the cost of their training. Part of this same directive offers modest grants to encourage farmers to keep farm management accounts.

All the directives pre-suppose that the member governments will bear a major share of the cost. The Community will for most purposes pay only 25% of monies spent in this direction. For the directive concerned with the cessation of farming, up to 66% of the costs may be claimed from FEOGA (Fonds Européen d'Orientation et de Garantie Agricole) in certain backward regions of the Community. The Commission's financial estimates for 1974-76 [2], published

1. u.a.=unit of account.
2. SEC (73) 3743 final.

12

in October 1973, give some idea of the level of expenditure likely to be involved, at least up to 1976. In 1974, only 15 m.u.a. were expected to be spent on these three directives. By 1976 the figures foreseen were 112 m.u.a.

Even when allowance has been made for the leverage effect of this Community contribution, the total weight given to structural reform still seems small. The Mansholt Plan of 1968 had foreseen structural expenditure reaching an annual rate of 2500 m.u.a. In fact it seems likely to continue to be rather less than 10% of all FEOGA expenditure.

Problems of poverty are especially acute in hilly and mountainous regions. These areas, which are often of great natural beauty, are ill-adapted to modern farming techniques and are in danger of becoming depopulated. In November 1973 the Council approved a directive on "less favoured areas." Special assistance may be given to farmers in not more than 2 ½% of any member state. Farmers in such regions may receive an annual payment based on the number of stock or area of crops and additional aids for investment on the farm or in the development of a craft or of tourist facilities to be carried on simultaneously with the farm business.

The greater precision with which problem areas are to be defined, the readiness to offer differential aids among farmers and the inclusion of support for non-agricultural rural industries represent important innovations in the Common Agricultural Policy. Such policies demonstrate an interface between the established CAP and the evolving regional policy of the Community. In 1972 the Commission proposed the establishment of a European Regional Development Fund. One of the main purposes of this proposal was to stimulate non-agricultural employment in poor agricultural regions. Discussion on regional policy proved protracted and the size of the proposal fund seemed small in relation to the acute regional differences in the prosperity of the Community. In the autumn of 1974 agreement was reached and the Community's regional policy will in future supplement the structural aspects of the CAP.

Both regional and structural policies are facilitated by the activities of the European Social Fund. In 1972 the Council decided to grant assistance from this fund for schemes designed to improve the employment and the geographical and occupational mobility of people giving up farm work. This extension of the role of the Social Fund should relieve the agricultural budget of part of the costs associated with the retraining programme. Taken together with changes in the CAP and the new regional policy, it represents a more balanced and coherent approach to the problems of rural poverty than existed in 1970.

Evolution within the Community

Within the context of changed world markets and developments within the Community, longer-run changes in agriculture have continued to take place. Agricultural employment in the Six, which had totalled 16.2 million in 1958,

13

had fallen to 8.4 million by 1972. Despite the smaller labour force, output continued to rise, an index based on 1961-65 reaching 123 by 1971. These changes implied a substantial improvement in agricultural productivity. Indeed, productivity on farms was growing more rapidly than in most other industries.

Agricultural trade has grown, especially between member countries. The figures below suggest that the effects of the Community on patterns of agricultural trade have been more pronounced than its impact on industrial transactions.

Table 1

The Growth of Trade in the EEC of Six
1964-1971

	Exports			Imports		
	1964	1971	% change	1964	1971	% change
Total	42,562	99,860	235	44,910	98,247	221
To/From Six	18,383	49,217	268	18,054	49,117	272
From Nine	21,576	54,830	254	21,691	56,012	258
Agricultural Food Products						
Total	4,951	11,918	241	12,156	20,818	171
To/From Six	2,487	7,784	312	2,491	7,791	313

Sources: Basic Statistics of the Community EEC 1972
Newsletter of the Common Agricultural Policy, January 1974.

Changes in farm size still lag behind the need to create larger self-contained units capable of employing modern farming methods to best advantage. The average size of holding in the Six increased at a rate of 3% per annum in all member countries except Italy during the 1960s. Holdings of less than 20 hectares decreased in number, whilst the number of those over 50 hectares grew. Such statistics give but a pointer to the true complexities of structural change. In some countries there was a tendency for the proportion of part-time farms to increase. All countries gave aids to encourage the consolidation of fragmented holdings and the amalgamation of small farms. In some of the remotest parts of the Community, there was a tendency for land to fall out of use, or be used much less intensively, as many of the rural population sought employment off the farm.

During the 1960s these changes in agriculture took place in an environment of falling real prices for most important agricultural goods. Since 1972 this trend has been offset for some farmers by the pressure of rising world cereal prices, but even in 1972-73 the prices received for wheat, discounted for changes in the cost of living, were lower in all member countries than in 1958-59. For most of this period cattle prices were a notable exception to this trend, being especially firm in France and West Germany. In 1974, however, cattle prices fell sharply as the market encountered a period of temporary oversupply.

14

In terms of the value added in agriculture, the fall in real prices tended to offset increased productivity. Community figures [1] suggest that the value of output per agricultural labour unit was increasing in all member countries in 1964-70 and 1966-71, but only in Italy, the UK, and, from 1964 to 1970, in Belgium was the increase faster than that per working person in non-agricultural sectors. The implication seems to be that for much of the Community the gap between farm and non-farm incomes had tended to widen by the end of the decade. For cereal producers increased prices since 1972 may have reversed this trend but for the majority of farmers it probably remains true that although incomes have risen they have not improved relative to income from other employment.

The Rise In World Agricultural Prices

Changes in the CAP and the development of the Community's own agriculture have been overtaken by the increase in world prices. If world prices remain permanently higher than in the past a greater contribution to food supplies will be needed from the Communities own agriculture. If the recent changes herald a period of greater instability in world markets the CAP will have to give increased emphasis to maintaining stable conditions for Community producers and consumers. Much more then depends upon the future course of world markets.

The level of cereal prices is central; both as human food and as the basis of much livestock feed, they influence a wide range of agricultural prices. The table below gives some indication of the development of cereal supplies from 1969-1973. It is apparent that world output has continued to grow despite setbacks in some regions. The most important producing areas are North and Central America, Asia and Europe including the USSR. Production in the United States and Canada is especially significant since it provides a substantial proportion of grain available for sale in the world market.

Table 2

World and Regional Cereal Production 1969 to 1974
(Million Metric Tons)

	World	Northern America	Western Europe	Oceanic	Africa	Latin America	Near East	Far East	Europe and USSR
1969	1,197	242	134	15	42	64	43	207	217
1970	1,213	215	128	13	42	70	41	221	234
1971	1,316	276	148	15	43	73	44	217	242
1972	1,273	263	148	12	45	68	47	206	235
1973	1,372	274	150	18	38	76	41	236	287
1974	1,337	238	158	17	43	86	46	220	272

Sources: 1969 to 1971: F.A.O. Production Yearbook, Vol. 26, 1972.
1972 to 1974: F.A.O. Monthly Bulletin of Agricultural Economics and Statistics, Vol. 23, No. 10/11, 1974.

1. Agricultural Incomes in an Enlarged Community, SOEC, 73, 900.

The price level in world markets is much influenced by relatively small shifts in the rate of growth of production and consumption which result in changes in the quantities of exports or imports. The acute phase of price increases stems from very large cereal purchases by the USSR and China in 1972. This development in the market is not yet fully understood. Some authorities see it in a once-and-for-all movement to a higher price plateau, others regard it as a fluctuation, admittedly large, but one which will in due course provoke a downward movement in prices to levels much more like those which prevailed in the late sixties and early seventies. This issue is so central that further discussion of some of the main elements is necessary.

(i) *Trade policy of the USSR*

Soviet grain production in 1972 was 20-25 million tons below the level of 1971. Soviet planners had anticipated a larger harvest than in 1971 and needed this to meet the demand of their growing livestock sector. In China, grain production was ten million tons below planned requirements. The Indian wheat crop declined and there were, too, crop losses in a number of other Asian and African countries. Shortfalls in grain production in the Soviet Union were not new. The extremities of weather mean that, although, over the past decade, a very large increase has taken place in Soviet grain production, output in any one year remains uncertain. A new element in the 1972 situation was the decision of the USSR to cover its grain deficit by imports. In earlier periods, shortages had been dealt with by reducing consumption. This involved cutting the number of livestock as well as reducing deliveries for human food. Since the USSR's grain output is likely to remain variable, it might be argued that a continued readiness to import grain will result in periodic and sizeable additional demands reaching the world market. In general, this would tend to force prices up. It would also lead to less stable world prices.

Before this analysis is accepted, some qualifications must be noted. In 1972 the USSR bought grain at prices much below those which have since prevailed. It must be questioned whether at higher world prices equivalent imports would be made. Again, dependence upon large and irregular purchases of grain imports might be thought to leave the USSR economy in an unduly exposed position. By a marginal moderation in the growth of livestock output in the years when grain harvests were good, more substantial stocks could be accumulated for use in less favourable periods.

(ii) *Production by the agricultural exporters*

Since the end of the Second World War, agricultural production has risen substantially and more or less continuously. In the 1960s annual rates of increase for the world as a whole were around 2.7%. This was not evenly distributed around the world but all countries achieved considerable and sustained increases in output. From time to time acute shortages arose in one or other of the developing countries as crop failures associated with the vagaries of weather

16

occurred. Such shortages could be covered by drawing upon the surpluses of the developed world. Apart from such emergency relief, programmes of "Food Aid" which ensured a more regular supply of food were evolved and operated, notably by the United States. So dependable were these supplies that it was sometimes contended that they encouraged the recipient governments to give too little attention to their own agricultural industry. An optimistic outlook on future food supplies was further encouraged by the so-called "Green Revolution." New varieties of wheat and rice evolved in Mexico and the Philippines, respectively, promised to increased very rapidly and very substantially the output of these staple food commodities in many tropical underdeveloped countries. Since the yields of the new varieties were often several times these of traditional types of cereal, it seemed: that for a few years at least there was a prospect of abundant food supplies.

This prospect was discouraging for agricultural exporters. The growing self-sufficiency of some traditional import markets, notably in Europe, and the expectation that the developing countries would be able to produce more of their own needs encouraged traditional agricultural exporters to limit their production. Policies of supply management helped to ensure, for example, that wheat production in the United States, Canada and Australia declined from an average of 66.5 million tons in 1966-70, to 61.4 million tons in 1970-72. But by the time that the present sharp rise in cereal prices began, in mid-1972, the United States Commodity Credit Co-operation held large stocks of feed grains and American farmers were receiving set-aside payments for taking some 60 million acres out of production.

This situation, which was based upon expectations of low world prices, contains substantial possibilities for the expansion of output. The question is whether production will be allowed to increase (or can be prevented from increasing) to a level at which involuntary stocks accumulate. The expressed intention of the US government is to avoid such a development. In the Agriculture and Consumer Protection Act of 1973, target prices for the next two seasons were fixed at levels considerably below the contemporary market price level. It is on the basis of these prices that the US government will guarantee wheat, grain maize and cotton [1]. Government payments to make up the difference between market and target prices will, however, be limited to $20,000 per farm on each of these main crops. In effect, this places considerably more risk on the shoulders of the producer.

Events seldom match expectations. If prices in the world market had remain at the levels experienced in 1973-74, there seems little doubt that commercial motives alone would have ensured a very large increase in output. Prices have now fallen and it remains to be seen whether farmers will reduce their output. Undoubtedly, lower prices will create problems for farmers who had undertaken investment and incurred costs predicated on a high price level. It is at

1. Wheat $2.05 per bushel (60 lb.), grain maize $1.38 per bushel (56 lb.) and cotton 39 cents per lb.

least posisble that steps to stabilize the market could become a political necessity. A policy which was formulated in times of high prices and prosperity might need to be changed and stocks might once more begin to accumulate.

(III) *The growth of world demand for agricultural exports*

On a worldwide basis, trade in agricultural goods has grown in recent years, despite agricultural protection. As might be expected, the rate of growth in other types of trade, raw materials, manufactures, etc., has been more rapid, so the proportion of total trade attributable to agriculture fell from some 30% to 20% during the 1960s.

A growing volume of agricultural imports is needed first, to satisfy the demands of countries where rising incomes are enabling consumption levels to outstrip local production and, second, to meet the needs of low income countries where the rate of growth of population exceeds that of food supplies. The two situations are quite different.

As income levels rise, countries produce more. They are thus able to use some of this extra production to import food or other goods for domestic consumption. No problems arise so far as payments are concerned, provided exchange rates are at appropriate levels. The more important obstacles in the path of a rapid increase in food imports are the battery of protective devices used to shield domestic agriculture. Inevitably, it is the developed countries, which account for a relatively modest share of the world's population, that dominate world trade. In 1969, for example, Western Europe, the United States, and Japan accounted for about two thirds of all world food imports. Such imports not only supply goods which, because of climate, cannot be produced by the importer's agriculture (pineapples and bananas in Europe, for instance), they also enable domestic agriculture to expand livestock output by importing feedingstuffs, principally cereals and oilseeds.

This pattern seems to be well established so that, in densely populated areas, as economic development takes place, a growth in agricultural imports must be expected. However, there may also be an expansion of exports from those developed countries where the application of more capital, better technology and more specialisation enables agricultural goods to be produced in excess of domestic requirements.

In recent years, Japan has been the most notable example of a rapid growth of food imports associated with rising levels of per capital income. The density of population there means that improved standards of diet can be met much more readily by imports than by extra domestic production. Although the Japanese situation is unique, it is likely that as other densely populated regions attain higher levels of per capita income, food imports will grow. At the moment, however, there are few signs that the densely populated Southeast Asian countries have yet reached, or are about to reach, this state. It is possible that some oil-exporting countries may devote more revenue to food imports, but these regions are, on the whole, sparsely populated and appear to concentrate wealth

18

in relatively few hands. Certainly, economic development must be regarded as a factor tending to increase demand, but this seems more likely to be a gradual than a sudden factor.

In contrast, the needs of the densely populated poor countries can arise very suddenly. A crop failure may endanger the lives of millions of people. To provide food on commercial terms from the world market requires foreign exchange. For all low-income countries, this is scarce and needed to buy imported capital equipment if development is not to be delayed. For some low-income countries, available reserves of foreign currency may not exist on a scale to meet food requirements. The supply of food to meet these pressing needs will then depend upon the willingness of richer countries to make deliveries on concessional terms. In a low-priced, over-supplied world market, such deliveries cost relatively little and help to relieve downward pressures on market price. In a world in which a commercial outlet exists at high prices, gifts of grain are more costly, tend further to raise prices and may be less readily forthcoming.

Taking into account changed policies of agricultural exporters, the new involvement of the centrally planned economies in the world market and the growth in demand for grain in both commercial and "famine relief" markets, it by no means follows that the balance of supply and demand will support prices at the heights reached in 1973-74. Table 3 shows how substantially agricultural production has grown in the twenty years from 1952 to 1971.

Table 3
Rates of Increase in Agricultural Production
(per cent per year)

	F	WG	I	N	UK	West Europe	World
1952-1958	2.6	2.8	3.8	1.9	2.2	2.2	3.3
1958-1965	4.2	0.7	1.8	1.6	5.0	2.6	2.2
1965-1971	2.9	4.2	1.8	5.1	2.6	3.0	2.9

Source: Agricultural and Food Statistics for the Enlarged Community, M.A.F.F., 1974.

Although these gains have not been evenly distributed over time or geographically, they have in general been greater than the growth in population. In Europe, for example, population has grown at some 1.0% per annum, agricultural production has risen by 2% to 3%. It seems unduly pessimistic to believe that the era of expanding food output is at an end. Given more capital and the application of known technology on a larger scale, let alone the discovery of new technical improvements, continued growth seems attainable.

The one clear lesson of recent experience is that the future course of world prices cannot be predicted. FAO studies based on recent trends indicate that food production is likely to grow more rapidly than population in developed countries and less rapidly than population in developing countries. Should this prove to be the case, a reform of trade mechanisms will be needed if the productive capacity of the wealthy countries is to make a more adequate contribution to the food needs of poor countries. It does not, however, mean that the price level in world agricultural trade can be foreseen. The probability that centrally planned economies will seek to replace deficiencies in their own production by imports, the low level of carry-over stocks to meet needs for "famine relief" and to support expanding livestock industries suggest that whatever the longer-run trend in prices, markets are likely to prove more unstable in the next decade than they were in the years between 1962 and 1972.

The disruption of the Community's policy for agriculture since 1970 has come about mainly as the result shocks from the unforeseen and substantial rise in world prices. Recent indications that agricultural prices are falling from their highest levels do not necessarily imply a return to the lower and more stable price regime of the 1960s. It seems therefore reasonable to explore ways in which arrangements for international trade might be improved and greater stability secured for agricultural markets. Stability is desirable as an end in itself. It is too a pre-condition upon which the Community and the world might proceed to reduce the impediments to freer agricultural trade. A reduction of fluctuations in international markets should be seen as a basis for developments in the Common Agricultural Policy which will lead to a more efficient use of Community resources and the establishment of a common market in agricultural goods which is freed from distortions.

Recent events have created a greater awareness of the importance of secure food supplies. There is an understandable tendency to associate this with a greater degree of self-sufficiency within the Community. To undertake policies which encouraged complete self-sufficiency would at this stage be a mistake. Extra security would be purchased at a high cost in terms of resources and lower living standards. International trade still affords the prospect of lower-cost supplies and the opportunity to use resources in Europe to best advantage. The first task must then be to attempt to ensure that through an agreed set of rules international trade can be stabilized and security of supplies attained. Only if such an approach fails should the Community proceed to deliberately increase its own self-sufficiency in food supplies.

The Stabilization of World Agricultural Markets

Introduction

Discussion of improvements in world agricultural markets is timely. Negotiations within the framework of the General Agreement on Tariffs and Trade (GATT) are now starting. In the past such negotiations have made little progress in improving agricultural trade. Many governments, anxious to retain freedom to support their own farmers, have been content to exclude agriculture from the area of discussion. When, as in the Kennedy Round, agriculture has been included progress has been slight and the resulting agreements of little effect in encouraging world trade.

In 1975 there is a unique opportunity for a fruitful discussion of agriculture. In this the Community may play a leading role. Since enlargement it has become very much the largest importer of food in the world. The terms upon which it allows imports and exports to take place affect all world traders. Its attitudes must then have great influence on the success or failure of trade negotiations. In the largest food exporting country, the United States, there are also indications of a changed attitude to international trade. The recent sharp increases in world food prices have contributed to domestic inflation there. The outcry occasioned by the suspension of soya bean exports in 1973 has created a greater sensitivity about the effects of such policies on the reputation of the United States. There is thus a common concern for greater price stability and the assurance of reliable supplies and markets in the world's largest importer and exporter.

The proposals made in this chapter link the questions of access to markets and stability of world prices. As was indicated in the Atlantic Institute study of 1970, the independent pursuit of internal stability through protectionist policies makes the world market less stable, its prices more depressed, and so justifies even greater degrees of protection. Because protection prohibits low-cost supplies from entering the market and finances subsidized exports, any shifts in production, which may be quite modest in relation to total world output, are reflected in an artificially limited world market. The inevitable result is a very large fluctuation in prices.

Attempts to negotiate a more satisfactory and agreed way of stabilizing prices may not succeed. It may be necessary to fall back on "second-best" solutions which may involve regulated and limited access to Community markets. At this stage, however, it would be premature to resort to such methods until the current opportunities for an international solution have been explored.

The International Framework

Instabilities in world commodity markets have been a matter for concern over many years. Various schemes to bring about more orderly arrangements have been suggested and for some products, International Commodity Agreements have been attempted. The record of such schemes is discouraging. Since World War II, international commodity agreements have been negotiated for five commodities—wheat, coffee, sugar, tin and olive oil. With the exception of tin, all these agreements have ceased either to operate or to have any real substance.

The difficulties are formidable. Commodity agreements that attempt to stabilise prices between reasonably narrow bands tend to fail if a trend in price is established. Should the trend be upward the exporters feel they are losing, whilst, in so far as price is held down, production may be discouraged forcing the underlying equilibrium price to an even higher level. Eventually it becomes worthwhile to break the agreement. If in contrast the price trend is downwards, then importers receive a similar incentive to drop out of the scheme or evade its terms. Commodity agreements that divide the world market between exporters, or, by agreement, between exporters and importers, tend to freeze the pattern of production. The result is that low-cost producers feel a growing sense of frustration because of their inability to expand at the expense of higher-cost suppliers. Agricultural commodities are in competition both for markets and resources. An international arrangement which seeks to maintain a high price level for one commodity may encourage its replacement by others (saccharine for sugar for example). If an arrangement raises the price level to producers there may be an embarrassing tendency for supplies to run ahead of demand unless some system restraining production is applied. Finally, arrangements to stabilize agricultural markets are really applicable only to those commodities which can be stored at low cost. Grains and coffee seem suitable candidates. Livestock and livestock products are not.

Recent experience has increased the desire for price stability but events have made the prospects even less encouraging. Not only have commodity markets become less stable but the international monetary system shows increasing signs of stress. The re-distribution of purchasing power as a result of the increased price of oil has greatly added to present uncertainties. The form in which oil exporters hold their wealth must influence many market prices. In so far as some is invested in food commodities it may create a new and as yet unpredictable element in the market. Interest has therefore increased on devices to limit price fluctuation.

Stability demands that there shall be limits to upward as well as downward price movements. For the world as a whole such stability may be attained through stock holding; provided sufficient supplies are held to meet periods of shortage and sufficient funds are available to accumulate stocks in times of surplus, prices may be contained within some specified range. The situation facing individual countries is different. Confronted by unexpected shortage, a country may increase its imports, and, if it wishes, keep internal prices down by subsidies. Faced by rising world market prices, an exporting country may limit exports and so hold down its own prices. In periods of oversupply, countries may maintain their price levels by imposing taxes on imports and subsidising exports. In effect, such policies rely on other countries to hold stocks to cover periods of shortage and to absorb when surpluses tend to depress prices.

Policies of this type, when combined with attempts to protect domestic agriculture, distort the world trading system upon which they rely to maintain internal stability. Instead of stocks forming a valued and profitable part of a world trading system, as they might if trade moved freely and there were a good understanding of the future course of production and consumption, they are accumulated reluctantly during periods of surplus. In Europe, for example, the term "butter mountain" has been used to describe such an involuntary stock of butter. In periods of high price the situation is reversed, stocks are discovered to be "essential" and countries scramble to safeguard their supplies. In each situation the action of national governments, focused on internal stability and the protection of domestic agriculture, tends to exaggerate price fluctuations in world markets, forcing prices down when they fall and up when they rise.

It is therefore proposed that there should be an international approach to the management of buffer stocks. This would enable prices in world markets to be more stable and diminish the problems of maintaining stable domestic prices. As a result, there would be less need for the types of national agricultural policies that disrupt world trade. More stable prices would also tend, in the longer run, to increase production in lower-cost areas and enable the world's agricultural resources to meet more adequately world food needs. The effort should begin now, through a gradual rebuilding of stocks from their present low level.

An internationally co-ordinated approach to stock holding is seen as a supplement to the normal commercial transactions of world trade. Established trading patterns respond well to the complex day-to-day needs for goods to move from country to country. What is envisaged here is a framework within which such activities might continue without the extremes of booms and slumps which have characterised agricultural markets in the past. At the same time, an internationally co-ordinated system of stock-holding is likely to be less costly for the world as a whole than if individual countries seek to safeguard themselves from the risk of crop failure by creating national stabilization stocks. Because there would be some pooling of the risks of crop failure in various countries, the total stock required to provide a given level of security would be smaller.

The scheme outlined in the following paragraphs seeks to capture these benefits. Although it is hoped that many countries will participate, the system can be operated by any number of governments provided they are prepared to obey the rules. The proposal does, however, contain devices to protect members from the actions of non-members. The scheme is described in six stages:
— principles for determining the level and location of stocks
— operating the stock
— financing the policy
— relations with internal agricultural policies
— relations with the "rest of the world"
— the coverage of the scheme.

(I) *Principles for determining the size of the stock*

If there were perfect knowledge of future levels of production and consumption, the task of deciding upon an appropriate level of stock would be relatively simple. Stocks would be accumulated in high output years so that their sale in years of scarcity, at a price which recovered the costs of storage, just emptied the stock. In an uncertain world it is much less easy to establish an appropriate level of stocks. Private businesses are unlikely to hold stocks longer than are needed to maintain the current rate of activity. Stocks are expensive to hold, they represent substantial sums of capital and are vulnerable to unpredictable fluctuations in value. To remain competitive it is necessary that the individual business sells at a price corresponding to current input costs. If raw material prices fall after a firm's stocks have been bought, losses result. Thus most enterprises seek to avoid taking a speculative stock-holding position. Those who do speculate are, in most cases, seeking a fairly rapid turnover. Where prices are moving around a recognised level, this behaviour may have a stabilizing influence; where changes take place which destroy the "recognised price level," private speculation may make instability worse. Once an upward trend is perceived there is an incentive to withhold goods from the market anticipating higher prices. Thus the speculator tends to accumulate stock in periods of scarcity. Conversely, when prices develop a downward trend, there is pressure to liquidate private stocks as soon as possible in order to avoid losses. Such behaviour contributes to the collapse of the market and accentuates the downward price movement.

Public stock-holders are not under these pressures and should accumulate stocks on a falling market in order to release them when prices turn upwards as a result of a shortfall in supplies. To succeed in dampening down excessive price movements, the public stock-holder has, however, to choose an appropriate size of stock. Too large a stock will involve unnecessarily high storage

24

costs. Too small a stock will be incapable of restraining upward price movements in a situation of scarcity. The size of stock must also reflect the degree of price stability required. If all that is desired is a smoothing of price movements around upward or downward trends, then small stock may be adequate, buying and selling prices adjusted fairly readily. If, in contrast, it is desired to fix prices around some particular point, then the minimum size of stock would be large and the volume required would grow as the underlying disequilibrium between the "fixed" price and an "equilibrium" price increased.

A recent study by Casley, Simaika, and Sinha [1] draws attention to some of the key elements in a public stock holding policy. For a series of hypothetical policy decisions they illustrate the probability of success (i.e. that the stock does not fall below zero), in relation to a variety of factors. These include the size of the initial stock, the relative rates of change in production and demand, the variability in output and the extent to which changes in output are met by calling upon or accumulating stocks. Their work confirms that success is more likely where stocks are high initially and where the stock does not seek to replace the whole of any deficit or absorb the whole of any surplus.

Table 4

Low and high instability indices
of cereal production 1952-1972

Selected Countries with Instability Index less than 10	Index	Selected Countries with Instability Index 20 or above	Index
Denmark	8	Canada	28
United Kingdom	8	Australia	43
France	8	USSR	20
United States	9	Argentina	22
India	8	Norway	21
Pakistan	9	Sweden	20
		Ghana	146
		Somalia	111
		Tanzania	32
		Congo	25

Source: Casley *et al., op. cit.*

The appropriate level of stock for an internationally agreed system must allow for the differing degrees of variability in output experienced in various countries and for the extent of stability which it is intented to provide. Table 4, which is based on Casley *et al,* indicates the wide range of instability in cereal production among various countries from 1952 to 1972. If from an international

1. D. J. Casley, J. B. Simaika, R. P. Sinha "Instability of Production and its impact on Stock Requirements," *F.A.O. Monthly Bulletin,* May, 1974.

stock, the whole of the deficits were to be made up or the surpluses absorbed, of a country with high variability, then there would be a net transfer from more stable countries. In the language of insurance, all countries would be paying the same rate of premium but the benefits would be systematically distributed in favour of some. Such a policy might be deliberately chosen, if it seemed to benefit poor countries, but this would have to be argued on more general grounds than the promotion of agricultural stability.

It is therefore proposed that the size of a jointly organised international stock should be related to the variability of output and the size of output in each participating country. The aggregate stock of all members would be determined on the basis of the past variability of output for the group as a whole. This would be smaller than the size of stock needed to cover each individual country separately since there would be a pooling of risks. The share contributed by each country would vary in proportion to the volume and uncertainty of its own production and its past level of consumption.

A simple arithmetic illustration using arbitrary numbers may clarify this proposal.

Table 5
Participating Countries

			A	B	C	D
(I)	Average output over ten years		10	15	25	50
(II)	(a)	Maximum output in any one year	12	16.5	32.5	52.5
	(b)	Minimum output in any one year	8	13.5	17.5	47.5
(III)	Variability as a % deviation from average		20	10	30	5
(IV)	Size of independent stock (see notes)		2	1.5	7.5	2.5
(IV)	Size of pooled stock (see notes)		1.5	1.1	5.5	1.9

Explanatory notes to table 5

(i) In each country the average level of output over the past ten years.

(ii) a & b maximum and minimum levels of output in this period.

(iii) Variability expressed as a percentage deviation from average output.

(iv) The size of independent stocks needed to ensure that consumption could be maintained at the level of average output in each year depends upon the discrepancy in the most extreme year and the probability of its occurence. In this table the simplifying assumption has been made that there will not be more than one maximum or minimum crop in ten years in each of the participant countries. Thus, if each held the stocks indicated in row (iv), consumption could be maintained on average levels in the year when output was on its lowest. This is a major simplification since probabilities of good or bad outcomes would vary among countries and mean that they would require larger or smaller stocks if they were to achieve an equal degree of security. It is assumed that the probability of good or bad outcomes is independent between countries.

(v) The size of a pooled stock would be smaller because the chances of all participants simultaneously experiencing maximum or minimum outputs are is the product of the probabilities of each country taken in isolation. In terms of the illustrative figures used here, the chances of an aggregate output as high as 113.5 or as low as 86.5 are one in 10,000. Hence a pooled stock, fixed, say, at ten, would give even greater security to participants than the sum of the independent stocks recorded in row (iv).

This table assumes that the internationally shared stock is as available to countries in need as nationally held stocks. In part this is a question of logistics. Stocks must be physically accessible to the places where they are needed. In fact, moving agricultural commodities is an expensive and time-consuming activity so that the total size of a pooled stock needed to give equal security to separate national stocks would be increased. Distribution is only part of the problem of availability; there is, too, the question of political willingness to supply goods according to the rules. Unless the participants A, B, C and D are confident that stocks held anywhere in the system will be made available when needed, the scheme cannot operate.

The size of the stock required also depends upon the degree of risk countries are prepared to leave uncovered. The table as it stands implies that the stock will be adequate to meet shortages anywhere within the system. In practice, we cannot have complete certainty about the "variability" factor, nor is it likely that countries would wish to meet the cost of avoiding all cuts in consumption, should very exceptional losses of output occur.

The table makes no mention of the cost of holding stocks. In any real situation this is a crucial element. Some commodities store well at low cost. Others can be stored only with the aid of expensive capital equipment and tend, even when well looked after, to deteriorate in taste. It is necessary that stocks held internationally should be limited to products for which the costs

27

of storage do not exceed the benefits to the participating countries of the stability they provide.

The illustrative table assumes that, apart from year to year variations in output, there is no long-run change taking place in the level of production. A more realistic framework would have to incorporate assumptions about the rate of growth in output and consumption and allow for increasing the size of stocks and redistributing the weighted contributions of each country.

The suggestions made so far may be summarised as follows: national stocks on an internationally agreed basis should be set up for commodities where the benefits of stability outweigh the costs of storage. (Stocks in any one country would, if need arose, be accessible to all other participants in the scheme.) The size of stocks should be determined by the overall variability in output for the participating countries as a group, and an agreed political decision about the degree of risk it is acceptable to tolerate. The contributions of each member to the group would depend upon a weighting system reflecting its own volume of output plus the volume it consumed and its variability in production. A procedure would be agreed for varying the size of stocks in relation to established trends in the volume of output.

It is proposed that stocks should initially be accumulated in their country of origin. The advantages of maintaining stocks where they are produced are substantial, but there is a need, too, for stocks to be held where they can be moved into use quickly should the need arise. Importing countries need to safeguard their own situation and are invited to do so by participating in an internationally co-ordinated scheme. Stocks financed by such countries are likely to be held within their frontiers. The commodities stocked may be imported from other member countries or bought from their own producers. Some errors in stock estimation are almost inevitable and must be allowed for within any stock holding policy. However, it seems likely that confidence would be increased if an impartial review body were to report the production, consumption, trade and stock levels of all participants. The review body, which might be based on one of the existing international organisations—e.g. GATT, FAO, OECD—would have no powers but would report to the participant countries as a group. If there were a deliberate attempt to understate or exaggerate stocks, action would be a matter for discussion among the countries taking part in the scheme. Given this safeguard the advantages of having jointly arranged stocks seem likely to exceed those of an internationally owned stock.

(II) *The operation of an internationally co-ordinated stock*

The object of the internationally agreed stock scheme is to improve the operation of the world market, not to replace commercial activity by bureaucratic processes. Within a framework in which there is a secure outlet to the world market and a certainty of adequate supplies to meet the needs of importers, extreme price fluctuations are unlikely to take place. But if advantage is to be taken of the healthy working of the market, the gap between the prices at which goods are brought into stock and the price at which they are sold to the commercial market must be sufficiently wide to allow normal trading relations to continue. It is also necessary that these price levels should be adjustable in relation to longer-run shift in consumption or the costs of production. Three phases of operation must be considered, the build-up to agreed stock levels, the operation of the policy at these stock levels, and ways of modifying the desired level of stock.

In the initial phase it is essential to avoid forcing prices higher at a time of scarcity by buying for stock. A further stimulus to prices would do little to increase output but would compel more poor consumers to leave the market. Production is more likely to increase if there exists confidence among farmers that sudden price collapses would not occur. The "buying" price for stock holding should initially be set below the peak of recent prices but above the estimated cost level of most farmers in substantial producing countries. This would encourage continued expansion of output while the relatively high market price would restrain the growth in consumption.

The scheme becomes partly operational when the stock accumulated at this price in one country reaches the designated level. At the point all other participants may buy from the stock holding authority of the country whose stock is "full," at the buying price (which will be below the usual commercial price) plus a fixed handling charge. In effect if production in a participant country exceeds its consumption, commercial or concessionary export and stock requirements, the goods may pass at the buying price into other member countries' stocks. Since it is likely that in the initial period surplus stocks would be too small to meet all requirements, a formula dividing supplies among participants in proportion to their basic stock requirements might be employed. Thus in the build-up period, both farmers and exporting countries would be assured of a minimum price for all they can produce.

In phase two, when it is assumed that stocks have reached the required level in all participating countries, the scheme becomes fully operational. The participating countries fix a selling price to traders within their frontiers. This will be a price which allows for the costs of storage and handling. It will be a price ceiling for the market fixed above the normal range of commercial price variation and designed to operate when shortages are severe. At this stage a continuous assessment has to be made of the stock levels in each country. If a relative shortage develops in one area, then it will be made up at the "buying" price plus handling charges from other participating countries. If at the designated buying and selling prices a relative surplus develops in some centre, then it will be shared, at the buying price, among all participating countries on a key which relates to the stock levels agreed for each centre. The effect of these manœuvres is to make the pooled stock effective in ensuring supplies and in maintaining prices within the designated range. At the end of the stock year an inventory of all stocks is prepared. If stocks for the group as a whole exceed the desired level, the buying and selling prices for the following production year

29

would be cut. If total stocks fall below the level required, buying and selling prices for the following production year would be raised. The amount of the price adjustement should in principle relate to the supply elasticity for the commodity among participating countries as a group. In reality, too little is known about such elasticities and the scheme would have to proceed by experimental price shifts in the indicated direction. The object should be to make prices move sufficiently frequently for each step to be fairly modest. Once the price was agreed, however, producers would know that it was firm for the next production period. Apart from adjusting prices in the light of changes in the actual stock levels, it may be necessary to modify the price level to take account of inflationary shifts in producers' costs. Thus, assuming stocks were within the range in which no action was required but inflation had raised costs by some ten per cent, it is likely that prices would have to be raised in order to maintain the same level of output in the ensuing production period. It seems better to anticipate this adjustment than to run stocks down and have to make a larger adjustment in a following year.

The third operational phase takes place when it is necessary not simply to adjust the prices to maintain stocks at agreed levels, but to take account of changes in the appropriate level of stock. Such changes might become necessary because of long-run shift in the level of production or demand or because the variability of output changes. For most products it seems probable that output will tend to increase. The variability of output will be affected by two conflicting forces. Better techniques, provision of irrigation water, improved seeds, etc., may diminish the vulnerability of yields to weather, pests and disease. At the same time increased output may press production into more marginal regions where the number of years in which adverse weather significantly reduces yields increases. It seems likely then that the required overall level of stocks will be increased over time. The increase will, however, occur at different rates in differing countries. In order to update the distribution and level of stocks, use might be made of a rolling average. The number of years included must be long enough to include varying seasons—but not so long as to slow adjustments unduly.

(III) *Financing international stocks*

The benefits of this scheme for jointly organised stocks are security of food supplies and relative stability in food prices for those who participate. In effect, the amount of stock needed to provide a given level of security is smaller than would otherwise be the case and agricultural trade is enabled to move more smoothly. Benefits accrue to the public as a whole rather than to individual business. By stabilizing food prices, one major inflationary pressure may be avoided. In modern industrial communities trade unions resist reductions in the purchasing power of wages by campaigning for higher nominal wages. In so far as they are successful, labour costs tend to be increased and manufacturers must raise final selling prices to maintain profitability. When food prices fall there is no tendency for a symmetrical reduction in the level of money wages.

30

As a result instability, especially in food prices, tends to be inflationary. Deflationary policies, whether of a fiscal or monetary character, may be required to contain these inflationary pressures. Such policies reduce both consumption and employment. Their cost to society as a whole includes not only low output from idle men and capital, but also the social and emotional distress experienced by those who become unemployed. If stock-holding can reduce the extent to which such deflationary measures are needed, the community as a whole benefits.

Gains of this character do not figure in the financial accounts of industrial businesses. They provide no incentive for the private sector to hold stocks in order to stabilise prices. Indeed, any firm which attempted to do so would encounter severe risks and ultimately make large losses. The private yield on such stocks may be negative but the public yield is positive. There is then good reason for the financial cost of a stock policy to fall on the public purse.

Public stocks may, in principle, be financed out of taxation or by the extension of central bank indebtedness. For commodities which are used up during the year, the appropriate method of finance is short or medium-term credit. Commodities which are not used up represent an addition to reserves. Such reserves may be held against the issue of central bank money. This process is not inflationary since the flow of money matches the flow of goods whose prices are thereby held constant. If when the commodity is taken out of reserve the corresponding amount of central bank indebtedness is extinguished, the net effect on the price level will remain neutral.

The publicly held stocks envisaged in this proposal have the character of investment. Although the actual items held in stock will have to turn over from year to year to avoid deterioration, the overall level of stocks is over the run of years likely to be constant. It is therefore suggested that the reserve stocks should be financed in each country by central banks issuing appropriate amounts of new money. The running costs of the stock must however be financed in other ways. Agricultural commodities involve substantial storage costs. For example, the annual cost of storing grain in the United States appears to be about 30 cents per bushel. In other countries where conditions at harvest or during the storage period are less favourable, the annual running cost would be higher. To finance this charge from central bank sources would be inflationary. The costs of storage, deterioration and handling must then be a call on taxation.

A numerical illustration may give some notion of the sorts of magnitude involved. In 1973, world wheat and course grain production totalled some 1052 million tons. If we assume that the degree of price stability required could be attained with a world stock of 10% of annual production, total stocks would have to be about 105 million tons. Purchased at a floor price of $100 per ton, total outlay would be $10.5 billion. If it is assumed that the annual cost of maintaining this stock amounted to 10% of the total value of the stock, then the recurrent change falling on taxes would be of the order of $1 billion. This would be accompanied by an increase of some $9.5 billion in central bank lending. Although such numbers are formidable they must be seen against the

31

background of a total GNP well in excess of $3000 billion in industrial countries. The actual costs of internationally co-ordinated stocks would of course depend upon the decisions taken by governments. It seems likely, however, that a worthwhile degree of stability could be achieved for some important commodities at a cost to taxpayers which is modest compared with that of current agricultural policies in most developed countries.

The financial arrangements envisaged require that each participant country shall be responsible for building up its own stock. The total financial outlay would be smaller than for independently held stocks giving equivalent security. Initially stocks would be bought within each country so no foreign exchange burden would be created. As the stock became fully operational countries which had not acquired their share of the total would buy at the buying price plus a handling charge. This would require a foreign exchange expenditure, but the stock would retain its value in world markets and would have been bought at prices no higher than needed to ensure an adequate sustained level of production. If when the stocks were full, more was produced in a participating country than was required, imports would be shared among participants. This process would enable prices to be maintained in the current year at some greater cost to importers than would otherwise apply. However, the reduced buying prices in the succeeding year would prevent those imports from becoming burdensome. In the converse situation, when stocks fell and production was less than currently required, the importers would gain from continued supplies at the agreed price. In subsequent years the exporters might recoup this "loss of foreign earnings" by the assured higher price which would be announced early enough to enable them to expand production.

The scheme as such makes no special attempt to help developing countries by weighting financial responsibility in relation to the varying level of per capita income among countries. Security in food supplies and stability of prices is at least as important to low-income countries as for those who are richer. It is true, too, that the provision of finance for a stock is more difficult for poor countries than for rich and that any undertaking to purchase goods for foreign exchange is especially onerous. These are the problems of poverty and they could be relieved by the provision of aid from richer countries, possibly from those with newly aquired oil revenues. By contributing to the buildup of stocks or by holding larger stocks against such needs in low-income countries, developed countries might provide worthwhile assistance without depressing internal price levels, and so discouraging domestic production in poorer countries. To participate in the scheme, however, the stocks held by low-income countries should be available, on the same basis as other countries, for use elsewhere and entitled to supplementation when the need arose.

(IV) *Relations with internal agricultural policy*

Relations between domestic agricultural policy and the internationally pooled stocks are crucial. There is a danger that a country might attempt to exploit the scheme through manipulation of its own domestic policy. There is, too, the certainty that each government must be able to satisfy its own electorate about the soundness of the scheme and its compatibility with national interests. Solutions which require detailed interference with agricultural policy may avoid the first group of difficulties but they are unlikely to be acceptable to the producers and consumers in every participating country. There must be assurances that an international scheme will not be abused and at the same time freedom of action for individual governments to meet the needs of their own producers and consumers.

A fundamental premise of a co-ordinated stock scheme is that there shall be international buying and selling prices. These might allow for geographic variations in transport, handling and storage costs, but they would remain international prices moving up and down in all countries as overall stocks exceeded or fell below requirements. In practice, the buying price would imply a floor price for producers. Local production which was surplus to requirements would be saleable within the scheme at that price. Internal policies which encouraged the expansion of output beyond domestic requriements would result in a growth in the exports which other participants were required to buy. To some extent, such policies would be discouraged because as total stocks exceeded requirements prices would fall. However, this would not prevent an exporter who extensively subsidised production from pushing prices down, depressing output in other countries, unless their governments also provided subsidies, increasing market share, and gaining foreign exchange from other participants. An importer who pursued similar policies of domestic support would also cause problems for other members. By reducing imports, foreign exchange would be saved, the stock levels would tend to rise, depressing the international buying price, and so compelling other countries either to subsidise their producers or to cut the prices they received. Problems would arise should an exporter or group of exporters exercise an effective monopoly in the market. By cutting output through internal quota schemes stocks might be prevented from rising. The resulting increase in the buying price would not result in a growth in output but a growth in the revenues of exporters.

For the scheme to work fairly it would be necessary for participating governments to agree not to provide support, over and above the stability represented by the buying price, nor to indulge in subsidies on major items of variable cost in order to raise output. Such a restraint would need to be matched by an agreement not to restrict output, through for example, quotas or acreage withdrawal programmes. The proposals made in this study would remove the need to artificially restrict output. Supplies which could not be sold in the commercial market would be assured of an outlet at the current buying price for taking into stock. Only in later seasons would this price be reduced and then for all producers, not just those in countries which at prevailing prices tended to have a surplus.

An international buying price would be unacceptable in countries where production difficulties are especially severe or where past policies have resulted in a structural pattern which raises costs. In the long term, farmers faced by such difficulties might be helped to reduce costs or assisted to leave the industry. This would inevitably take several years especially where initially there was little alternative employment to that provided by the farm. Where many farmers fall into this category it may be impractical to safeguard their welfare through supplementing income from farming by additional payments from public funds. To accommodate this need it is suggested that such countries apply a fixed tariff over and above the international buying price. This would maintain higher internal prices but, if the overall stock level required a cut in the buying price, farmers in "high cost" countries would also face lower prices. This fixed tariff would initially be negotiated among all participants. There should be, too, a time-table for its gradual elimination. This time-table might reflect the varying opportunities for countries to provide non-agricultural employment. In the case of low-income countries where adjustments were not possible in the foreseeable future, the point at which any cuts in tariff took place might be postponed indefinitely.

In order to allow goods to be exported from countries which imposed a fixed tariff, some aid would have to be given to exporters. It is proposed that this should be provided at the same rate as the fixed tariff and maintained at the same level for exports to all destinations. In this way the scheme would allow trade to continue without the disruption of markets caused by variable export subsidies.

Some governments are reluctant to use price cuts as a means of restricting output when prices seem likely to fall. This reluctance should be reduced in a system in which price cuts are modest and sudden collapses ruled out. However, it might be reassuring to make provision for some acreage withdrawal or diversion programme within the framework. The vital feature of any such programme should be that reduction in output should not be limited to low cost producing areas. Thus cuts in the acreage of any crops should be shared out among the participant countries by international agreement, not imposed by unilateral action.

Such restraint would be unworkable unless steps were taken to safeguard the incomes of farmers when prices fell or acreage was cut. The extent to which it is felt necessary to compensate farmers for price cuts depends upon the social conscience of the community and its ability to pay. It might well be that no compensation need be offered to large, relatively wealthy farmers affected by a gradual price reduction, whilst smaller producers qualified for full compensation. Decisions on such issues must be left to the individual governments, provided only that any amount paid to offset the effect of a fall in the buying price does not give an incentive to increase output produced in subsequent years.

(v) *Relations with the rest of the world*

The suggested international stock policy is in principle open to any number of countries. Both exporters and importers stand to gain. Since each country is responsible for its own share of the stock, few problems arise provided all participants obey the rules. It cannot, however, be assumed that all countries would participate. The wider the coverage of the scheme the greater is likely to be its contribution to a more orderly and efficient world market. All countries who are prepared to obey the rules must then be welcome members. This includes the USSR and China, who have become important world traders in grain, although they may in the event prove unwilling to accept the restrictions such a scheme implies. There may be difficulties, too, in extending the scheme to developing countries for whom both the problems of finance and of inadequate storage facilities may be acute.

Although assistance in building stocks might be a worthwhile form of "aid," richer countries might well prefer to hold larger stocks themselves and provide more emergency relief from time to time, rather than hand over control to the governments of poorer countries.

In practice this may limit the applicability of the scheme to the developed market economies. Despite this, a stabilization policy would not be unattractive. For cereals, at least, agreement does seem possible between the major free market importers, Japan and the EEC and the principal exporters, the United States, Canada, Australia and Argentina. All these market economies have experienced discomforts from destabilized world prices and the prospect of sharing the costs and benefits of greater stability among themselves could prove attractive.

If the international stock policy is to work it should be freed from disruption arising from sales or purchases by non-participating countries. So far as unwanted deliveries threaten to depress the price the participating countries could protect themselves by a variable import levy, related to their own buying in price, and applicable to trade with third countries. To prevent third countries from de-stabilizing the system by large purchases which force prices up, export licences, which might be withheld if stocks fell below a specified level, could be employed. In effect, the participant countries would trade with the rest of the world on terms which were consistent with internal stability. Freer trade would be dependent upon a willingness to observe the rules which ensured stability.

Apart from defending the scheme from instability the participants may also wish to give aid where famine threatens countries outside the scheme. For this to be possible it may be helpful to designate a contingency stock which the participants would seek to build up over and above the amounts required for security and stability amongst themselves. The location and finance of this stock might be a matter for agreement on a different basis than the main terms of the scheme. For example, finance might be related to GNP and thus would be broadly in line with per-capita income levels and contingency stocks held in locations where they might be readily deployed among vulnerable countries.

(VI) *The coverage of the scheme*

The practicality of a stock-holding policy depends upon the cost of keeping the commodity in a good and wholesome condition. Modern techniques of food preservation enable consumers to enjoy perishable products out of season. Such methods as freezing, freeze drying or canning are expensive. They change the character of the product and require substantial fixed equipment. As part of the apparatus for meeting a regular commercial demand for food they perform a valuable stock-holding function but they are ill-adapted to meet sudden gluts in supply or to provide rapid relief where conditions of scarcity or famine prevail. This means that several categories of agricultural produce must be excluded from the type of arrangement proposed. Meat, fruit and vegetables are clearly unsuitable. Stocks might in principle operate for more storable commodities such as sugar, coffee or oilseeds. It would be a major step forward if an internationally agreed system of holding central stocks, particularly wheat, could be established. Cereals provide an important part of the diet of poor people. They also have a central role in livestock production. Major upsets in cereal prices communicate their effect to all parts of the agricultural industry. Fortunately, cereals are storable.

The experiences of past schemes makes it apparent that facile optimism about proposals to improve the working of the world market in any agricultural product is misplaced. It also shows, however, that a world market which is subjected to uncontrolled dumping and to undisciplined purchases creates problems for any nations. For poor countries these may take the form of hunger or even starvation. For richer countries the main problem may be unstable prices. The approach to the improvement of the world market suggested in this study is based on the principles that only those who wish to join need to obey the rules and that the rewards they reap are distributed, over time, among the participants. It is proposed that the Community should support a scheme for cereals and that it should seek especially the co-operation of the United States and Japan. If this could be secured, a relatively stable element would have been provided in a crucial area of the international agricultural framework.

If international agreement cannot be reached the Community will have to continue to insulate its domestic markets from instabilities originating beyond its frontiers. In such a situation free trade in agricultural commodities is likely to prove impossible.

The method of financing stocks outlined in this chapter might, however, still make an important contribution to the working of the Community. In 1973 intervention purchases and export restitutions accounted for almost three quarters of the EEC's expenditure on agriculture. If this system were replaced by buying at intervention and holding accumulated stocks against central bank credit, expenditure from the budget of the Community would be dramatically reduced. Payments from FEOGA would be needed only to defray the costs of storage facilities and the loss in value due to any deterioration in the products stored.

Since agricultural expenditures account for about 80% of the total Community expenditure, this change in the method of finance of stocks would transform the operation of the Community's budget. It would release resources for the support of incomes, and for structural and regional policies. In particular, it would greatly reduce the cost of the policy to net importing countries such as the United Kingdom, Germany and Italy. Those budgetary problems which tended to dominate discussion at the summit conference held in Dublin would very largely disappear. The anxieties expressed at that meeting by the British government were based on assumptions that the future relationship of world prices and EEC prices would be broadly that established in the 1960s, and that the Community would pursue agricultural policies which were of the same type as those now in operation. If through international agreement world prices and Community prices can be brought closer together, one source of anxiety will have been removed. If, by holding stocks against central bank credit the cost falling on the budget can be cut, the "burden" of the CAP to the UK will fall still more. Thus the mechanisms outlined here may contribute both to greater stability in agricultural markets and to a more acceptable balance of benefits within the Community.

The Community's Contribution to Food Supplies

The proportion of food it is desirable to produce within the Community must depend upon assumptions about the future price level in world markets and the costs of production in Europe. In so far as schemes to create greater stability in world markets permit the Community to trade more freely with the rest of the world, the degree of self-sufficiency will become an automatic outcome of economic forces. It seems unlikely, however, that for all products sufficient stability will have been achieved through international agreement to allow unrestricted trade. For those for which agreement is not reached, the decision about how much to produce must be made by the Council of Ministers and implemented through the CAP.

The provision of an adequate supply of food is essential for any society. The concept of what is adequate varies. In strict biological terms the minimum amount needed to sustain healthy human life may be provided in a variety of different ways. Europeans are accustomed to a diet that goes far beyond the minimum. A wide variety of foods are consumed, but there is relatively little year-to-year variation in the consumption of individual foods. In the past decade, consumption of cheese, meat, fats and fruit has increased more rapidly than that of other products, but in no case has per capita consumption grown by more than 4% per annum. In a similar period the per capita growth in gross domestic product was 4.9% per annum. Contraction has taken place in the quantity of potatoes and cereals consumed, but the annual rate of decline is modest, less than 2%. Because the quantities consumed tend to be inflexible, fairly minor variations in the amount of agricultural products marketed can generate wide fluctuations in price. Such price variations are disconcerting for consumers as well as for farmers. More than a quarter of total consumer expenditure in the Community is on food. Sharp price increases reduce real income especially among poorer households who spend a larger than average proportion of their income on food. Attempts to safeguard real incomes may have far-reaching de-stabilizing effects on the economy.

For European goverments, then, an adequate food supply means not only one which affords the nutritional minimum necessary for survival but a supply which will sustain present patterns of consumption without disruptively large price fluctuations. This is a much more ambitious goal. Left to itself, the market tends to be unstable. Agricultural and trade policies must counter this and attempt to ensure that the combination of imported and home-produced agricultural goods reaching the market is fairly constant and yet capable of response to match evolving demand. The CAP regulates both the terms offered to Community farmers and the conditions upon which imported agricultural goods may enter the Community. It must, therefore, accept major responsibility for ensuring adequate food supplies.

In the past, one of the main criticisms of the CAP has been that it stimulated excessive domestic supplies, particularly of cereals, milk and sugar. The system of price support it uses requires that domestic production which cannot be sold at or above the price level approved by the Council must be removed from the market. This process has accounted for most of the expenditure under the policy. The costs have been very considerable, as the table below makes clear.

Table 6

Estimated Expenditure on Export Restitutions and Domestic Intervention 1967/68-1974

	Export Restitution	%	Domestic Intervention	%	Total	%
Cereals	3131.3	43	2603.4	23	5734.7	31
Milk	2199.1	30	4522.3	40	6721.4	36
Sugar	745.0	10	732.7	7	1477.7	8
Olive oil, oil seeds	38.8	1	2163.8	19	2202.6	12
Other	1133.6	16	1281.6	11	2415.2	13
Total	7247.8	100	11303.8	100	18551.6	100

Notes: Annual estimates by the Community of its anticipated incurred expenditure excluding re-entries due to the operation of the CAP.

The figure for 1974 is provisional.

Source: MAFF EEC Agricultural and Food Statistics, June 1974.

Production at a level that involves export restitutions is particularly damaging. Domestic intervention, although costly, is more acceptable. In some cases, olive oil for example, payments to support producer prices may have the character of regional aid distributed among some of the more needy of the Community's farmers. For other products excessive supplies may be absorbed within the Community in non-competing home markets. For example, wheat may be de-natured so as to be fit for use in animal feed but not for bread making. Losses are involved in this process but the bulk of the value is retained within the Community. The accumulation of stocks may itself help to stabilise domestic prices.

In 1973 and 1974 the CAP maintained lower and more stable prices for some food products than prevailed in the world market. At a time of international scarcity, production within the Community has ensured secure food supplies for the EEC and supplied profitable exports to the world. At contemporary world prices the CAP did not appear so protective. It may be claimed to have been vindicated against earlier criticism. However, the role of the CAP in relation to food supplies must depend not on the present scene but on the probable future pattern of world markets and the potential for agricultural production within the Community.

In chapter II, the uncertainty surrounding any attempt to predict future world food supplies was emphasised. Against such a back-cloth it seems imperative to consider the contribution which the agriculture of the enlarged Community could make, not only to feeding the European population but also as a potential exporter of food. Such an analysis cannot, however, deal only with the physical potential for production. It must consider, too, the costs involved. To channel resources into high-cost agricultural production in Europe, if this discourages lower cost production from taking place elsewhere, actually reduces the world's supply of food. If agricultural expansion is to take place where scarce resources yield the largest volume of useful output (i.e. where costs are low), then the goods produced must have access to a market. If every developed country pursued a policy of encouraging agriculture to the point of self-sufficiency even where extra production involved high costs, then investment in low-cost exporting areas would be unprofitable. Such an international misallocation of resources would add to the risks of food scarcity.

The extent to which the Community seeks fuller self-sufficiency must then be related to its capacity to reduce production costs. At first sight, there seem good grounds for believing that substantial reduction in costs is possible. Europe is well-placed to produce more food at low cost. Natural conditions in the Community are favourable for agriculture. It has a high proportion of usable land, some of it highly productive. Its climate is free from excess of heat or cold. Over most of its area the amount of rainfall is satisfactory and reliable. Distances to markets are short and the proximity of a sophisticated manufacturing sector ensures a ready supply of reasonably priced machines, chemicals and the other necessities of modern farming. The type of technology that has raised yields in recent years has been most readily applicable where there exists an educated labour force and an abundant supply of capital. In these respects Europe compares well with most of the world.

There exist, however, severe structural problems. There is a proliferation of small farms often fragmented into several "parcels" of land. This may be attributed to the traditionally protectionist policies for farming. More sympathetically, it may be seen as one outcome of the long-settled character of Europe and the dominance of a legal tradition which divides estates among the family, rather than passing them intact to the elder son. The effect is to raise the costs of agricultural production.

Costs are increased by the excessive size of the agricultural labour force implicit in this small farm structure. Modern farming methods achieve high labour productivity by increasing the amount of output per worker. Small farms find it difficult to apply such techniques. The small farm which continues to employ a full-time farmer and, in many cases, members of his family, must suffer from high labour costs per unit although wages and profits are low. There have been very substantial reductions in the size of the agricultural labour force since the Community came into existence. There has also been a modest shift towards larger farms. Public policy especially in France and Germany has aimed at farm consolidation and the prevention of further fragmentation. These developments help to create a lower cost and more competitive agriculture in the Community, but they are as yet incomplete.

In European terms, low-cost agricultural production does not mean low output. The favourable location in relation to markets and the good natural conditions of production imply that low costs are attainable where intensive use is made of agricultural resources. Thus, yields of crops compare favourably with those in other parts of the world. The livestock sector, in some parts of the Community at least, achieves high densities of stocking and good rates of converting feed into meat, milk and eggs. Such methods have enabled output to continue to rise despite the reduction in the labour force, the re-distribution of farm land and the relative decline in real prices over most of the period since 1958. In real terms this represents a substantial reduction in costs per unit of output. The character of the CAP made such expectations alarming. Greater surpluses of wheat and sugar threatened to make the budgetary cost of the policy grow. Growing attention was given to the need to avoid surpluses. Schemes were introduced to persuade dairy farmers to switch to beef production. The price of coarse grains was raised relative to that of bread grains. The case for quota schemes which would limit either the amount produced, the amount marketed or the extent of the Community's liability was argued. It was noted that large farms which already received adequate incomes contributed more than proportionately to production and thus to surpluses. In this context, schemes which offered higher unit prices to small producers were sometimes advocated.

In a world threatened by shortage, suggestions to limit supplies seem folly. It is even more absurd to cut output by discouraging large, low-cost producers in order to keep high-cost farmers in existence. The CAP is to be criticised not so much because it generates periodic surpluses as because it tends to retain in business farmers who cannot produce at low cost. Maintaining prices to preserve income levels compounds the problem. Farmers can only earn the protected income by staying on the farm. At the same time, their land cannot be re-structured into more efficient units which would permit satisfactory incomes to be ensured at modest prices by enabling low cost production to take place.

41

There is a tendency for low cost producers to expand output provided there is any reasonably stable price environment. New improved methods often allow output from existing resources to be expanded at modest cost. This extra output adds to income even if prices fail to keep pace with inflation. For example, agricultural production continued to expand through the 1960s in both the Six and the UK, despite falling real prices for farm goods. Although the systems of support differed and prices were higher in the Community than in Britain, farmers in both areas continued to invest in new and improved methods. Any explanation of this process must include personal, technical and economic factors, but the implication seems to be that given a prospect of stable or even slowly declining margins, the more progressive farmers will continue to innovate and cut production costs.

There then are grounds for believing that the output of agriculture would grow if the CAP directed resources towards lower cost producers. Both imports and exports of agricultural products might increase but overall the Community would become more, rather than less, self-sufficient. Such a policy demands changes in the way the CAP is presently operated. It is likely to result in a different balance between prices, giving relatively less to bread grains and more to livestock. It will require renewed emphasis on structural reform and on agricultural advice and research devices to accelerate the movement of land into larger, more competitive farm units and to help the agricultural labour force adapt to the need for fewer but more skilled workers. The CAP itself has to operate within a framework of regional and economic policies upon which depends the creation of new employment opportunities for those who leave agriculture.

Agricultural Prices and the Confidence of Farmers

The CAP remains an essential feature of the Community but there are grounds for believing that recent events have weakened the farmers' confidence in effectiveness. The failure of livestock prices to keep pace with feed costs has reduced profits on many farms. The continuing rise in the cost of machinery and chemicals purchased from other sectors has eroded the benefits of high prices to cereal producers. In countries in which currencies have depreciated, the operation of monetary compensatory amounts has tended to keep agricultural prices below their value in other parts of the Community.

The restoration of confidence among farmers is important if there is to be an expansion of low-cost production. Output may be increased by the application of new methods which enable more efficient use to be made of existing resources. Such innovations almost always require fresh investment by the farmer, who will be disinclined to undertake improvements if the prospect of profit is highly uncertain.

The severity of the recent decline in margins has led to demands for offsetting price increasees for farm products. Such increases which might be regarded as a form of indexing CAP prices are not without problems. The nature of the price support provided through the CAP means that higher prices for farmers would raise consumer prices at the time that inflation was most troublesome. Rates of inflation vary between member countries. This implies that price increases related to the average rates of inflation would result in unjustified rises in consumer prices in countries which had below-average rates of inflation. Although farmers' costs are affected by the general price increases, some enterprises are particularly susceptible to the price of one or two items. For example, 70% or more of broiler and egg producers' costs are feed. If the price of one of these inputs rises more than average, compensation for general inflation might not restore profitability. However, if prices were allowed to rise to fully offset feed costs, it might not be easy to reduce them when prices fell, given the present framework of price determination in the CAP.

These difficulties suggest three ways in which the operation of the price guarantee aspects of the CAP could be modified to provide more confidence among producers and greater flexibility in response to changing circumstances.

First, in reaching its annual decision on agricultural prices, the Council of Ministers should take a view of the margins farmers might expect to receive for particular products, rather than the price alone. Although it would be helpful to have accurate data on existing magrins, this is not crucial. If in the light of past performance and expected market conditions, it seemed that at current prices and costs more would be produced than could be sold without intervention on export subsidy, the margin would be reduced. If shortages were feared, margins would be widened. Such adjustments are inexact but they would tend to push production in the right direction. In order to reassure farmers that massive year-to-year reductions in margins would not occur, some maximum amount by which margins could be reduced in any one year would be established by the Council. Thus, even where a reduction in output was needed farmers would be sure that the year-to-year change would not suddenly destroy the profitability of their investment.

The second modification designed to create confidence concerns the maintenance of margins between the Council's annual price "fixings." Farmers, like other private business men, cannot expect to be shielded from all risks. They must in the interest of the Community economise in inputs which have become more expensive. At the same time, violent swings in prices or costs, arising from factors totally outside any individual farmer's control, may destroy farm enterprise even though at normal cost price relationships it is efficient and profitable. One characteristic of much innovation in farming methods is to make farmers more dependent upon purchased inputs and to require them to concentrate their activities on a smaller range of products. Such changes permit farms to make fuller use of technology developed in other sectors and to achieve greater economies of scale within from businesses. In general, this means that production costs fall. Farms of this type are, however, more vulnerable to adverse shifts in input or output prices. If these are extreme they may be forced out of business. The more backward, low-output, multi-enterprise small farm with the minimum of purchased inputs may in contrast survive such adverse price movements even if this means reducing the farm household's consumption. From the Community's viewpoint the price fluctuation which eliminates low-cost producers and allows high-cost farmers to survive is damaging. There is then a case for limiting the extent to which margins are allowed to deteriorate between the annual reviews made by the Council of Ministers. One possibility would be to make an automatic adjustment in prices when an agreed list of costs had risen or fallen by more than 10%. The price adjustment would not be complete but it would ensure that efficient producers did not find their businesses suddenly becoming totally unprofitable. Adjustments of this character would not require a Council decision but could be made by the Commission and the Management Committees. Because downward as well as upward adjustments would be automatic, consumers would be safeguarded and there would be a tendency to stabilize production.

The confidence of farmers should be increased if the CAP ensured that margins on major products would be protected from catastrophic changes as a result of inflation, and if the adjustment from year to year were restricted to stated proportions. Within such a framework, investment should be encouraged, and as a result of greater efficiency the margin needed to sustain any particular level of production should decline over time. In other words, costs might be expected to fall.

Recent experience has, however, indicated the weakness of the present CAP arrangements for supporting livestock prices. There are a diversity of ways in which livestock and livestock products are treated. For poultry and eggs, market prices are allowed to fall until the market is cleared. For pigs, intervention purchase occurs at prices which are low compared with those normally expected to prevail. Intervention in the beef market occurs much closer to the "guide" price, and for milk, intervention takes place in butter and skim milk to keep internal prices near to the "target" price. Intervention purchase and the accumulation of stocks of livestock products may be justified if it adds to the total value of the product through maintaining prices at times of glut and keeping prices down by supplying the market when conditions of relative scarcity recur. If the selling price covers the costs of the operation, it is clear that the system has made the market work better. Even if the stock cannot be re-sold at a profitable price, it may be justified if the benefits of any stabilizing effect exceed the cost of holding the commodity. For products which store well the costs of holding for stabilization may be easily borne. However, most livestock products require specialist and expensive storage facilities. Marginal additions to stocks which can be handled by existing installations may cost little, but if more than this is required, storage of goods purchased at intervention is likely to prove very expensive. In extreme circumstances, lack of physical facilities for slaughter and storage may even make the system break down. Should this happen, the farmers' confidence in the CAP is likely to falter. If to maintain internal prices the product is ultimately dumped abroad at prices much below those of intervention, this involves real and potentially large losses to the Community.

The third proposed development of the CAP's price policy is designed to avoid the unintentional accumulation of very large intervention stocks of livestock products which can only be disposed of with the aid of export subsidies. It has two aspects. First, it is suggested that the gap between intervention and target prices for milk and beef be widened, so that the intervention takes place at levels which will just cover variable costs and interest on fixed investment for efficient producers. The Management Committees might retain discretionary power to intervene in order to steady markets at somewhat higher prices if these purchases seemed likely to be self-liquidating as a result of subsequent price rises. At the lower intervention price the Community would be required to purchase as at present. The second proposal is that goods purchased at intervention in excess of any desired level of stock should be resold within the Community. The recent sales of beef to pensioners at reduced prices point the way. Such schemes should be held in readiness, so that the first benefit of any unexpected surplus in supplies would go to those most in need. If sales through these channels prove insufficient to clear the market, the commodity concerned should be sold back to the commercial market. It is recognized that this would depress prices, result in larger deliveries to intervention and involve the intervention agency in losses, which would fall on the Community's budget. Such expenditures would be embarrassing to the Council of Ministers and cause them to seek to avoid policies which tended to over-expand production. Ultimately the taxpayer would have to bear any losses on these transactions. But provided the general tendency of the policy was not to promote continuous over-expansion by maintaining too-large margins in the long term, such expenditure would be infrequent and would represent a response to periodic crises in the livestock sector. At the same time the benefit of extra supplies would be enjoyed by Community consumers rather than by other countries. Because there would be no massive accumulation of stocks, the farmers' fear of a sudden breakdown in the price support system would be removed.

Milk causes more problems for the CAP than any other livestock product. It is the largest single item in livestock output and, taken together with beef, which is often a by-product of the dairy enterprise, accounts for about 60% of animal production in the Community of Nine. Milk production is especially important in the economics of small farms, many of whom have few alternative enterprises. It is thus a product of social and political as well as of economic significance. Fixing margins for milk producers involves numerous complex interactions. For example, buoyant beef prices may stimulate expansion in milk production in response to higher calf prices. Again, milk may be sold in many different manufactured forms. Over time, the appropriate price differentials for

45

manufactured milk products may require raw milk to be used for different proportions of butter, cheese and skimmed milk powder production. Changes cannot happen quickly and in the interim, shortages may force prices up or surpluses cause stocks to accumulate. Given the sensitivity of the milk market to so widespread a range of demand factors and the uncertainties of output stemming from year-to-year weather variations, it is most unlikely that any reasonably trouble-free method of organising this market can be devised.

The suggestions made in this study—fixing margins in relation to overall developments in supply and demand, providing some stability in margins against very large fluctuations in prices or costs and allowing the market greater scope to find commercial outlets before mandatory intervention occurs—are designed to promote confidence among farmers and foster lower cost production. By selling intervention purchases within the Community, future "butter mountains" would be avoided. Either the surplus would become a "stabilizing stock" or it would be sold initially to those in need. This would not remove the problem of the milk sector. Indeed, the process of encouraging low-cost production would itself tend to increase the difficulties of many small high-cost farmers. Thus, social and political pressures would be intensified. It was the contention of the 1970 Atlantic Institute study that such social pressures should not be allowed to distort production through the maintenance of high prices. Prices could only be reduced if effective action were taken to protect the more vulnerable members of the farming community. To meet this need, it was proposed that compensation should be paid if prices were cut. This analysis retains its validity. The extent to which milk production can be made to be more sensitive to economic requirements then depends on the credibility of alternative methods of safeguarding farm incomes. These are discussed later.

The Process of Structural Reform

The programme of structural reform within the Community should now give greater priority to reducing the cost of production. As it stands, structural policy is an amalgam of national measures and Community directives. There is in detail considerable variety in the policies pursued but their goal is common: to create holdings which can provide an income for those who work on farms equivalent to that of workers in other industrial sectors in the same locality. There can be no doubt that by raising the productivity of labour and of capital such schemes contribute to lower-cost production. There is, however, a natural wish to create as many "viable" holdings as possible. This approach tends to multiply the number of holdings which survive and make them less adaptable to changed price-cost relationships. In the short term they may remain viable. In the long run when a different pattern of agricultural output becomes appropriate, farmers

46

on such holdings may be unable to adapt or to apply a new technology. They then become high cost producers and may encounter severe income problems. Structural reform should then be mainly justified in terms of its ability to raise incomes through lower costs.

There is no more effective instrument of cost-reducing structural reform than the prospect of lower prices and tighter margins. Faced by such expectations the incentive for those farmers who have an earning capacity outside agriculture to leave the industry is increased. Those who remain are under pressure to adopt new cost-reducing methods, whether these are introduced as a result of enlarged holdings, consolidated farm land or the application of capital. Structural programmes, whether as part of the CAP or as national aids, can then attempt to assist such farmers. But they are not always easy to apply.

Some of the difficulties encountered may be illustrated. Improved farming methods require larger farms. Increasing farm size through structural reform represents an inescapable threat to existing land users and may involve some changes in the way in which land is owned. Deep divisions exist about the "right" form of land ownership and tenure. In some countries the rights of land ownership are carefully preserved. In others the tenant's position may be more heavily safeguarded. Some countries rely on voluntary agencies and the operation of the market to bring about land reform. Others give special pre-emptive rights to statutorily established reform agencies. Within a Community in which traditions are so different, it is unlikely that any single common approach to the problem of increasing farm size can be agreed.

Larger farms and improved methods require, too, fewer, and more skilled farmers and farm workers. Unlike most other businesses, farming has remained a family enterprise. The selection of new entrants has owed more to the accidents of birth than to systematic training and testing. Although this process appears archaic in a modern science-based industry, there are strong reasons for its survival. More than most businesses, farming is geographically dispersed and farm workers have considerable independence of action. To co-ordinate and control such actions by conventional bureaucratic process is expensive and may be ineffective. Family farming provides its own strong motivation. Again, farm work is a long-term undertaking. Good husbandry yields dividends years ahead. Neglect may impose no immediate penalties. For the family it may be sensible to take a long-term view which would seem irrelevant to an individual concerned only with the immediate problems of pleasing his masters.

The constraints on structural policy on a Community level are real. At the most, one can look for a partnership involving the farmer, the member governments and the Community. Progress is unlikely to be rapid and there is an ever-present risk that structural policy may enable high cost units to survive. One of the Community's main responsibilities seems then to be to ensure that structural aid itself is not allowed to overrule the operation of the market.

Advice and Research

Better production techniques represent a hopeful means of producing more at lower cost. Public policy helps at two levels, the finance of research and the provision of extension services. Scientific research into agriculture usually requires large institutions and expensive equipment. Its results are uncertain and, even when helpful, difficult to measure. In all countries therefore public research expenditures must from time to time be scrutinized in terms of their value to the public. Such reviews may lead to more effective research. The Community as such plays a very minor role in research but it should discourage any tendency to make indiscriminate cuts in the amount of support provided. International communication already takes place between professional bodies and through journals. A marginal improvement might result from more generous Community aids to help research workers within the Community meet in order to discuss common problems. The Community could also give some supplementary aid to research programmes which were promising but unlikely to secure adequate assistance from national governments.

Extension services operate in all Community countries. There is a great variety of organisation but in most countries advisers tend to emphasise the considerable gap between the best-known practices and those applied on many farms. Within the limitations of known technology, there are opportunities for improving the output of agriculture in Europe. The Community's contribution to extension work is presently limited to funding part of the cost of training socio-economic advisers. It is clearly an aspect of public policy in which detailed intervention from Brussels would be unlikely to succeed. Much must depend on activities which are locally controlled. However, it might be one of the more constructive ways in which financial support from common funds could supplement national efforts in the more backward regions.

We may summarise the present discussion as follows:

The contribution of Community farmers to the Community's food supplies must be assessed in the light of the world situation. If international agreements along the lines outlined earlier in this study are acceptable, then the problems of the internal price level will be simultaneously settled and farmers will be assured of a reasonably stable price for their product. If a more stable international environment cannot be obtained, the Council of Ministers must periodically assess the world food supply situation and determine its policy for Community agriculture in the light of its judgment. By providing greater confidence about margins, by promoting structural reforms which reduce costs and by encouraging the discovery and application of new methods, it may add to the Community's food supply at modest cost. World food prices seem particularly uncertain in the next few years, but an increase in domestic food production at low cost seems likely to be a welcome contribution to food supplies in the Community and in the world at large.

The proposals outlined here for ensuring that the Community's agriculture makes the best possible contributions to the EEC food supply do not envisage any fundamental change in the CAP. Prices are fixed by the Council of Ministers with the possibility of adjustment between annual "fixings" in order to ensure that they have the effect intended. Structural reform and agricultural improvement still depend primarily upon member states. Intervention is still the first means of maintaining the internal price level. Each of the innovations has a CAP precedent. The price adjustments of September 1974 represented an attempt to restore margins between annual "fixings." The schemes for subsidised sales of butter and beef represent a use of a "fall back" device for supporting livestock prices without accumulating excessive stocks. What is new is not the machinery but the attitude to its use. The CAP is seen as an instrument to ensure adequate food supplies at moderate and stable prices. It is a food policy as well as a farm policy.

The Agricultural Common Market and National Policies for Agriculture

The Common Agricultural Policy operates within a Community in which the policies of member governments continue to have an important influence on the agricultural and food industries. In general terms, it sets prices for agricultural commodities, ensures that they can move freely between member countries and contributes towards structural reform policies. Much still depends, however, upon decisions taken by member states.

Two areas of special sensitivity are discussed in this chapter: farm incomes, and border taxes and subsidies or the so-called monetary compensatory amounts.

The Common Agricultural Policy and Farm Incomes

An àgricultural policy which is directed towards the efficient use of resources within the Community will not ensure satisfactory incomes for all those currently engaged in agriculture. The Mansholt Plan of 1968 recognised that a lasting improvement in the living standards of the agricultural population required massive structural changes in the industry. The Atlantic Institute Study of 1970 accepted this analysis but drew especial attention to the need to adjust prices in order to remove existing surpluses and foster a healthy pattern of new investment. Such a price policy could only be undertaken if there existed an alternative means of protecting the incomes of those farmers who faced lower prices. The study proposed a device of this character.

The changed circumstances since 1974 have in no way destroyed the underlying logic of this argument. Although higher world prices have made it unnecessary to reduce nominal prices, rapid inflation has already cut the real value of CAP prices. Faced by lower real incomes, farmers now seek higher nominal prices. Indiscriminate price increases which fully offset inflation would, however, simply reproduce the imbalances between the prices of agricultural products which existed in the 1960s. Inevitably, surpluses would re-appear as soon as world prices turned down and expenditure on market support would tend to rise to very large amounts. If the Council of Ministers is to use the CAP to promote a more efficient agriculture within the Community, it must be able to reduce the margins on products which are in over-supply as well as expand those for which an unsatisfied market still exists. Whether within a more stable world market or in order to optimise agricultural production within a Community

50

which still has to insulate itself from disruptive fluctuations in international trade, there must still be freedom for prices to be moved downward as well as upward. Such freedom cannot be claimed at the expense of depressing still further the living standards of some of the least affluent of the Community's citizens. There remains then a need for an effective form of compensatory income payment. Since 1970 the Commission has published a study on *Agricultural Incomes in the Enlarged Community* [1]. This makes a valuable contribution towards understanding farm income problems as they affect agricultural policies. Some of the more important points it makes can be mentioned.

First, it indicates that in the period 1964-1970, farm incomes grew less rapidly than other incomes in all member countries except Italy and the UK [2]. A second feature of this report was the evidence it provided showing regional differences in agricultural incomes within the Community. The report suggests that during the 1960s farm incomes were rising more rapidly in the better than in the worst-placed agricultural regions. Thus the distribution of income within the agricultural industry may have become even more unequal. At the level of the individual farm business, the Commission's study confirms the long-held conviction that as farm sizes, measured in terms of units of production, increase, income per Year Work Unit tends to rise [3]. The study shows that incomes seem to be lower among older farmers. Since more than half the farmers in the Community are 57 or more years old, it may well be that there is a concentration of poverty among people of pensionable age. There exist, too, market differences in the incomes earned in different types of farming or "technico-economic orientations." Farms in the classes described as "bovines," "granivores-herbivores" and "herbivores-granivores" had in 1970 revenues per Year Work Unit less than 60% of those in the class "general agriculture."

The Commission's study does much to clarify discussion of farm incomes. It shows that not all farmers are in need. The large farmers, those whose farming is only a secondary source of revenue and those situated in the more prosperous parts of the Community, do not appear to suffer hardship. In contrast, farmers in disadvantaged regions, the small farmer and the older farmer do appear to have very poor incomes compared with most of the Community's people. A policy designed to bring about a lasting improvement must operate in three key areas, the redeployment of the agricultural labour force, the reorganisation of the physical resources of farming and the development of backward rural regions.

Natural circumstances may assist the redeployment of manpower. The age distribution among farmers is heavily skewed towards older men. Many such farmers have no successors; when they retire their land is likely to be available

---

1. SOEC 73 900.
2. Since in this period the UK had much lower prices than the Six, this information is at least consistent with the view that high prices in themselves may not improve the relative incomes of farmers.
3. Year Work Unit: the work of one person for at least 280 days or 2380 hours per year.

for enlarging other holdings. The passage of years will then reduce the number of farmers and, if the evidence of the Commissions's report proves right, allow a more technically competent group of farmers to take over. The development of part-time farming represents a relatively painless way of reducing the amount of labour employed. In the short run it raises income; in the long run, the proportion of time spent on the farm may fall. As the generations change, many part-time farms seem likely to disappear. Apart from retirement and an increase in part-time farming the rate of migration from agriculture depends upon the creation of suitable jobs in other sectors. This is a function of economic growth and is outside agricultural policy. To some extent the movement of manpower may be eased by policies which direct industrial investment to rural areas, but the scope for this must not be exaggerated. If such rurally located plants are not competitive or are unable to rely upon continued government subsidies, they may fail, leaving pockets of unemployment. Provided a flow of suitable jobs exists, expenditure on retraining farm workers and on vocational guidance may accelerate the redeployment of labour.

The reorganisation of farm land must depend on the existence of satisfactory arrangements for those whose land is absorbed by other farms or taken out of use. The governments of most European countries have attempted to counter the excessive fragmentation of farms and to enlarge holdings to a more viable size structure. Larger farms allow modern farm enterprises to operate nearer their optimum scale; therefore costs per unit of output tend to fall. Larger farms can attract and reward good quality trained farmers and farm managers. Such farmers are better able to assess new innovations and are more likely to succeed in their application. Larger farms are also capable of more flexibility in their technico-economic orientation. This makes them better able to withstand temporary setbacks in some lines of production and also more capable of adapting their emphasis to longer-run changes in relative profitability. From the Community's point of view the progressive reorganisation of the physical assets of farming is of great long-run importance. It offers not only higher incomes for those engaged in farming, but also the prospect of less costly farm production.

There are some regions of the Community, the mountainous and hilly areas especially, in which the future of any agricultural activity seems doubtful. The process of farm enlargement, the application of modern farming methods and the introduction of very skilled management seem unlikely to allow a satis-factory income to be earned from farming in such regions. Inevitably the popu-lation tends to leave, local communities break up and the regions may become desolate. The agricultural output of these areas is not needed to meet the Community's food supplies. If it were, prices would rise to cover production costs and the process of depopulation cease. The justification of continued agricultural activity must then rest on a judgment that for non-food reasons it is important to keep such areas populated. Many such reasons may be offered. Farming may keep the countryside open for leisure activities; it may help to preserve the environment, it may safeguard some precious rural, cultural characteristics. It may be desired to keep a population in an area for strategic reasons. Policies which are intended to assist agriculture in disadvantaged areas must then be justified in special terms and should employ devices which support the incomes of those producers it is intended to help. This rules out price policies.

The process of structural reform and the use of discriminatory aids to support "less-favoured regions" may help towards an improvement in farm incomes in the longer term. Success in raising the incomes of most of those engaged in farming must, however, depend upon the pace at which new opportunities are created outside agriculture.

Within the Community, decisions about the direction of the economy remain with the governments of member countries. Inflation, incentives to investment, the overall balance between public revenues and public expenditures are but a few of the crucial policy areas in which there exists no common policy. Since the level of employment is greatly influenced by such decisions, it is clear that the Community cannot control the rate at which new jobs appear. Regional policy may make some contribution, but the limited amount the Community is to spend in this direction suggests that its immediate influence over the distribution of industry will be small. As a result, the policies which exist within member countries may remain the most important instruments by which new employment can be directed toward rural areas.

It is the object of the Community to create an integrated European economy within which goods and resources are free to move. The management of such an economy by nine separate governments seems likely to become more, rather than less difficult as economic interpenetration proceeds. Only concerted policies relating to issues such as employment and inflation are likely to avoid growing stresses between the members. Concerted policies, however, are cumbersome to negotiate and likely to reflect the shifting political situation within member countries rather than the needs of the Community. There is then a strong case for a closer economic union within which central issues of economic management would be decided on a common basis. Part of this process would include monetary union and measures to assist those parts of the Community which were least able to compete. Given such authority the Community might properly accept responsibility for the income level of its citizens.

Economic union seems, however, less attainable now than appeared to be the case during the 1960s. Divergent trends in member country economies have made the maintenance of fixed exchange rates impossible. In some quarters there is a greater tendency to stress the separate national identities of member states and to view the Community almost wholly in terms of national self-interest. This is disappointing for those who take an idealistic view of European Unity, but if the Community is unlikely to attain control of economic and monetary policy in the member states, it cannot accept sole responsibility for maintaining personal income levels.

53

Agricultural incomes have been an exception to this rule. Since the Community has taken authority to determine the level of farm prices through the CAP, it cannot evade responsibility for changes in incomes that modifications in its price policy may bring about. If member states were allowed complete freedom to raise the incomes of their own farmers, competition within the Community might be severely distorted. In the more prosperous member countries, where the opportunity cost of the farmer's labour was higher, greater income supports would be justified. There would, however, be an incentive to give excessively generous income subsidies. If too much were given, agricultural production would tend to be continued where costs were high and cut back in poorer countries where costs were low—the precise reverse of the changes which would be in the interest of the Community as a whole.

The extent to which the incomes of the agricultural population can be raised depends not only on the prices fixed for farm goods but, in the long run, even more upon the creation of new jobs off the farm. The Rome Treaty, article 39.1 (b), foresees an improvement in farm incomes as a result of increased productivity and the optimum utilization of all agricultural factors of production. The CAP may make a contribution to increased productivity through creating a stable framework within which investment in improved methods will be encouraged and structural reform accelerated. It must do so in cooperation with the policies of member governments in other sectors of the economy.

A widespread improvement in the relative incomes of people in agriculture compared with those of workers in the rest of the economy is unlikely to be attained quickly. In the meantime, the Community needs freedom to use a flexible price policy to regulate agricultural production and to permit a better relationship between domestic production and the world market. Before flexibility can be exercised, arrangements which will maintain farmers' incomes despite adverse movements in prices are required.

There may, from time to time, be irresistible pressures on the governments of member states to relieve hardship in depressed rural areas. Such aids must be encouraged on humanitarian grounds but the Community should ensure that they do not distort agricultural production or trade. Aids of this type are likely to be financed initially from national budgets, as are most social payments made in other sectors of the economy. As the Community develops the activities of its own Social Fund, this may enable it to play a more active part in helping poor people within the EEC, in whatever industry they work. It would also facilitate a common approach to the problems of economic adjustment within the Community. The proposals made for income compensation in the 1970 report provide a pattern which is still relevant. For example, it could be used in present circumstances to compensate vulnerable farmers for cuts in real income resulting from any failure to adjust CAP prices for the full effect of inflation. More generally, it affords a device which could enable a policy designed to reduce agricultural production costs to take place without personal

54

hardship for many existing farmers. Because it gives aid in a way that does not stimulate increased production, it avoids many of the worst distortions associated with national aids to agriculture.

The new method of financing stocks through credit as proposed in Chapter III creates new possibilities for the Community to play a more positive role in income support and structural reform. Because budgetary expenditure on export subsidies and stock holding would be reduced, the CAP would be enabled to do more to help promote improved efficiency in agriculture and to relieve the poverty of those whose incomes were least satisfactory.

In the period of rapid price inflation experienced since 1972, member governments have tended to increase their own aids to agriculture. These are sometimes directed towards specifically structural policies but they often are of a more general character, for example, tax reliefs or subsidized fuel costs. The introduction of such subsidies represents a setback for the CAP and it is tempting to conclude that it is fruitless to try to control the policies of member governments. Attention should, it might be argued, concentrate on trade between member countries and the implementation of measures to prevent gross intra-Community dumping. Such discussions might centre on the appropriate level of border taxes or subsidies. Despite its attractions such a move would be defeatist. It would be a grave setback for the longer-run development of the Community. Differential national aids would almost certainly be more generous in the rich than the poor member countries. As a result, the division between the rich and poor countries would widen and the prospects of close links within the Community be seriously impaired.

It remains necessary therefore to control all national aids, which may differ in degree and type according to local traditions and the character and needs of local agriculture. The Commission already investigates such aids. This monitoring function is vital to the health of the Community. It should be continued and its results made public. Increasingly such as the one proposed in the 1970 report, national aids should be limited to those which are neutral in terms of their effect on production. Where national aids which do affect production are used, by promoting structural reform, for example, they should be limited to those which fit within the framework of Community policy. This does not require a uniformity of method inappropriate in so diverse a situation, but it does require that agricultural production should be steered in a direction which is consistent with the interests of all member countries.

Border Taxes and Subsidies

Trade of all types has expanded markedly during the Community's early life. Between 1964 and 1971 total exports grew by 135%, total imports by 121%. Agricultural trade also grew: exports by 141%, imports by 71%. Intra-Community trade has grown rather more quickly than trade with the rest of the world: important evidence of the effect of the Common Market. Trade in agricultural products has apparently been even more influenced than trade in other goods. Intra-EEC agricultural exports rose by 212% compared with 141% for agricultural exports as a whole, and intra-EEC imports by 213% compared with 71% for total agricultural imports.

This very large increase in agricultural trade between member countries is regarded as a major achievement and is highly prized by those who export agricultural products. The higher prices maintained by the CAP for intra-Community trade added to their earnings during the 1960s. Had all exports been sold at world prices, substantial subsidies from national funds would have been needed. Alternatively, painful cuts in domestic agriculture would have been inescapable. More recently it has been the turn of agricultural importers to benefit. Export levies have kept some agricultural prices below world market prices and supplies which might have been consigned to the world market have been available for consumption within the Community. These are important advantages in an uncertain world and should strengthen awareness of the mutual gains provided by the CAP.

Although the CAP does ensure that, to a greater degree than before, goods can move between member countries, all is not plain sailing. Regulations concerning health and hygiene, national tax systems and rigidities within food marketing systems all limit movement. There are no short cuts to the removal of these obstacles. Given the will, the harmonisation of regulations and tax systems and improved marketing information may gradually create a market within which products may sell as readily in another Community country as in the country of origin. Even so, it is likely to be a very long time before a single market exists within the EEC. Differences in traditional methods of taxation and in health regulations often reflect real differences in the circumstances of each country. For example, a policy of vaccination against foot-and-mouth disease may be helpful in countries where it is endemic; in countries which are normally free from the disease it may add to problems. There is a need for flexibility and common sense in the pursuit of harmonisation, lest the process of creating a single market become a source of disunity within the Community. At the same time, the Community must not lose sight of the goal of creating a competitive market throughout this area.

The most evident impediment to a single market for agriculture in the Community has not arisen from lack of harmonization but from monetary problems.

Since 1968, variations in exchange rates have been frequent and substantial. The pound sterling has floated downwards since the UK entered the Community. The Deutschmark has consistently increased in value. Governments have been unwilling to implement the price changes necessary to keep the prices received by farmers uniform in terms of units of account. Instead, the system of border taxes and subsidies—or MCAs—has been introduced to allow for differences in prices and to prevent speculation in agricultural goods.

Taxes are imposed on imports to countries whose currencies have risen in value and on exports from countries where the currency has depreciated, and subsidies are granted on imports to devaluing countries, as well as on exports from revaluing countries.

In principle this system permits trade between member states to continue at the unit of account prices fixed by the Council. In practice it allows countries to have different internal price levels, it re-creates the frontiers which a common market should remove and it involves immensely complicated administrative problems for the Commission, the customs authorities and private traders. Since traders have to contend both with uncertainties about money exchange rates and with uncertainties about changes in the way MCAs are administered, margins must be widened and consumer prices raised. Costs are incurred by national governments and by the Commission, who have to work out the MCAs and monitor their operation.

The Community has accepted border taxes and subsidies because no other instrument seemed likely to cope with the problem of changes in exchange rates without greater disruption to the flow of trade. An alternative to MCAs would be a system of taxes or subsidies provided within the member country. For example, a country which devalued might allow goods to enter at CAP prices but provide a subsidy to consumers equivalent to the depreciation of their currency. The subsidy would have to be paid not only on imported items but also on domestic production. If it were not, home produced goods would tend to flow to other Community countries. Conversely, a country whose currency rose in value might continue to import at CAP prices, but provide a subsidy for farmers to maintain their prices unchanged. Such schemes are cumbersome, expensive, likely to generate anomalous situations and unlikely to be capable of introduction or modification quickly enough to keep pace with the frequent changes in exchange rates. If, however, the relation between EEC and internal prices is to be adjusted at the frontier, then border taxes and subsidies are inevitable. On balance, their disadvantages seem less than those of alternative schemes to produce the same end

The Commission is anxious to reduce and eventually eliminate MCAs. Ultimately it is hoped monetary union will make such devices unnecessary. At present, however, stresses arising from the oil price increases and the higher prices of food and raw materials suggest that changes in the rate of exchange between member country currencies are likely to be a recurrent feature of economic life in the imminent future. At this stage it seems that the introduction of a single European currency would have to be accompanied by arrangements to make very large transfers from strong to weak member countries. If this were not done high levels of unemployment might occur in the less competitive regions of the Community. Neither large financial transfers nor higher levels of unemployment are politically acceptable. One must then conclude that monetary union is at this stage an aspiration rather than a practical possibility. There is thus a prospect of compensatory amounts becoming a lasting feature of the CAP.

This is not a satisfactory situation. It represents an internal contradiction. The object of compensatory amounts is to prevent the adjustments in consumer and producer behaviour which changes in exchange rates are intended to bring about. As a result the extent of adjustment needed in other sectors, and in other countries, in order to attain equilibrium is enlarged. For example, a country which revalues but applies compensatory amounts prevents a contraction in its own agriculture. Resources which would otherwise have moved to other activities remain on the farm. At the same time, because the volume of production is maintained, the opportunities for other countries to export to the strong currency area are reduced. Thus other currencies are weakened and the capacity of revaluation to achieve a better balance between exports and imports impaired. Countries which devalue but apply compensatory amounts equally tend to frustrate the purpose of the adjustment. Consumption and imports are maintained, domestic agriculture is not encouraged; indeed, since costs rise it may be discouraged.

The paradox of this procedure is demonstrated by the fact that if countries applied the compensatory amount method to all transactions, non-agricultural as well as for agriculture, the capacity of exchange rate changes to restore balance to a country's external payments would be destroyed. Agriculture is treated as an exception for three reasons. First, food prices are a sensitive political issue and their increase may have a more than proportional inflationary effect. Second, the agricultural sector provides employment for many poor farmers whose incomes it is wished to protect. Third, to operate without compensatory amounts, the CAP requires that all official prices be adjusted at once and by the full extent of the parity change. In other sectors price changes resulting from changed parities occur less rapidly and may not involve a shift corresponding to the whole of the changed value of the currency.

In present circumstances monetary compensatory amounts seem inevitable. Used to buy time whilst more fundamental measures are taken to check inflation or safeguard vulnerable groups of farmers, they may have a valuable smoothing effect following changes in exchange rates. They should not, however, become permanent, allowing different internal price levels to persist indefinitely in member countries. Nor should they so defer the consequences of changes in exchange rates as to encourage governments to resort too lightly to devaluation or revaluation. Two steps are now needed, the gradual elimination of existing MCAs and a marked diminution in the extent to which new MCAs will be allowed to offset the discomforts of exchange rate manipulations.

To deal with existing MCAs it is proposed that the Community should gradually reduce the proportion of the difference between prevailing levels of exchange and Smithsonian parities which member countries are allowed to offset by border taxes and subsidies. At the moment, no MCAs are payable for adjustments up to 2 1/2%. This margin of nil adjustment would be progressively increased, say at six monthly intervals, so that the level of MCAs on changes greater than 2 1/2% would gradually fall. During this period governments would have an opportunity to give other forms of aid to poor farmers or vulnerable consumers and to take steps to counter inflation. To clarify this suggestion the principles involved are illustrated in the Table below. The numbers used are purely notional.

Assumptions:

(a) Initial Smithsonian parity 2°0 u.a. per member country currency unit (e.g. £)

(b) New exchange rate 1°5 u.a. per £

(c) At outset full devaluation covered by MCA

(d) Each six months the amount uncovered rises by 5% of initial exchange rate.

Table 7

Period		MCA [1]	Per cent of change from initial parity covered by MCA	Per cent of change from initial parity not covered by MCA [2]
Year I	Months 1-6	0°5 u.a.	25	0
	Months 7-12	0°4 u.a.	20	5
Year II	Months 1-6	0°3 u.a.	15	10
	Months 7-12	0°2 u.a.	10	15
Year III	Months 1-6	0°1 u.a.	5	20
	Months 7-12	Nil	0	25

Notes:
1. MCA=Subsidy on imports from other members and tax on exports to them per unit of the devaluing currency.
For revaluing countries the direction of taxes and subsidies would be reversed.
2. Internal price levels of member states must be changed where MCAs are inadequate to cover changes in exchange rates.

Applying this method, the MCA existing in Year I would be eliminated by the end of Year III. At the same time, the member country government would have been under increasing pressure to provide other forms of assistance to groups adversely affected by the implicit price changes.

Application of this principle would gradually eliminate existing MCAs. To cope with future parity changes it is suggested that MCAs are limited to two thirds of the difference between the existing and any new rate of exchange. They would then be subject to the gradual elimination process suggested for existing MCAs. This change would compel governments to take into account from the outset some of the discomforts from allowing their currencies to appreciate or depreciate. It would not remove altogether the smoothing effect of MCAs where the case for a new exchange rate was very strong, but it would contribute marginally to the case for stability when such were being considered. Greater stability in exchange rates between member countries would help the smooth working of the Community, not least of the Common Agricultural Policy.

The implication of this second suggestion combined with the gradual widening of the extent to which changed rates of exchange are not offset by MCAs are illustrated by an extension of the previous table.

Additional assumptions:

(a) In Year IV there is a further devaluation leaving the rate at 1°25 u.a. per unit of member country's currency (£)
   (i) The new parity is 37 1/2% below the initial Smithsonian rate
   (ii) The new parity is 0°25 u.a. below the previous level
(b) Rule 1 for the gradual elimination of MCAs implies that any change in parity up to 25% of the initial level is not eligible for MCA treatment. Thus, only 12 1/2% now qualifies for MCAs.
(c) Rule 2 for new exchange rate changes requires that any new MCA must not cover more than two thirds of the total devaluation. Thus the MCA or a change of 0°25 u.a. must not exceed 0°165 u.a.

Table 8

Period		MCA [1]		% of change from initial parity covered	% of change from initial parity not covered by MCA
Year IV	Months 1-6	Rule 1	°25	12 1/2	25
		Rule 2	°165		
	Months 7-12	Rule 1	°15	7 1/2	30
		Rule 2	°165		
Year V	Months 1-6	Rule 1	°05	2 1/2	35
		Rule 2	°165		
	Months 7-12	Rule 1	Nil	0	37 1/2
		Rule 2	°165		

1. The effective MCA is the lower of these calculated by either rule. The rule suggested for new MCAs has the effect that compensation is initially below the point equivalent to that paid on existing departures from Smithsonian parity. The process of gradually reducing MCAs ultimately reduces them below this level, in the second half of Year IV in terms of the figures used in the illustration. By the end of Year V all MCAs have once more been extinguished.

Detailed rules for the elimination of MCAs would be agreed by the Council of Ministers at the outset. Once they have been decided, the progressive elimination of MCAs would be assured although the device would still exist as a method of easing the process of adjustment implicit in any future changes in exchange rates. The smooth working of the CAP would be eased if the percentage by which MCAs were reduced was relatively large and the step-by-step increases frequent. There must, however, be a real opportunity for governments to take other steps to cope with the problems facing farmers when currencies are revalued or consumers when currencies depreciate. By ensuring that exchange rate changes are allowed to work in agriculture these changes should help production to be relocated within the Community in response to economic forces. To prevent such changes is to perpetuate the situation in which no truly common market for farm goods can exist within the Community.

Conclusion

Agricultural policies are made by governments for their own people. International repercussions of decisions about domestic farming policy are often regarded as of secondary importance. The European Community in creating the CAP has had to contend with complex internal problems. A single internal market has had to be reconciled with the need to attain a balance between members and to shield poorer farmers from a decline in their incomes.

The changed world outlook since 1972 has made this tendency to economic isolationism inappropriate. No longer can it be assumed that world prices will be below CAP prices or that there exist abundant supplies to make up any deficiency in EEC output. As the largest world trader in food, the Community must consider both the opportunities and the hazards of the new situation. The contribution of the Community's agriculture to food supplies has grown in importance. At the same time there is a greater need for the Community to exercise its influence towards a more stable and rational system of world trade.

This study has attempted to contribute to this re-appraisal. It stresses the importance of an international solution and suggests means by which this might come about. Greater stability in food prices is in the interests of both exporters and importers but it is likely to prove elusive unless there is some co-operation on stock-holding among the major trading countries. Such co-operation can provide more stability with lower physical stocks. The necessary condition is good behaviour among all who seek to benefit both in terms of their internal policies and in terms of their own stock-holding operations. Although this may limit the number of countries who are able to work together, it does not seem unlikely that in current circumstances some of the major developed market economies would be willing to accept the constraints of greater co-operation as a price for more stable prices.

The Community must safeguard its own food supplies and if this cannot be done through international agreement, it may require an increase in self-sufficiency. Even within a framework of co-operation it seems likely that additional European farm output would be welcome, provided it is secured at low cost. Expansion of this nature is a long term project requiring new investment on farms, this structural reform of the industry and the introduction of new technology based on research. Increasingly, the role of the CAP must be to create an environment within which these processes can take place. Although the details of structural reform must depend on national governments and the role of the CAP in research and extension is minimal, by its price policies and by its co-ordinating function the Community can still exercise a strong influence. Provided prices are set at reasonable levels, the accumulation of unwanted stocks may be avoided.

A short-run surplus situation should not be thought of as grounds for subsidising exports. If stocks become too high then prices must be lowered and agricultural resources directed to different activities. For livestock, this study suggests that where large surpluses arise prices should be cut to clear the market. Initially, reduced prices might be limited to poorer consumers, but if necessary the Community should not shrink from more general price cuts.

This study argues that the problem of low farm incomes cannot be appropriately handled within the context of the CAP alone. Neither prices nor structural policies are adequate to deal with the need to create employment in other sectors and to maintain incomes for those who although their earnings in agriculture are poor cannot find other jobs. In the long run, as the Community assumes control over economic policy, it must accept responsibility for all incomes, agricultural as well as others.

For the present, however, the framework within which developments in the level and distribution of incomes in agriculture as in other sectors are determined depends on the decisions of member governments. In so far as the Community has taken practical steps to raise farm incomes, these have been mainly concerned to maintain the level of agricultural prices. This is a bad way to help low-income farmers, most of whom have relatively little to sell and thus gain only minor benefits from the high prices. It is, too, a socially undesirable way of helping farmers because it benefits mainly large farmers, many of whom are relatively rich, and imposes burdens on poor consumers who spend a larger than average proportion of their incomes on food. However, the Community does have a special responsibility to ensure that adjustments in agricultural prices, which it controls, do not result in severe hardship for those farmers who are affected. It still needs a method of compensation for price changes. The Community has the additional duty of supervising national aids to farmers so that they do not conflict with the concept of competition within the Community. As the Regional Fund and the Social Fund increase their activities, the Community may be able to play a growing part in the longer-term improvement of farm incomes. At this stage it must not disguise from the member states their own responsibilities in these matters.

The CAP has made a great contribution to the development of the Community but in recent years agricultural policy has tended to exemplify disunity rather than convergence among members. The difficulties arise because of changes which have taken place outside the CAP itself. Rapid inflation has so raised farmers' costs as to encourage governments to resort to national aids and special tax reliefs. The enlargement of the Community has created problems in relation to the financial equity of the Budget, a Budget dominated by agricultural expenditure. Changing parities have restored frontiers and generated the complications of compensatory amounts.

The proposals made in this study should help to restore a convergence of interest between member countries. By removing border taxes and subsidies although in a gradual way and with new transitional arrangements if future changes of parity take place, the unity of the agricultural market will be restored. Within such a reunited agricultural common market internal free trade will take place and the principle of comparative advantage be allowed to operate. By protecting margins from dramatic changes as a result of cost increases, there will be no need for unilateral government action to counter the impact of inflation on farmers' incomes. By making prices responsive to the needs of the Community for farm production in the light of supplies available both from the world market and from EEC producers, the balance between exporters and importers, consumers and producers will be maintained. In these ways, the development of the CAP may bring about more harmony between members and a deepening commitment to the concept of a Community.

Europe's Economic Security

Non-energy issues in the international political economy

WOLFGANG HAGER

Introduction

It has become commonplace to say that we are living in an age of economic interdependence. Since World War II, the volume of global trade has grown at a rate almost twice as fast as that of global output. International capital movements have increased greatly, and so have movements of workers, skills, and technology. The interpenetration of national economies has proceeded to such an extent that now, in some European countries, trade accounts for upwards of half of gross national product. Even in the United States, long regarded as one of the world's most closed economies, the ratio of trade to GNP has presently reached above 7 percent.

The interdependence of the world economy was both a cause and a result of the design of the postwar economic order. The architects of the Bretton Woods twins (the IMF and IBRD) and the GATT genuinely believed that free trade and investment were vital instruments of world peace. With markets equally open to all, nations would have no need to resort to the weapons of economic warfare as they had in the 1930s. The tide of economic nationalism would be stemmed, and with it the forces of political and military nationalism as well. Hence the principles of liberalism, multilateralism, nondiscrimination, and reciprocity that were built into all of the postwar economic institutions. In turn, these principles fostered a rapid growth of flows of goods, funds, and factors across frontiers. All countries participated in the international division of labor, and all had some share in the resulting gains of income and productivity.

But as Dr. Hager emphasizes in this informed and perceptive study, interdependence has two sides. One is the welfare benefit from efficient factor allocation, economies of scale, and accelerated economic growth. The other, darker side is the threat to national economic security. As Richard Cooper has written, interdependence restricts national autonomy "by embedding each country in a matrix of constraints which it can influence only slightly, often only indirectly, and without certainty of effect". As interdependence grows, so too does the matrix of constraints. And as the constraints grow, so too does the feeling of a country that it is not interdependent but, rather, *dependent*—conditioned by outside events and unable to determine its own fate.

Dependence has two aspects. First, it implies a high measure of sensitivity to external forces: dependent economies are unable to avoid being influenced by events elsewhere. And second, it involves a high measure of vulnerability, that is, irreversibility of impact: dependent economies are unable to override the influence of events elsewhere. Together, these mean that foreign economies have an implicit veto power over the capability of domestic decision-makers (private or official) to direct the evolution of the local economy. Options for behavior— the essence of security—are lost.

Not that dependence is necessarily shameful, or even painful. Dependence is simply the price one pays for the benefits of a division of labor—the logical corollary of interdependence. This is as true of the individual family as it is of the family of nations. All participants are dependent to a greater or lesser extent.

But there, of course, is the catch: "to a greater or lesser extent ". Like Orwell's equals, in any system of interdependence, even though all participants are dependent, some may be more dependent than others. This also is as true of the individual family as it is of the family of nations. Interdependence can be *asymmetrical*—some participants being dependent in many respects, others in just a few. It is when such asymmetries become pronounced that feelings of insecurity begin to grow.

Feelings of insecurity are nothing new to the less developed countries of the world. Dr. Hager remarks the *dependencia* debate of the fifties and center-periphery arguments of the sixties. LDCs (*) have long chafed under the "rules of the game" of the postwar economic order. For many of them—despite much evidence to the contrary—liberalism, multilateralism, and all the rest are simply so many chains that bind them into relations of "neo-colonial" dependence and exploitation. Income and productivity may gain, they argue, but their own share is far too small—and even the "crumbs off the table" are purchased at the price of lost autonomy. Such arguments are of course what lie behind LDC demands for A New International Economic Order in the seventies.

Now it is the turn of the Western World to experience growing feelings of insecurity. A variety of historical circumstances have combined to threaten the autonomy of the advanced industrial nations—including, not least, the collective efforts of the LDCs themselves. The rich are discovering that interdependence is a two-way street: OPEC has demonstrated that there are also asymmetries in the international economy favoring the poor. The time is ripe, therefore, for reconsideration of the problem of western security and world resources. Dr. Hager's study could hardly come at a more opportune moment.

Dr. Hager makes his focus Western Europe, reviewing the issue of economic security from the perspective of trade relations, and provides a comprehensive analysis of European dependence on foreign markets and sources of supply.

(*) Less Developed Countries.

Broad in scope, his discussion is also deep in insight. His conclusions warrant serious consideration. Like the recent Atlantic Paper by Miriam Camps on *"First World" Relationships: The Role of the OECD,* this Atlantic Paper makes an important contribution to the expanding world debate on global economic management.

Benjamin J. Cohen

Associate Professor of International Economic Relations,
Fletcher School of Law and Diplomacy Tufts University
and
Visiting Research Associate,
Atlantic Institute for International Affairs, Paris.

Foreword

The sense of crisis in the world economy that has made economic security an issue in the 1970s is clearly linked to the collapse of the postwar monetary system and the energy crisis of 1973. This essay deals with neither of these issues, for no better reason than that enough has been said and written about them already. Instead, this essay deals with trade questions linking these with concerns arising out of the present world recession: the management of the economy, and the prospects for long-term stable growth. After a discussion of the nature of economic security, and the domestic economic parameters that are vulnerable to outside economic influence, the essay turns to the various ways in which Europe's dependence on the world market represents a threat to economic security in the short and long term. This part of the essay therefore questions the somewhat unthinking consensus that has seen the economic and political security of the West linked to an ever increasing economic interdependence among nations. The last part deals with the security of Europe's supply of raw materials, again linking this issue with the broader concerns of international economic management in general.

The author would like to thank the Atlantic Institute for International Affairs for its support of this study.

Paris, Bonn, November 20, 1975
Wolfgang Hager

Economic Security

Paradise Lost

A foreign, economic, or finance minister looking at his agenda in the mid-seventies must think with regret of the straightforward sixties and fifties. By comparison with today, this was a simpler world, and certainly a more ordered one. Domestically, the goal of getting richer, although not the only aim, had an overriding priority; it thereby simplified foreign economic policy. Getting richer meant maximizing efficiency, efficiency meant maximizing market forces, and this in turn provided a basic complementarity that made economic exchanges among nations into positive sum games. The international economic system conceived in the mid-forties and put into operation by the late fifties seemed to fit the straightforward, uncomplicated goal structure of the times.

François Duchêne has aptly called this world of great hopes and intellectual certainties a *belle époque* [1]. The habit of international co-operation and the growing skill of bureaucrats and politicians in the art of international communication are perhaps the most enduring legacies of this brief period—little more than a decade—when the great dreams of the planners of the postwar system, the Harry Dexter Whites and the John Maynard Keyneses, were realized.

Yet that system, or rather the truncated version which smaller men were willing to accept, [2] suffered from two major flaws. One was the limited scope of its institutions and their limited capacity for discretionary, innovative, and managerial action. These tasks fell, by default, to a single country, the United States. The system would function as long as the United States had the power and will to make it function. And this power depended not only on a substantial margin over others in the assets of international politics, wealth, and military power, but also on the limited need to use that power. As in all political systems, leadership of the Western world depended on the consent of the led. This consent could be lost either because leadership was used not in the pursuit of global welfare, or because it was abused to serve national goals of the leading power. This was clearly the case when the country in charge of the world's money debased the coinage. But consent could also be lost, because the consensus on values, which had reduced international negotiation to a debate on tactics rather than on strategy, broke down.

1. *The Crisis of International Cooperation,* Triangle Paper, No. 1, 1973.
2. Cf. Richard Gardner, *Sterling-Dollar Diplomacy,* Oxford, 1956.

For here was a second flaw in the system: its values did not correspond to the broad development of practical political economy within the participating countries after the war. Its economics in many ways were those of the pre-World War I days of the gold standard, and perhaps equally important, worked best if its constituent parts adhered to equally classic concepts of *laissez faire*. Instead, the system came to consist of welfare states and welfare cases. In the welfare states ever broader conceptions of social security meant an increasing involvement of the state in conjunctural management; in the maintenance not only of full employment but, increasingly, of security of tenure for all in their chosen occupation; in maintaining certain types of industry, in creating others, and in influencing the location of such industries, etc. In the language of welfare economics, the state—not from a theoretical base but under the pressure of practical politics and the shared perceptions of its citizens—began to cope with the "externalities" of market economics, to pursue the broader public goals which are not automatically satisfied through the "invisible hand," the aggregate effect of the sum of microeconomic decisions. Older, nineteenth-century ideas of welfare—taking care of those too weak and unable to cope in an otherwise healthy world of competition—blended imperceptibly with the newer needs. This ensured a remarkable similarity between right- and left-of-centre policies.

To most international economists, the new tasks of the state seem irritating and illegitimate impediments to the achievement of a richer and more perfect world. The new instruments—regional policy, industrial policy, environmental legislation, subsidies of one kind and another—are summed up under the dry term "non-tariff barriers," to be put in the dock in multilateral trade negotiations. Capital controls, the attempt of governments to have a say over where national savings are to be put to productive use, are dismissed as retrograde steps which prevent the efficient allocation of factors.

It is the gradual rejection of the central legitimizing concept of the liberal world order, the maximization of global welfare (in the narrow sense of monetary wealth), which has perhaps struck the most mortal blow to the old system. The first to reject this concept in words—though all had in deeds—were the developing countries. These were later joined by the raw-material exporting countries, including those that are members of the OECD. Under the global welfare maximization model it was seen that unequal gains from a liberal world order could be rationalized by a thesis, unassailable on theoretical grounds, that every one would be better-off if factors were allocated more efficiently. A partial critique of this system was attempted with economic arguments, notably the infant-industry argument, but most of the critique has been based on (a) the empirical evidence that the simple efficiency criterion of the global model led to substantial "externalities" (the "wrong" sort of growth occurred—socially regressive and with the priorities set by outside forces); and (b) that the equally simplistic assumption of the model, that is, the existence of an atomistic international market place, was patently absurd. The issue of unequal power is the common theme of the successive critiques of the prevailing system: from the *dependencia*

72

debate of the fifties, to the centre-periphery arguments of the sixties and the debate on multinationals.

One of the most attractive features of the classic postwar system was its guarantee of equality, as the strong and the weak were submitted to the same rules. The new heresy dismisses the formal equality of opportunity as irrelevant and judges the performance of the system by the equality of results. Besides— and a very important besides—the strong retained the ability to interpret the rules, and if these no longer suited them, to change the rules.

The sixties saw the great achievements of trade liberalization and the phenomenal growth of international investment, but the value of power came to intrude explicitly into the simple world where every nation lives under the law. Interest groups began to form: UNCTAD and the European Community in the field of external trade. Their example was successfully followed by the Lomé Associates, who in the recent negotiations with the Community reaped the full benefits of solidarity. The Andean group with some success began to strengthen its negotiating position vis-à-vis foreign capital. But the breakthrough seemed to have come when the success of OPEC opened up an important new source of power: raw material power. With its help, international negotiation moved explicitly away from the allocation of marginal advantages within a given system, and turned to the constitution of the system itself. The founders of the postwar system had talked about the new international economic order which was to replace the chaos of the thirties. A generation later a new constitutional debate was started: However, the demands for A New International Economic Order, for most Western governments at least, spelled the loss of any order at all.

The inherent disadvantage of revisionism, indeed synonymous with it, is the necessity to change and, more often than not, to break the rules of the past. Those with power can usually gain consent, however reluctantly given, for a change in rules. Such was the case in the Smithsonian Agreement which ratified the inconvertibility of the dollar; such was the case, more or less, with the Community's Mediterranean policy, [3] which breached the anti-discriminatory principles of GATT. Those with less power will find it necessary to act unilaterally, to break the rules, and to present their partners with *faits accomplis*.

Badly handled, a period of revisionism is one in which contracts cease to have validity, a period of uncertainty and of great danger. Economic security as an issue is linked to the crisis of the international system.

In many ways, therefore, the appropriate level of analysis is the international system, not Western Europe. Indeed, much of the analysis which follows deals with global issues. Yet, as was argued earlier, the very roots of the crisis stem from a national as opposed to a global definition of interest. While neither Western Europe nor the European Community represents a nation, they do form a group with distinct and common interests, with comparable problems, with

3. Cf. Wolfgang Hager, "The Community and the Mediterranean," in Max Kohnstamm and Wolfgang Hager, eds., *A Nation Writ Large?*, London, MacMillan, 1973.

common societal and economic characteristics, and with instruments for common action in the field of foreign economic policy.

There is a contrary school of thought which argues with the help of impressive evidence, that the global crisis, which is the symptom of the deeper, constitutional crisis—oil, the recession, the world monetary system—has rendered the Community obsolete as a framework for problem-solving. The Atlantic system —witness the formation of the International Energy Agency, the intensified monetary co-operation in the OECD support fund and in the Group of Five, the intensive consultations on conjunctural policy—has regained an importance for Europe in the field of economic policy unparalleled since the days of the Marshall Plan. For long-term issues of truly global significance—food, the oceans, future energy supplies, and the welfare of the Third World—the United Nations and its present and future agencies (World Bank, IMF, FAO, etc.) seem predestined to play a role much larger than in the long years of seeming decline.

Yet the Community has not become any more obsolete than the nations that compose it. The key question is not where issues are ultimately dealt with, but at which level interests are formulated and brought to bear in the larger bargaining process. The Atlantic world is a trilateral world, with Japan, the United States, and the European Community as distinct geographical entities and distinguishable economic and political personalities. Each of these lives in symbiosis with developed partners: Japan-Australia, the United States-Canada, and the Community with the members of the old OEEC. Inevitably, they maintain specially close relations with the three developing regions to the south of each of them.

To adopt an *a priori* global perspective is legitimate and useful. The work of the Club of Rome and other initiatives seek to change our consciousness towards a broader view of the world community. In practise, however, taking the global view either leads to utopian calls for global redistribution on a massive scale and to special pleading for the developing countries, or, in the form of appeals to the requirements of global interdependence, the global view becomes a device for a conservative maintenance of the status quo. Similarly, taking an *a priori* Western or Atlantic point-of-view is to preempt a good deal of the analysis through a normative choice. For the constitutional crisis of the world economic system is above all the crisis of the American-centred postwar system. In the difficult choice between conservation and reform, and in the difficult debate on the nature of reforms, Europe must make up its own mind before trying out its ideas on its partners.

This task is uncomfortable and unfamiliar. The *Pax Americana* was, for the most part, a happy state of affairs for Europe. Within the OECD world, a strong central source of intellectual and political initiative and political guidance provided (and continues to provide) a bracket for the unruly diversity of the nations. Toward the Third World, the maintenance of an order congenial to Western interests provided a security shield to Western Europe in ways so subtle that it was taken, erroneously, as a state of nature.

The nature of economic security

It has become fashionable to assert that, in international affairs, economic security now has become as important as military security. This judgment implies that both these types of security can be measured by a common standard. It may be useful to use the analogy of military security in order to find a suitably narrow definition of economic security. Very broadly, we can distinguish three levels of military threat: physical annihilation through a nuclear exchange; conquest; and the loss of an independent foreign and domestic policy through fear of sanctions by a likely aggressor.

The closest equivalent to nuclear annihilation would be mass starvation as a result of inadequate food supplies. It is useful to remind ourselves that increasingly marginal groups in marginal developing countries live under this threat, and indeed suffer from its execution. For Western Europe, barring a military catastrophe which falls outside this analysis, mass starvation through lack of external supplies is unthinkable. The self-sufficiency ratios of the EEC are over 100 % for edible grains, and about 85 % if feed grains are included. The EEC is self-sufficient in potatoes, sugar, all vegetables, dairy products, and, for practical purposes, meat. It imports over one third of its fish—not a very crucial item in its diet—and has very low self-sufficiency ratios of only about 50 % in citrus fruit and 40 % in fats and oils. In the latter category, however, Community consumption is three times the world average. [4]

To the extent that agriculture is dependent on imported fuels and fertilizers, a failure of these supplies would cause a fall in food production. However, since agriculture would be a high-priority sector in any supply crisis, and since this sector consumes considerably less than the self-sufficiency ratios of the above-mentioned inputs, this most extreme threat to economic security need not be considered in greater detail.

There is, however, a real if partial equivalent to conquest the second type of military threat mentioned above. Apart from the loss of independence in general, one reason countries have feared conquest since the time of Napoleon is the likelihood of an enforced change in the social and political system. Richard Cooper, writing on Resources and National Security, [5] defines security as "the capacity of a society (nation) to enjoy and cultivate its culture and values." I would prefer a slightly more operational definition: *Economic security is threatened, when external economic parameters are changed in such a manner as to produce a strain on the sociopolitical system of a nation which leads to its break-down.*

Unlike military conquest, a change in our system through outside economic forces can come about only through the intermediation of domestic forces. A threat to economic security is therefore not only a function of the magnitude of

4. Hans Michaelis, *Memorandum über eine europäische Rohstoffversorgungspolitik*, 1972, p. 35 and 40.
5. Richard Cooper, *The Middle East and the International System: Part II*, "*Security and the Energy Crisis*," Adelphi Paper No. 115, Spring 1975.

an external economic influence, but also of the strength of the sociopolitical system which is confronted by such a challenge.

When the multiple crisis of the world economy developed in 1973, many observers at the time feared that the social contract in several European countries would not be able to take the strain, and that consequent mutations in their systems of government would occur. Popular Fronts, and corporatist and even military regimes were seriously discussed at the time. A pessimist may feel that it is too early to say they were wrong for, unlike threats to military security, those to economic security may work as a delayed-action bomb. The social contract, badly damaged by a set of reverses which have undermined the confidence and solidarity of the citizen in the prevailing form of sociopolitical organization, may limp on, only to break down years after the mortal blow. A historical example of this phenomenon was the German hyperinflation of 1923. It helped to weaken the resistance to the next misfortune, the depression of the early thirties, and thus contributed to the rise of National Socialism

A more than academic problem concerning our definition is raised by the difficulty of assessing what constitutes a breakdown of the system. How does one distinguish it from a successful adaptation to an external challenge, e.g. the command economies of the Western democracies during World War II? Ultimately, this is a normative question, and different individuals will choose different elements of our present system which they consider essential: the rule of law, parliamentary democracy, a measure (which?) of free enterprise. For practical purposes, however, one can argue in terms of a broadly shared consensus in Western Europe, although that consensus partially excludes for instance the Communist and neo-Fascist voters in Italy, Communist voters in France, and the far left of the British Labour party.

It is commonplace to point to the fragility of the particular system this consensus seeks to preserve: the pluralist, democratic welfare state. One particular characteristic of this system is of particular relevance to a discussion of economic security, i.e. its high dependence on the satisfaction of a substantial majority of its citizens, indeed of all its citizens who are organized to express their interests. This need is partially a function of democracy as such, partially a function of the complex interdependence of the modern industrial state, which gives small groups, e.g. electricity workers, a virtual veto over public policy, and partially a result of the success of governments in achieving a quarter century of expanding and shared prosperity. Tolerance for economic reserves has thus been lowered by a shift in our values which has raised expectations of an indefinite continuation of this state of affairs.

Expanding prosperity, however, has had a further effect. By increasing the total "cake" available for distribution, it has disguised or at least eased the struggle over the distribution of wealth and opportunity. Already before the present crisis it was becoming clear in a number of countries that redistribution had reached a stage where serious social conflicts were likely. Wage demands even in Germany well in excess of productivity gains, and the abandonment

76

of the Dutch system of nonconflictual wage bargaining, which had been in operation for decades, were evidence that this trend was becoming universal in Western Europe. Another, more subtle indicator was inflation, a progressively less effective instrument used by governments to create the illusion of expansion and to avoid hard choices by borrowing on the future.

Western Europe, therefore, had become economically vulnerable by its internal dynamism, independently of any actual threat materializing from the outside. Two hypothetical examples illustrate to what extent economic security as defined here depends on these perceptions. If, through a series of economic reserves, the Western European population suffered a halving of their standard of living, they would return to the not uncomfortable level of 1960. But the process of getting there would surely produce intolerable strains on the same system, which in 1960 was considered most successful. The second example argues that there is a possible exception. Most threats to economic security are, in contrast to military threats, diffuse, difficult to diagnose and rarely the result of an overtly hostile act. Economic reserves are therefore primarily seen as a failure of domestic government, and by extension, of the system of government. However, a wartime blockade though representing a serious threat to welfare, is likely to constitute less of a threat to the *system* than more marginal but diffuse threats. Governments have clearly recognized this, as they, at least publicly, blame present recession on the price rises forced on us by the oil producers. This is at best a very partial explanation.

Lastly, a word about the third type of military threat mentioned above, which causes the loss of an independent foreign policy (and possibly some loss of domestic sovereignty) not by conquest, but by the threat of conquest. This too has its equivalent in the field of economic security: what Finlandization is to military security, Arabization may be to economic security. Of course, in the latter case, there can be no question of a total loss of the freedom to conduct one's preferred foreign policy, but rather a modification and adaptation of existing policy on a narrow range of issues, notably Israel. These, though important in moral terms, are not central to Western European national interests. These very same issues, however, are central to the foreign policy of the American ally: hence the core of European foreign policy is indirectly touched. Arabization moreover, has meant interference in the domestic social system through the attempt to exclude Jewish banks from subscribing to international bond issues to finance Arab projects, thereby forcing banks to practice racial discrimination; and through trade, discrimination against firms having important financial and trading links with Israel.

The price of failure

In order to evaluate the relative gravity of different sources of insecurity stemming from the global economic environment, we have to return briefly to the domestic economy affected by it. External parameter changes can affect all four key policy targets of the Western welfare state: employment, price stability, growth, and the balance of payments. Whether these changes are relevant to economic security depends, inter alia, on their magnitude and the speed with which the parameter change occurs: together these determine the magnitude of economic adjustment and social strain imposed.

Thus unemployment very quickly affects the social climate, since it not only hits one particular group—the industrial workers—disproportionally hard, but also a well-organized group with historical sensitivity to this particular form of welfare loss. Some observers now dismiss this sensitivity as atavistic, since unemployment has ceased to be the economic disaster of the past. This more relaxed attitude is beginning to be shared by some trade union movements; but if it is to take hold, unemployment must be a transitory phenomenon. Long periods of unemployment, for instance if the present recession should last well into 1976, as some pessimists predict, could bring back social strains, which so far have been surprisingly muted in Western Europe. A prolonged period of high unemployment could also follow from a massive effort at structural adjustment imposed by changes in the cost patterns of industry (e.g. through changes in the prices of raw materials, or by the need to transfer industrial activity to powerful producers of commodities, or in the context of a more active development strategy in general). Since such adjustment would largely involve a rise in productivity, and individual workers would suffer relatively short periods of unemployment combined—in some countries at least—with retraining schemes, this source of unemployment may be less dangerous to economic security. If unemployment is sensed very quickly, reduced growth *per se* produces its effects on the social climate more slowly. As was mentioned earlier, the struggle over distribution in Western Europe was eased because the total "cake" available for distribution grew steadily larger. Once the cake ceases to grow, the struggle for distribution changes character. It no longer involves sharing out the gains from growth, but taking something away from someone so as to leave him not relatively, but absolutely, worse off. The strains produced by this process in the short term will be small if the better-off submit to this redistribution, as seems to be the case in present-day Britain. The argument becomes more complex through the fact that reducing the income of the better-off may, in practice, reduce personal savings in favour of consumption. This means that investment for future growth does not take place, thereby laying the basis for future conflict. It remains to be seen what will happen in another country which is a candidate for a long period of slow or no growth, namely Italy, where the middle classes strongly resist a redistribution of income. A quite different issue of great complexity is posed by the prospect of permanently lowered growth rates as predicted by certain analysts of long-term economic cycles. A rise in real living standards by the population, of 2 % annually, could be experienced as stagnation and, in time, could build up an explosive degree of frustration. On the other hand, slow growth is probably a prerequisite for sucessful long-term problem solving, since fast growth may in the future outrun our technical and social capacity to deal with it. In a whole number of areas, notably energy and the environment, slow growth provides an essential commodity, i.e. time.

The third target, price stability, or if we add a negative sign, inflation, may contribute to economic security in the short term. "Inflation has in a true sense been the safety valve of political stability, the unseen hand which temporarily accommodated the imperatives of political survival to the imperatives of economic supply by debasing the coin in which infulfillable political pledges were made." [6]

Inflation does not necessarily stem from domestic demands for redistribution, e.g. via an expansionary monetary policy to accommodate high wage demands, but also from external demands which would require a loss of domestic income. One such case was the Vietnam war. Another was the recent oil price increase crisis. Both, in the final analysis, were financed over the printing presses.

It is by no means empirically verifiable that inflation is dangerous to society. In Brazil, for instance, inflation works quite differently from the way it does in most welfare states. It keeps the real wages of workers low or declining, and heavily subsidizes investment through negative interest rates. In the industrialized countries, inflation is often accompanied by a rise of labour costs in total GNP, and a decline in investment. In the one case, inflation allows rapid growth (with some help from the police), in the other low growth. A somewhat similar case can be made for France on the one hand, and Britain on the other. What then are the dangers to economic security stemming from inflation? Most broadly, inflation undermines confidence in one basic contractual instrument, not only economically, but, as regards society in general, money. As Robert Roosa puts it, "As the sense of norms is impaired by the continuous erosion of values in the marketplace, there must inescapably be a degenerative influence on the mores of political and social institutions." [7] Whether this fear is justified is impossible to prove, not least because inflation coexists with, and is often a symptom of, a whole range of domestic malfunctions. Certainly the reference to Germany's hyperinflation of 1923 tells us little about the comparatively modest inflation rates of today. We do know, however, that inflation produces a redistribution of incomes from those with power to affect prices and wages to those who have little power. Precisely because of this power differential, however, such regressive redistribution may have to go a long way before causing conflicts which endanger the system; old-age pensioners do not topple governments.

The fourth policy target—the balance of payments—affects economic security indirectly through impairing a country's capacity to pursue the first three targets. Correcting a balance-of-payments deficit in practice not only means a reduction of domestic demand in favour of exports, but a slowdown of growth in general and an increase in unemployment. A classic balance-of-payments squeeze, therefore, affects quite quickly the variable "social contract," which

6. Peter Jay, *The Times,* September 1975 (Review Supplement).
7. "Controlling Inflation during Recession," *The Atlantic Community Quarterly,* Spring 1975, p. 102.

may serve as shorthand for our definition of economic security. Of course, there is no need to institute corrective policies as soon as a sharp deterioration in the balance of payments occurs. Some of the most important institutions of the postwar period, notably the IMF and the General Agreement to Borrow, have precisely this task of allowing nations, through the extension of international credit, to defer the moment of truth, and or to allow time for the least disruptive method of correction. Since the oil crisis, such international credit facilities have proliferated, the most notable addition being the $ 25 billion support fund of the OECD.

In addition to the short-term halt of growth and the increase in unemployment, measures to correct a negative balance of payments have a more pernicious long-term effect on both growth and employment. For one important part of domestic demand that is discouraged during a squeeze is investment, so that long periods of slow growth and unemployment follow even after the actual deflationary measures are lifted. This has been consistently the experience of Italy and Great Britain.

The international environment affects these policy targets chiefly through the operation of two markets, for goods and for capital. The countries at the southern periphery of Europe, in addition, are dependent on foreign labour markets as well. The following sections of this essay will deal primarily with factors affecting trade, and with the impact of trade insecurity on general economic insecurity.

The Insecurity of Exports

Trade dependence and conjunctural management

From 1953 to 1972, world trade grew at a mean annual rate of 8.9 % per year —almost twice as fast as the world economy.

This average hides a consistent slowdown in the growth of world trade between 1968 and 1972, when growth fell from 13 % to 6 % annually.[1] In 1973, however, world trade grew by a nominal 37.3 %, and in 1974 by an estimated 44 % to reach the staggering figure of $ 800 billion. [2] Of this, 60 % is accounted for by manufactured and semimanufactured goods, the remaining 40 % by commodities, of which roughly a third share each is represented by food, industrial raw materials, and fuel, respectively. From 1973 to 1974, the developing

---

Table 1

Share of world trade by country and region

Country/region	1973	1974
Industrialized countries of which:	72.2	67,5*
United States	12,5	12.3*
EEC	37.3	34.2*/**
Japan	6.6	6.8*
Germany (Fed. Rep.)	12.0	11.1*
France	6.3	5.7*
Italy	4.0	3.8*
Great Britain	5.4	4.7*
Developing countries of which:	18.3	24.5**
OPEC countries	7.0***	13.0**
Eastern bloc	9.5	8.1****

  * IMF estimate on the basis of figures for the first three quarters of 1974.
  ** IMF estimate on the basis of figures for first half of 1974.
  *** Estimated on the basis of IMF statistics.
  **** Estimate on the basis of data provided by the GATT secretariat.

Source : UN Yearbook of International Trade Statistics (various issues) and IMF Internaitonal Financial Statistics (various issues): From Hajo Hasenpflug, "Revolutionary Changes in World Trade", *The German Tribune,* February 1975.

---

1. *UN Economic Survey of Europe in 1972,* p. 23.
2. Hajo Hasenpflug, "Revolutionary Changes in World Trade," *The German Tribune: Economic Affairs Review,* 2/1975.

countries increased their share of world trade from under one fifth to almost one quarter. The industrialized countries and the Eastern bloc account for seventenths and less than one tenth, respectively. The EEC accounts for over one third of world trade.

A crude indicator of the importance of foreign markets to domestic economic activity is given by the share of exports in total gross domestic product. The figures below refer to goods only, leaving out other items of the current balance.

The figures are for 1973, before the 44 % growth of world trade in 1974.

Table 2

Exports as share of GDP, 1973

	percent
Belgium (BLEU)	47.6
Denmark	22.3
France	14.0
Germany (Fde. Rep.)	19.4
Ireland	32.8
Italy	16.1
Netherlands (BLEU)	47.6
United Kingdom	17.6
TOTAL EEC*	22.09
United States	5.5
Japan	9.1

* Sum of GNPs/Sum of exports (including intra-EEC trade).
Source: OECD-Observer, No. 74, p. 23.

Throughout the postwar era there has been broad agreement—at least among the industrialized countries—that the growth in foreign trade, i.e. the growth of interdependence, represented a great asset to prosperity. The recent past, however, suggests that the role of trade is more ambivalent. On the positive side, we expect a general welfare gain through trade from the consequent efficient factor allocation, the possibility of greater specialization, and the economies of scale permitted by larger markets. In the particular historical context of the last two decades, the fast growth of trade relative to economic growth in general, has been a motor for the latter.

Another asset to domestic welfare provided by trade until recently was the smoothing of variations in the business cycle. For most of the postwar period, these were "out of phase," especially on both sides of the Atlantic. Neo-Keynesian conjunctural management thus had powerful assistance from the fact that a domestic slump tended to be compensated for by buoyant external demand; conversely, inflationary pressures were mitigated by a fall in external demand.

Yet markets can represent a threat to economic security in two ways. One is through a reversal of the historically beneficial effect of variation in global demand on domestic demand management. The other stems from the dependence on the import policies of trading partners.

The emergence of global demand variations of such a magnitude that offsetting domestic measures of conjunctural management become insufficient, completely alters the cost/benefit analysis of foreign trade. It is no accident that the synchronization of world business cycles and the emergence of a dominant global business cycle are occurring only now. The integration of the world economy was far less complete before the Kennedy Round, the growth of the Eurodollar market, and the growth of international production which had occurred by the late sixties. As late as 1967, a severe economic downswing in Germany coincided with the period of excessive demand stimulation in the United States (1966-1968) associated with the Vietnam war. Since then we can observe a surprisingly short-term world business cycle with an increasing amplitude. The synchronization was still incomplete in the mild downswing of 1969-1970. It became apparent in the worldwide boom of 1972-1973 and in the even deeper world recession of 1974-1975, to be followed by an anticipated global upswing in 1976-1977.

In order to evaluate the new cost of interdependence, it may be useful to compare the orders of magnitudes with the welfare gains from free trade. During the long debate over Britain's membership in the Common Market, the welfare gains of trade liberalization were estimated by membership advocates at a once-and-for-all effect of between 0.5 and 1 % of GNP. Victoria Curzon, an ardent proponent of free trade, assessing the effects of more than a decade of British membership in EFTA, on exports, arrives at a figure of 0.0041 % of GNP. [3] She goes on to say that it would be wrong to conclude from this that the whole EFTA exercise was of no significance, since "most economic policies rarely deal with magnitudes which are very much larger: they are always 'peanuts' when compared to GNP."

Yet for countries that depend for 20 % or 30 % of their total GNP on external trade, the welfare losses from this trade dependence can (in a single year) be a multiple of the long-term gains of free trade. *The crucial relationship that determines a country's vulnerability to recessionary impulses from abroad is the rate and magnitude in the fall of external demand compared to the total compensating demand that can be created domestically.*

Germany's recent economic difficulties provide an illustration. In 1975, world trade showed an estimated decline of 5 %, German exports of 9 % in volume terms. [4] Of the total recessionary shortfall in demand of some DM 60 billion, 40 billion were accounted for by exports. Put differently, the fall in exports caused a 4 % drop in GNP. A fall in demand of this magnitude seems to dwarf the government's capacity to create demand through the classic Keynesian instrument of deficit spending. By mid-1975, the public sector deficit stood at 70 billion DM, 6 % of GNP; this was caused, among other things, by falling tax revenue and increased unemployment payments due to the recession. Yet even this deficit only kept the recession from getting worse; it did nothing to cure it.

3. Victoria Curzon, *The Essentials of Economic Integration: Lessons of the EFTA Experience,* London 1974, p. 304.

For that, another 40 billion DM of government spending would have been necessary. Instead, in September 1975, the government decided on additional deficit spending of DM 5.75 billion whose purpose was not so much to stimulate the economy, but to avoid unemployment in the particularly hard-hit building sector. Assuming a multiplicator effect of $ 5 billion, where was the additional DM 30 billion worth of demand to come from? The general answer was: from the same world economy which so sadly failed to deliver (in fact to *demand*) the goods in 1975. [4]

Europe's lack of autonomy

The leading role of the United States in determining the business cycle in the OECD and beyond is to some extent puzzling. The United States accounts for only 12 % of world trade against the EEC's 34 %. The United States accounts for only 7 % of the EEC's exports, while more than half the EEC trade is with other members. The remaining EFTA countries, or the developing countries as a group, are each twice as important as export markets.

Table 3

Exports of the European Community in 1974
(in units of account and percent of total)

Destination	u/c	%
World	220,640	100
EEC intra	111,617	50.59
extra	109,023	49.41
OECD third countries	63,515	28.79
of which:		
EFTA	24,811	13.06
US	15,182	6.88
Japan	2,645	1.20
Developing countries	33,599	15.23
of which:		
Lomé countries	5,620	2.55
Arab League	10,039	4.55
Eastern Europe	9,461	4,29
Soviet Union	3,188	1.44

Source: Calculations based on *Statistical Telegram*, Eurostat, July 1, 1975.

Yet the American economy remains the single most important economy in the world. In 1973, its GDP of $ 1.297 billion almost exactly equalled the combined GDP of the Western European countries, $ 1.280 billion. Perhaps

4. *Sondergutachten des Sachverständigenrats zur Begutachtung der gesamtwirtschaftlichen Entwicklung zur konjunkturpolitischen Lage im August 1975,* Bundestagsdrucksache 7/1976, p. 5.

more important is the fact that the United States is the only economy in the non-Communist world which has preserved a large measure of autonomy in determining the domestic business cycle. This derives partially from the relative unimportance of external trade relative to total economic activity, partially from the fact that the United States manages the world's currency. It is the only country (apart from Japan with its own tight capital controls) that in a world of integrated capital markets, can set domestic interest rates relatively independently from external considerations.

In striking contrast, the Federal Republic of Germany, the largest economy in the EEC, with a share of world trade comparable to that of the United States (11.1 % as compared to 12.3 % in 1974) has never fulfilled its potential role as a motor for either world or European economic expansion. Hence Europe's dependence on the external environment is due, to a considerable extent, to the fact that this key economy looks to the outside world for the solution of its policy problems and does not see itself as an autonomous force that could help shape this environment. Two sets of figures give a rough indication of the considerable German potential for a reversal of its role from a derivative to an autonomous role in the international conjunctural context. Table 4 allows a comparison of Germany's public debt position with those of similar states, and hence the scope for expansion. The third column allows a comparison of reserve figures, i.e. a particularly crucial measure of autonomy.

Table 4

Public Indebtedness (1975) * +

	Public Indebtedness 1975 % of GNP	per capita in DM	currency reserves Dec. 1974 in million dollars
Federal Republic of Germany	25	4,135	32,720
Belgium	48	7,661	5,345
Denmark	13	2,291	935
France	12	1,745	8,851
Great Britain	80	7,051	6,939
Italy	48	3,409	6,941
Japan	14*	1,564	13,519
Netherlands	39	5,665	6,958
Sweden	39	7,593	1,734
Switzerland	24	5,268	9,011
United States	51	8,402	16,058

* Excluding the special budget.
+ Domestic and foreign debt, state and local.

Source: BMWI Tagesnachrichten.

To be a boom leader for the rest of Europe, Germany, according to a calculation by *The Economist,* would have had to create $ 25 billion worth of extra demand. [5] If that demand were to be created by direct government spending,

5. *The Economist,* August 2, 1975, p. 73.

(given the reluctance of consumers and investors to spend, such direct demand creation seemed indicated), this would have meant a doubling of the existing "neutral" deficit. In the event, the government, under heavy pressure from the opposition to do less, decided on one tenth of that figure (the 5.75 billion DM programme mentioned earlier).

This figure must be compared to a simultaneous French programme of $ 5.5 billion—almost three times the German figure—which had been preceded by a 15 billion franc programme in March 1975. Also in early autumn, the Danish government, in spite of huge public sector deficits, was forced to adopt a $ 0.7 billion programme, or 2 % of GDP. Similar measures were adopted in the Netherlands—all of them a multiple, in relative terms, of the German efforts. Italy and Great Britain, constrained by high inflation rates and a weak balance of payments, could do little. On the contrary, Britain was forced to raise the bank rate to protect the pound as the United States Federal Reserve, through a restrictive monetary policy, caused interest rates to rise.

The German programme makes sense in traditional domestic terms. A more expansionary policy would have preempted a part of future national savings for debt management. Growth today would have been bought at the expense of growth and inflation tomorrow.

Yet the terms of reference for the decision should have been neither traditional, nor exclusively domestic. For two years, since the oil crisis, most of the economies in the non-Communist world have limped along with the help of temporary expedients—international credits and a drop in real living standards. If external debts were to be repaid and internal social peace to be maintained, a speedy and *certain* resumption of economic growth was essential. By mid-75 it had become clear that more robust countries like the United States and Japan were going to choke off economic recovery at the first signs of rising inflation. It was also clear that the developing countries, having run down reserves and exhausted international credit lines, and with drastically reduced earning capacities due to the recession in the OECD countries, would exercise a contractive influence on the global economy in 1976. This was the moment for Western Europe to take control of the situation. With two major countries incapable of contributing to expansion—indeed, desperately in need of it—the task fell to the core countries of northwestern Europe. Here Germany may have failed its partners.

Ironically enough, the efforts to concert economic policies within the EEC and with the United States have been a prominent part of every summit meeting between Western leaders since 1973. In that year the fight against inflation became the rallying cry of the OECD. 1974 was a year of deep soul searching with the United States, and hence with OECD, trying to decide whether inflation or recession was the greater evil. Chancellor Schmidt took some pride in persuading the American government to relax its anti-inflationary policy—too late, as it turned out. As it happened, the following year a restrictive monetary policy by the Federal Reserve, reflecting the personal prejudices of Mr. Burns, undid what slight expansionary impulse could be expected from fiscal policy. In the summer of 1975, Chancellor Schmidt announced special efforts to co-ordinate EEC-wide reflationary measures, especially between Germany and France. If these meetings served any purpose, it was probably to inform the German government that the others were so desperate to inflate that they were willing to take chances—allowing Germany to proceed with a virtuous and responsible budgetary policy.

For the export-dependent economies of Western Europe, effective international demand management has become crucially important to economic security. Although co-operation with the United States and Japan will always remain important, the greatest opportunities—and the greatest penalties for failure—lie within Western Europe itself. Plans for an economic union have in the past excessively concentrated on achieving fixed exchange rates among the Community member states. Co-operation on economic policy is needed for its own sake. The new pathological properties of the international business cycle require an effective and ultimately a binding common economic management within the community. It should become an element in the European Union whose outlines will be decided in 1976.

Europe's trading partners

The future prospects of European export markets can best be assessed by looking at the various markets separately. Of relevance to economic security are three questions: What are the chances of export markets continuing to provide the dynamic, growth-inducing element of demand in the medium term? What are the chances for protectionism closing off export markets suddenly? Which markets are amenable to a policy of short-term quasi-Keynesian international demand management? From the standpoint of a single member country of the European Community, trading regions can be grouped as follows:

1. The member countries of the Nine.
2. The EFTA countries.
3. The United States and Japan.
4. Australia, Canada.
5. The Lomé and Mediterranean Associates.
6. The other LDCs.
7. The East European countries, including the Soviet Union.

The Western European trade area

Confidence in the continuation of free trade within the European Community stems not so much from the letter of the Treaty but from very considerable and balanced "interdependence."

Table 5

Intra-EEC trade as share of total trade

	Eur-9	B-L	Denm.	France	Ger.	Eire	Italy	NL.	UK.
Imports	47	66	46	48	48	68	42	57	30
Exports	51	70	43	53	45	75	45	71	33

Source: Eurostat. *Statistical Telegramme*, July 1/1975.

EFTA countries have similar trade shares with the EEC—although these cannot necessarily have reciprocal confidence in the much bigger EEC, for whom each EFTA country represents a comparatively small share of the market.

Confidence in the permanence of the intra-European free trade system, however, is also based on two further considerations. First, the European economic area is of a minimal size to sustain the specialization and the considerable economies of scale required by much of modern industry and technology. Secondly, in a world which will be dominated increasingly by bargaining over the international division of labour, the only substantial bargaining chip at the EEC's disposal is its unified 'internal' market. It is probably this argument, more than any other, which has provided an economic rationale for Britain's continued membership in the Community.

One concrete evidence of the differential quality of trade interdependence in Western Europe is the adhesion of a majority of EEC and EFTA members to the system of exchange-rate stabilization known as the "snake." [6] An international agreement for an eventual return to a stable exchange rate regime within the wider IMF context is unlikely. This means a perpetuation of a considerable cost differential in intra-European, as opposed to world, trading (the need for expensive forward exchange cover) which together with the cost of uncertainty —the dollar appreciated by 10 % in a single month in July of 1975—will act like a tariff.

Of course, as shown by the cases of Britain and previously of Italy and France, even the intra-European free trade commitment may prove too much of a constraint, if the system becomes unbalanced. In Italy's case the Community has shown itself flexible enough, at a time when Italy was running a trade deficit of $ 1 billion a month, to suspend the full rigours of the free trade commitment and to allow the imposition of an import deposit scheme. This, together with a savage deflationary policy, helped to eliminate Italy's non-oil deficit in eighteen months.

6. Apart from the member countries, Germany, Denmark, the Benelux countries, and, since July 1975, France, Sweden and Norway are "associated" members of the Snake; Austria keeps its currency unilaterally in line, and Switzerland is applying for membership.

There is a lively debate in Britain over the need for direct import restraints. [7] Because the case for such restraints made by the trade unions so closely resembles the classic beggar-my-neighbour argument, the macroeconomic dilemma which Britain faces is not always understood. Britain has a structural balance-of-payments deficit on current account (which is precariously balanced on capital account by Arab wealth: continued Arab preference for sterling is an act of reversible political charity). The only internationally accepted method of correcting this deficit is by domestic deflation and/or by devaluations. A worsening of the domestic recession would, under the present circumstances of stagnating world demand, fail to lead to a significant rise in exports. It would deal a possibly mortal blow to social peace in Britain, perpetuate underinvestment, and worsen the recession for Britain's trading partners. Devaluations, as Britain has already experienced with floating exchange rates, lead to dearer imports in the crucial short term (the downward stroke of the J-curve). The prospects for improved exports are poor. An international agreement allowing Britain to keep imports at a stable level so that it can risk a modest stimulation of its economy would end the wasteful underutilisation of Britain's human and capital resources and give some breathing space to the struggle over the distribution of wealth which is racking the country.

As Gordon Tether put it in the *Financial Times,* "If there is no provision in the international trade rules for allowing a country to take direct action to rehabilitate its external payments when the alternative is to let it drift towards disaster dragging the rest of the world in its wake, it is high time that it was created. [8]"

The British, Italian, and Danish cases show that the long-term outlook of the Community as a reliable and irreversible free-trade area does not, and perhaps should not, exclude short-term derogations to the free-trade principles. These will also in future be needed, if other instruments of economic management fail to assure the achievement of minimal policy targets.

The United States

Free trade between the United States and Western Europe is as much a political as an economic issue. Free trade and capital movements were to create objective bases for common interests, complementary to the common security interest, and reinforcing it in the eyes of foreign adversaries and domestic critics of the Atlantic Alliance.

American exports to Europe, moreover, have a uniquely political effect on the construction of European unity. Globally, the United States' demand for

7. An important contribution was provided by the National Institute of Economic Research in its quarterly survey of the world economy in March 1975.
8. *The Financial Times,* 2 July 1975.

lower European tariffs continues to be regarded as a threat to the Community's common external tariff. In the field of agriculture, American demands for greater access to the Community market for grains, puts pressure on the most developed area of Community policy, the Common Agricultural Policy (CAP). In the field of military procurement, where access to Community markets is directly linked to the security guarantee, American exports represent an obstacle to the achievement of a common European defense industry. The same is true for areas of high technology such as civilian aircraft and an EEC industrial policy.

While the composition of American exports—commodities plus high technology goods—gives them a double character of both complementary and substitutive trade, European exports to the United States are virtually all substitutive, i.e. in direct competition with domestic production in the United States. Whereas American exports to Europe may lead to conflicts on the governmental level, those of Europe affect in the first instance workers and industrialists—the classic sources of protectionism.

The battle of the liberal internationalist establishment against these forces is as old as the postwar free trade commitment itself. In the best of times, their victory was a narrow one and a number of developments suggest that the balance may tilt the other way in the not too distant future. First, the power of the international establishment has decreased; secondly, the executive branch has been weakened vis-à-vis Congress; thirdly, the trade union movement is now totally committed to protectionism.

The weakening of the traditional East Coast-based foreign policy establishment is partially explained by the Vietnam war, partially by the refocussing of priorities by one prominent member of the policy elite, Secretary of State Kissinger. He is concentrating, first, on direct accommodation with the Soviet Union and China and, more recently, on global issues such as food, energy, and the oceans. Taken together they make the promotion of interdependence through trade with the Western allies something of an irrelevant anachronism.

Since the broader foreign policy goals traditionally involved in the free trade issue have become less salient, the device whereby the executive initiated a major international trade negotiation whenever protectionist forces became strong, and thereby forced them into quiescence while negotiations proceeded, may not work for the present Nixon/Tokyo Round. That Round, it will be recalled, was the response to a slow deterioration of international trading practices since the Kennedy Round. On the American side, it started with imposed voluntary restrictions on textiles, steel, and other products. The Nixon/Connally shocks of 1971, followed with their import surcharge, export subsidy, and a devalued dollar. It peaked with the proposed Burke-Hartke bill which was eventually defeated.

Yet in order to win passage for the Trade Bill which would give the president authority to negotiate in the Tokyo Round, Congress, as part of its general efforts to increase its control over United States foreign policiy, greatly strengthened its supervisory role. Moreover, the discretionary powers given to the president were unusually double-edged. Sanctions against offending trading partners were given almost as much space as the positive discretion to liberalize trade.

There is evidence that attempts are being made to exploit the negative possibilities of the trade bill, especially as regards tougher application of antidumping laws and the imposition of "countervailing duties" in such sectors as cars, steel, floatglass and footwear: one fifth of EEC exports, or goods valued at $ 4.3 billion were under investigation in the autumn of 1975. [9]

The third shift in the domestic balance, the trade union commitment to protectionism, took place gradually as the competitive advantage of American workers, based on a monopoly of the high technology at their disposal, was gradually undermined through a wholesale export of that technology via direct foreign investment. With the support by the AFL-CIO of the Burke-Hartke bill (which called for restrictions on both foreign investment and imports and, less logically, on incoming foreign investments), the switch from the trade union support for free trade to a protectionist stance was nearly complete. The United Automobile Workers, the only group to hold out, faced with the simultaneous drop in domestic car sales of 20 %, a rise in imports of 16 %, and 200,000 unemployed car workers, are now vigorously lobbying for raised tariffs on all cars not containing at least 10 % American-made parts (with, the proportion to rise to 50 % by 1980). [10]

This broad outlook is still contradicted by most official American policy in the trade field. It is the United States which pushed most vigorously for the signing of a trade pledge in the OECD, when the sudden balance-of-payments deficits after the oil price rises evoked the spectre of competitive trade wars. If Great Britain signed this pledge and renewed it in the summer of 1975, this was at least as much due to the strength of American pressure as to the strength of the European connection. But, as conditions return to normal, and with a foreign economic policy increasingly in the hands of a mercurial, domestically-oriented Congress, a sudden switch of policy or a slow divergence between rhetoric and practice cannot be excluded.

Japan

The Community's position vis-à-vis Japan is the reverse of the American relationship: here, the Community is the potential protectionist. For Japan, the Community market is a marginal one, a situation which gives great latitude in its pricing policy. For many products, Japanese exports are characterised by a relatively fast initial growth, which then is stabilized at a moderate share of the

9. *Financial Times,* 2nd october 1975, p. 48.
10. "Us-Gewerkschaften kämpfen um die Basis: protektionistischer Druck wird verstärkt". *Handelsblatt,* 1-IV-1975.

total market. The demand for its products being established, direct investment often takes the place of exports. This does not apply to ships or motor cars. The growth of automobile exports to Western Europe, a competitive market with the greatest real product differentiation and the highest technical standards in the world, shows the absurdity of some substitutive trade. Unlike small-car exports to the United States, such exports serve no useful market function in Europe, and are bound to become uncompetitive within half a decade; exchange rate changes, rises in labour cost and in shipping costs will see to that.

By the same token—especially as regards high transport costs and the similarity of the products offered—Japan cannot, in the future, represent a dynamic export market to the Community regardless of the great potential wealth of Japan and a further liberalization of trade. At present, exports to Japan represent less than 3 % of Community exports. The future of Japanese-European economic co-operation lies in technological co-operation, and in reciprocal direct investment.

The Third World

A threat to economic security of a quite different order is represented by Europe's dependence on the markets of raw materials producers: Australia, Canada, the Third World, and COMECON. Despite their differences, they all conduct what is largely complementary trade with Western Europe. While substitutive trade—exchanging virtually identical products over large distances—could ultimately be dispensed with, provided the remaining economic space is big enough to allow specialization and economies of scale, complementary trade is absolutely indispensable. For, unless the raw-material producers buy European products, Europe lacks the means to pay for these raw materials. There is a general tendency, shared by all raw materials producers, to sell their resources increasingly in processed form. The 1975 UNIDO resolution calls for a 25 % share of world industrial production for the LDCs (as against 7 % now) and the so-called Corea Plan of UNCTAD; [11] both proposals stress the need for local processing. The wood producers of the northern hemisphere decreasingly sell raw timber and pulp, preferring to sell carpentry and paper instead. Australia insists, as a condition of supplying Europe with uranium in the future, on a transfer of technology and local processing. The Shah of Iran has hopes that, by the late eighties, his oil will be exported exclusively as the energy and chemical content of advanced industrial products.

The prospect of a world in which all raw materials producers process their own goods, leaving the industries of Europe and Japan bereft of supplies (the

11. *An Integrated Programme for Commodities.* The Role of International Commodity Stocks. Appendix III. Report by the Secrétery General of UNCTAD, TD/B/C.1/166, 13-XII-1974.

subject of the following section) and of markets, is not a very real one. While the ladder of transformation for a given product is not infinite, there are enough rungs on it for a substantial proportion of primary and secondary conversions to be handled by the raw materials producers themselves. Moreover, given the technical difficulties involved, the raw materials producers can hope to gain little more than a share of the *increase* in processing capacity needed. Since, in any event, an extension of such capacity in the industrial countries is increasingly difficult due to environmental reasons, the trend towards processing in raw-materials-producing countries (which tend to be less densely populated) is complementary to the domestic requirements of the heavily populated industrial countries. To the extent that plans for transferring raw-material processing will be successful (and hence complementary trade lost in favour of a semi-substitutive trade), this will not lead to an absolute loss of markets, but to an adjustment problem whose magnitude and pace will be much less severe than the adjustment problems suffered in the preceding decades (which were largely due to the exploitation of global labour-cost differentials).

One can, on the contrary, advance the opposite thesis: that the industrialization of the Third World, and hence its increased capacity to pay for the goods of the industrialized countries, would represent an indispensable dynamic asset which could help to sustain growth in Europe. To make this point one has to accept the plausibility of a macro-explanation of the current recession which goes beyond the argument, advanced earlier, that the recession is due only to the coincidence of short-term business cycles. Some economists, from Schumpeter to Kondratieff to Kuznets and Arthur Lewis, examined very long-time series and discovered the existence of long-term swings of between forty and sixty years in the business cycle. These they explained in various ways. For Schumpeter, these cycles were due to the different dynamics of innovation: new goods created new consumption needs, new markets, new forms of organization. Once basic innovations are made, others follow (echo effect). After a time, however, as Gerhard Mensch [12] has pointed out, in a recent updating of this school of thought, markets become saturated. Investment becomes pseudo-investment for product differentiation. The railway, electrification, the motor car, television, the jet, and petrochemicals were innovations which seem to follow this pattern.

If markets within the industrialized countries are indeed saturated (i.e. if there is no sector with growth rates dynamic enough to pull the rest of the economy along) then the prosperity of LDCs with their unlimited potential demand may be an asset to growth—even if that prosperity requires an initial transfer of existing wealth on the order of one or two percent of GNP from the European economies.

This relatively optimistic long-term outlook regarding trading opportunities with the LDCs must, however, be tempered by the bleak prospects for dynamic export markets in the short-term. The increase in oil and food prices has

12. *Das technologische Patt,* Umschau Verlag, Frankfurt 1975.

caused LDC trade balances to deteriorate even more sharply than those of the industrialized consumer countries. The cushion of reserves with which to finance imports is being exhausted, while extra lending from the oil producers and DAC countries only partially makes up the deficit. At the same time, the reduction of agricultural output as a consequence of higher input costs has increased the need to divert foreign exchange to food purchases that are primarily a North American preserve. Since 1972, the current-account deficit of the non-oil producing LDCs has deteriorated from an annual $ 9 billion to perhaps $ 35 billion in 1975. Total debt now stands at $ 120 billion and half of all new assistance is swallowed up by interest payments.

The fact that the LDCs have absorbed the greater part of the collective world deficit vis-à-vis the oil producers has exerted an important counter-cyclical effect in the current world recession. It has had a positive effect on employment in the industrialized countries, which would otherwise have had to be achieved through larger domestic budgetary deficits and deteriorating balances-of-payments. Nevertheless, this situation is unsustainable. Sooner or later the Dutch proposal for a partial cancellation of the LDCs' debt will need to be considered seriously. If it is forced on the industrialized countries through piece-meal bankruptcies, it will be impossible to reap the political effects of this gesture; much time will be lost through the cancellation of development programmes; and the collapse of North-South trade will prolong the worldwide recession. [13]

The short-term depressant effect of reduced earnings on LDC imports is, of course, partially counterbalanced by the increasing import capacity of the oil producers and their financial beneficiaries. In 1974, EEC exports to the Arab League members increased by 78 % (imports by 135 %). As regards imports by the oil producers, further impressive growth rates for imports have been predicted by, among others, the World Bank. A heavy question mark must, however, be set against these predictions since the physical and human limits on infrastructure seem to have been reached and surpassed even in a relatively advanced, well-populated country like Iran.

The ACP (Africa, Caribbean, Pacific) associates of the EEC represent a special case. Under the 1975 Lomé Convention, these countries have been granted access to European markets for (chiefly) agricultural commodities and foodstuffs against a very weak reciprocal trade commitment to Europe, namely guaranteed most-favoured nation treatment. Minimal earning power—and hence export opportunities for the Community—is assured by the export earnings stabilization scheme, Stabex (see below, p.127), as well as by more substantial amounts of direct aid. Of special importance among the ACP countries is the oil producer Nigeria, which accounts for two-fifths of ACP exports into, and a quarter of ACP imports from, the Community. [13] [14]

13. *Süddeutsche Zeitung*, 24-X-1975, p. 4.
14. Figures for 1974, in *Eurostat: Statistical Telegramme*, July 1, 1975.

The state trading countries

The state trading countries have in the recent past represented one of the fastest growing markets for Western Europe's and particularly Germany's industrial exports. Several reasons seem to indicate that this dynamism will be maintained in the future. The area as a whole (including China) has a combined GNP of about one trillion dollars, or one fifth of world output, but only one tenth of world trade. The persistent trade deficits of these countries with the West demonstrate their great import demand. Given the rise of raw material prices, notably of fossil fuels and gold, and given the need for Western Europe to diversify its sources of supply, commodity imports from the Soviet Union and Poland (coal and copper) can be expected to grow. Eastern Europe would hence enhance its capacity to pay for Western imports.

Against this must be set a number of considerations. First, even the Soviet Union imports considerably more than it exports. By September 1975, the USSR had borrowed heavily on the Eurodollar market to cover a deficit with the West estimated at $ 1.4 billion. To this will be added the heavy grain purchases, an expenditure that is to be repeated annually under the new United States-Soviet grain agreement. This means that even in future, Western European exports will depend on credits—at a time of increasing capital scarcity in the West.

In 1973, total credits granted for five years and more amounted to $ 10 billion, [15] or more than one year's worth of exports. To this sum must be added the swing credits accorded to the GDR by the Federal Republic, etc. Even where these export credits are not subsidized, they represent a diversion of domestic capital to the development of the Eastern economies to maintain the strength of the Community's export industries.

The medium-term outlook for the stability and growth of Eastern markets is uncertain. In spite of widespread assumptions to the contrary, the import of Western technology is marginal to the Soviet Union (which accounts for 40 % of Community exports to Comecon). According to a recent analysis, a doubling of Western trade would give the Soviet Union a productivity gain of 0.16 % of GNP. [16] Therefore the present trend towards increasing trade with the West can be reversed overnight if autarchic tendencies again get the upper hand in the Soviet Union. Unless the Soviet system changes drastically, this is bound to happen sooner or later when Western-carried-trade influence on the economy and on its organization reaches measurable levels.

The rise in raw material prices, which is slowly being carried over into the internal Comecon price structure, means that a much larger part of Eastern European exports will have to go east. There will be fewer goods available to

15. EEC Commission, *Information,* 347/x/75-F, p. 9.
16. Franklin D. Holzman and Robert Legvold, "The Economics and Politics of East-West Relations." *International Organization,* 1/1975, p. 281.

95

pay for growth-inducing Western imports. To this must be added the Comecon commitment to increase internal trade, entered into under the Complex programme of 1971 (and since confirmed) aiming at strengthening socialist integration.

Since Community trade with Comecon represents a modest 8 % of total third-country exports, nothing short of very high growth rates would allow this market to contribute to European economic growth in general. Such growth, however, would require increasing credits, plus an opening of European import markets to sensitive agricultural and labour-intensive products. In other words, Comecon trade competes for credit and markets with the demands both of our domestic economies and for the pressing requirements of the Third World.

Future trade problems

A look at the world trading opportunities of Western European countries in regional detail seems to suggest that the growth of substitutive trade within the OECD, which has been one of the prime stimulants of postwar economic growth, has probably reached its limits. The pattern of the future seems to be classic liberalism within all of Western Europe; substitutive trade stabilized through quotas and equivalent measures—safeguard clauses, voluntary restrictions, marketsharing agreements—within the rest of the world; commodity trade determined by contractual arrangements of one sort or another with the socialist, industrialized, and developing countries. Such contracts can cover price and quantity, credit conditions, investment and industrial co-operation provisions. Trade, under these conditions, might gain stability, though it might cease to expand relative to GNP.

The implications for the maintenance of economic security can be more easily put in normative than in predictive terms. Stable export markets depend to some extent on a stable flow of European resources to customers—through credits, through stable raw material earnings, and through stable export earnings by customers in general. This opens up new perspectives of international demand management with tools other than the (at present unusable) tool of global monetary control.

On the other hand, domestic demand management becomes more important if one ceases to see the international environment as a residual economic space with which to overcome one's problems. The proper definition of domestic in this context must be European. Not because the European record in this respect is brilliant, but rather because Western Europe will increasingly become a single market and is of minimum size necessary for a self-determined economic policy.

In a sense, therefore, Europe must become more consciously inward looking: first in order to take the responsibility for determining its own conjunctural cycle. This would enable it to discharge its responsibility to the many trading partners who are utterly dependent on a stable European economy. Secondly, if the assumption of largely stagnating trade is correct, Europe must find a substitute for the traditional growth-promoting role of international trade. Conjunctural autonomy is maximized if the trade/GNP ratio is minimized. Jacques Attali has recently pushed this view to its ultimate conclusion: exports could be reduced to the level needed to pay for raw materials and their immediate derivatives. Future growth in demand must come from a greater emphasis on domestic demand derived, for instance, from infrastructure investments which satisfy the new consumer preferences for quality of life goods rather than durables. The export sector should be oriented toward supplying high-technology goods required by the Third World. [17]

One need not go quite as far in order to bring about a better balance between economy and economic management. Means for reducing export dependence would consist of a gradual dismantling of subsidies to exports, i.e. of undervalued exchange rates where they exist; of export credits; of the restitution of value-added tax for export production (a truly incredible distortion of cost-patterns); and of industrial policies which favour the development of export-oriented (and -dependent) technology. The secular shift which can be observed in all mature economies, which decreases the share of manufactures relative to the service sector in total GNP, will provide a natural aid to this process.

If it is economic efficiency we seek to achieve through more international trade, there is much greater scope for such gains within the European Community and its associates: No less than 17 % of all goods and services consumed in the Community are publicly financed [18] and hence virtually exempt from the liberalization of the Common Market—in fact if not on paper.

For years, the European Commission has pushed for a rationalization of intra-EEC research and development and public procurement in the particularly restrictive and wasteful high-technology sector [19]. Its chosen instruments are industrial development contracts—for which companies in member states would bid competitively. Companies that secured such contracts to supply the Community with the needed equipment would receive a special status as common enterprises, with an advantageous tax system and other forms of subsidies. The programme combines elements of the Andean Group's approach to investment allocation with the American practice of having companies bid for large, publicly financed high-technology projects. Opposed by both Italy and Britain because of its competitive aspects, and by Germany because of its *dirigiste* possibilities, the programme, like so many others, has practically been buried by the Council

17. "La question de 1000 milliards". *Le Monde,* 21-III-1975.
18. "Die Wirtschaft und Schaffung eines enropäischen öffentlichen Auftragswesens." *Information Binnenmarkt,* 102/x/75-D 1975, p. 2.
19. For a development of the Community industrial policy, see "Principles and General Datelines of an Industrial Policy for the Community", *Bulletin Supplement,* 4/70; *Bulletin,* No. 5/70, pp. 58-64; 6/71, pp. 76-77; 4/73; 5/73, pp. 7-9; "Towards the Establishment of a Community Industrial Base". *Bulletin Supplement* 7/73.

of Ministers. Incidentally, the proposal shows, that elements of planning—the negotiated international division of labour which is slowly evolving globally as a substitute for the purely market determined division of labour—are not necessarily out of place even within the Community itself.

In this survey of trade opportunities, a relative decline of European trade with the two other great economic powers, the United States and Japan, has been accepted without too much regret. These three regions have a superb and unique ability to communicate with one another. Therefore, less crude forms of economic intercourse should become available in the last quarter of the twentieth century than shipping largely identical goods to one another over great distances. For many purposes, through direct investment or otherwise, the exchange of technology can take the place of trade. In pluralist societies, trade issues set important segments of national populations in opposition to each other, notably workers and farmers, and will increasingly become a source of friction within the OECD countries in general and the Atlantic Alliance in particular. Market access will become an increasingly scarce bargaining asset to be used for satisfying the welfare demands of the Third World and the political demands of raw materials producers. For those countries that have entered the post-industrial age, new forms of economic co-operation—joint projects in space communication, energy technology, urban transport, etc—are becoming more crucial to public welfare. The global problems of the future—world poverty, lack of resources and the oceans—will require the joint application of the skill and finance of the industrialized countries to solve them. It is to some of these problems that the following section addresses itself.

The Security of Imports:
the Raw Materials issue

In the early 1970s, a number of seemingly unrelated events appeared to shift the focus of trade concerns away from the preoccupations of the past decades, access to markets, and towards access to supplies. The publication of the study of the Club of Rome, *The Limits to Growth,* coincided with the onset of the great explosion of demand for goods caused by the synchronized world boom. Bad harvests in a number of countries and the disappearance of Peruvian anchovies added to the general impression that an era of scarcity was upon us. By 1973, tight demand conditions had their first repercussions in international economic relations. The United States, fearing a threat to its anti-inflationary pricing policy because of runaway world demand for feedstuffs, imposed a short-lived but long-to-be-remembered ban on soybean exports. The European Community, in an economically significant but little commented move, levied export taxes of up to 100 % on grain exports to prevent world demand from spilling over into the domestic market. Export controls for scrap became the rule world-wide. By late 1973 raw material prices had tripled and quadrupled. In October, finally, OPEC stumbled on the extraordinary pricing opportunities afforded by the global runaway demand situation.

The recession that followed should have banished the spectre of scarcity as quickly as it arose. Indeed, most raw material prices fell, but not by as much as could be expected. The two most crucial commodity groups, mineral fuels and grain, remained very high. Instead of being pushed back into its bottle, the oil power genie grew into commodity power. In spite of many learned articles proving the adequacies of world raw materials supplies, conservationist sentiment grew apace among producers.

In Western Europe the new uncertainty over raw materials supplies—for tomorrow and in the decades to come—produced virtually no policy response. The rule of when in doubt, do nothing, seemed to fit the case, for there were and are many more doubts than certainties. Since the end of the war, Europe had gradually outgrown the raw material base on which its industrialization had been achieved. Under the *Pax Americana*, it began to depend on raw materials produced in distant places, considering security of supply as a state of nature. A brief interruption in this frame of mind was caused by the Suez crisis of 1956. The realization that oil supplies—then a small part of total energy consumption—could easily be cut off led to the formation of Euratom. The Common Market was literally an afterthought to the central task of providing for joint energy security. By an accident of fate, just as the new institution had started to function, the United States adopted an autarchic energy policy. This caused the diversion of the newly discovered oil resources of the Middle East to Western Europe, at prices which killed nuclear prospects for over a decade.

By the early sixties, only the coal lobby still used the term "security of supply". But it was social policy, not security concerns, which saved European coal production from extinction. In this sector, as in others, the task of providing the raw materials for Western Europe was left to the multinational companies. If there were reservations, these applied to pricing policy, not to the ability of these companies to deliver the goods. In retrospect, one can only marvel at this confidence in the presumably indefinite capacity of private companies to exploit the resources of other countries. It was a confidence fully shared by these companies themselves which sometimes acquired operating rights valid until the end of the century and beyond.

The state of nature turned out to be the result of an accidental configuration of power. Prices seemed to be determined by the market, that is, production costs downstream, and consumer preferences upstream. And so they were—more or less—as long as a near-zero value was assigned to the resources in the ground, or, in the case of agricultural commodities, to land and labour needed for production. Yet commodity markets, more than any other, are dominated by small oligopolies—*de facto* monopsonistic buyers facing a number of countries, developed and undeveloped, eager to receive even small returns from their resources.

Without Western know-how and equipment to get them out of the ground, and without Western markets to use them, minerals were quite useless. Agricultural commodities, unlike food production, offered the chance to receive foreign exchange with which to build the future. It is not surprising either that much of the processing of raw materials was done in the consuming countries. Illiterate agrarian societies seemed hardly promising locations for complex machinery. By the time the rising expectations of the fifties and sixties had produced a universal desire for industrialization, worldwide production had set into the pattern denounced as unequal today. As the real opportunities of producer countries became apparent, however, the consumer countries, unwisely and for the sake of protecting a few tens of thousands of jobs, resorted to discriminatory tariffs and quotas to maintain their position.

Yet it would be foolish to argue that the industrialized countries owe their prosperity to the exploitation of the raw materials producers. That prosperity is due entirely to the value-added which technology, education, and deferred consumption have enabled them to achieve. Compared to the total wealth produced by our economies, commodities represent a relatively small proportion. In 1968, world mineral production amounted to about $ 80 billion, or 4 % of the combined GDP [1]. Fuel represented over 70 % of that figure, much of it produced in the industrialized countries themselves. Even if we include non-mineral raw materials notably rubber and fibres, the total share of non-fuel industrial commodities will scarcely exceed 3 % of GNP.

The following table gives the share of all commodities, including food, in gross value-added at factor costs for the Six. Since input-output tables are not often brought up-to-date, the figures apply to 1965. With the greater efficiency of materials use and the greater value-added, today's figures (except for energy) would be lower.

Table 6

Basic commodities: share in gross value-added
(EEC-Six, 1965)

	percent
Agricultural commodities	9.63
Other non-energy, including rubber	1.93
Fuels	7.92
Total	19.47

Source: Hans Michaelis, *Memorandum über eine europäische Rohstoffversorgungspolitik*, 1972, p. 27.

Of course, the value of materials is not the only indicator of their importance for the economy. Without them, the huge inverted pyramid of production that characterizes a modern economy would collapse. Since this is hardly at issue, the operational and more difficult question of relevance to economic security is: what shortfalls of what commodities would cause severe disruptions of the economy, and how likely are such interruptions?

Aside from the oil boycott, which seems to have exerted direct recessionary effects on the United States and Holland, and the British coal strike of February 1974, entailing similar consequences, we have had little concrete experience with the effects of sudden interruptions in supply. If we assume that oil, in terms both of importance and of the magnitude and duration of the supply interruption, represent the worst that could happen, then there is no great cause for alarm with regard to the other commodities. On the other hand, import dependence on oil or rather energy (60 %) is much lower than for many other materials (up to 100 %); and oil is the one commodity for which stockpiles exist. The 25 % production cuts imposed by some Arab members of OPEC (not Iraq and probably not Libya) are not of a different magnitude from the export cuts of 15 % and more agreed by copper, rubber, or tin producers in, admittedly, weak market situations.

Yet unless supply cutbacks of other commodities lasted very long, their effect—unlike that of energy—would probably be limited to single sectors of

1. *Annales des Mines*, p. 8.

101

the economy. The most vulnerable sector, with the greatest potential to affect the rest of the economy is steel. It requires iron ore, scrap, and small but crucial quantities of hardeners (cobalt, chronium, nickel, manganese, molybdenum, and vanadium) which, however, are in part mutual substitutes.

A very broad summary of the European Community's dependence on raw material imports is given in the tables below. The first shows the high proportion, sixty percent, of raw materials of total imports. Little of this trade is conducted according to standards of liberal market economies: prices, production levels, export and import quantities, and the degree of processing are determined by governments or powerful oligopolies. Non-fuel industrial commodities, however, account for only 19 % of imports.

Table 7

Commodities: EEC third country imports

	percent
Food, tobacco, etc.	19.4
Other agric. comm.	9.3
Ores and minerals	4.8
Fuel	19.8
Nonferrous metals	4.7
	58.0
Nonraw materials	42.0
All third country imports	100.0

Source: Hans Michaelis. Memorandum über eine europäische Rohstoffpolitik, 1975, p. 20 (rounded figures).

The following table gives the sources of raw material imports, including food products.

Table 8

Origin of EEC raw material imports, 1972

	percent
Industrialized countries	36.1
of which the United States	10.4
Developing countries	55.6
Centrally planned economies	8.3
	100.0

Source: Michaelis, op. cit., p. 20 (rounded figures).

The last table is based on a comprehensive evaluation of raw material dependence carried out by the European Commission [2]. Possibilities for substitution and recycling are indicated, as well as the trend towards local (extra-Community) processing and the political risk.

2. "Die Rohstoffversorgung der Gemeinschaft," Bulletin der Europäischen Gemeinschaft, Beilage 1/1975.

Table 9

Critical Raw Materials

Commodity	percent Dep.	Possibilities of Substitution	recycling	Political risk	Processing	Supply Security
Aluminium	56	good	26	no	yes	Satisfactory
Chrome	100	some	22	yes	yes	Risk
Copper	95	some	35	yes	yes	Risk
Tin	83	some	45	no	yes	Satisfactory
Iron	80	low	17	no	yes	Sufficient
Manganese	100	low	low	yes	yes	Satisfactory
Phosphate	99	minimal	low	yes	yes	Risk
Platinum	100	low	20	yes	yes	Sufficient
Wolfram	95	some	25	yes	no	Risk
Zinc	75	some	20	no	yes	Risk
Wood	17	low	24	yes	yes	Risk
Pulp	40	low	24	yes	yes	Risk
Paper	58	n.a.	n.a.	n.a.	n.a.	Risk
Veg. oil	78	good	0	no	yes	Satisfactory
Wool	80-100	good	·30	yes	no	Risk
Hides	40	some	0	yes	yes	Unsatisf.
Protein	80	some	0	yes	no	Unsatisf.

Source: Michaelis, *op. ci.,* p. 234.

Some of the judgments of this table will be explicitly or implicitly criticized in the following analysis. In general, the concern of the Commission, and hence the basis for judging the supply situation, is somewhat different from the economic security perspective of this analysis.

The characterization of proteins, hides, and wood products as critical materials points to this difference. The Commission is concerned that individual sectors of the economy—meat and dairy production, the shoe industry, and the paper industry—might be deprived of essential inputs. In its recommendations, autarchic measures for timber are noted as particularly urgent. The most detailed recommendations have been developed for this sector. In other words, the concerns are as much part of industrial policy as they are related to the viability of the total economy. From the more dramatic perspective of economic security as we have defined it, a slight (and healthy) reduction of protein intake, a less frequent change in footwear fashions, or a marginal decrease in printed output, e.g. advertising circulars, would easily cope with supply difficulties in the sectors mentioned.

Supply interruptions are only one source of supply insecurity. Equally worrisome, though as difficult to assess is the prospect of a gradual scarcity of supplies that would subject industry to a constant socially and economically costly adjustment burden with, at the extreme, an enforced change of life style for European society.

Natural scarcity

In economic terms, scarcity can be defined as the need to employ increasingly large amounts of other resources to obtain a given output of a commodity. When these amounts, and hence the price, are larger than any conceivable use would warrant, the supply of the commodity can be said to have run out. In an intermediary situation, consumption declines through greater efficiency of use, substitution, and the inability of certain consumers to pay. This latter case is of particular relevance to Third World countries. Already as a result of recent rises in the price of oil, grain, and fertilisers, the inability to pay has forced many LDCs to reduce imports and production of food to a level that is bound to increase starvation. In the longer run, rising real costs of primary commodities may make the inputs that are needed for the first stages of industrialization prohibitively expensive for LDCs, and hence destroy the hopes for such development. The most critical commodity in this respect is energy.

For the rich countries, a doubling of the real costs of commodities in forty years—which is a reasonable guess for minerals [3]—would lead to an acceleration of the present trend towards efficient resource allocation: in a decade when the United States GNP grew by 60 %, materials use grew by only 20 %.

Even if the ratio of commodities to GNP were to remain constant, we would have to devote 12 % instead of the present 6 % of GNP to commodities, or 0.14 % of annual growth incrementally—hardly a frightening prospect. Not surprisingly, many economists, aware of the successful adaptation of the industrial economies to drastically changed terms of resource availability in the recent past—the passing of the coal and steel age and the coming of the oil and plastics age; the revolutionary changes in the labour intensity of agriculture—dismiss concern about depleting resources as a fallacy based on the extrapolation of the status quo. They are supported by the geologists, who fail to see an absolute resource problem even at historical rates of increase in consumption, provided a higher price is paid to make up for the exhaustion of the most economic deposits. The exception is oil, which, at a price, can be replaced by coal-derived hydrocarbons from plentiful reserves.

A first doubt about this optimistic scenario comes precisely from the energy outlook. Because energy is crucial to the availability of all other commodities, we have to suspend our self-imposed exclusion of energy topics in this analysis. The best guess about total discoverable world reserves, which have remained constant for a decade, is about 2,000 billion barrels a day. Of that, 300 are used up and 700 are proven reserves. 1,000 billion remain to be discovered. At pre-energy-crisis rates of growth in consumption of 7 ½ % per annum, 2,050 billion barrels would have been consumed by the year 2000. [4] Even to sustain the more moderate expansion that is likely from now on, however, will

3. Cf. Callot, *Annales des Mines, op. cit.* p. 14.
4. I thank Caroll Wilson of M.I.T. for supplying me with this piece of arithmetic.

make huge demands on capital. One frequently used estimate raises the proportion of world GNP that must now be devoted to the expansion of oil supplies alone from the historical figure of 1 ½ % to 5 %! In addition, huge capital expenditures are needed for the development of nuclear energy and coal development. To this may be added perhaps fairly soon, solar energy, once the limitations of the other sources become evident. The great hope that fusion would begin to make an impact by the 1990s has receded to sometime in the first quarter century of the third millennium. This assigns a crucial role to the fast breeder. According to an often-cited Club of Rome forecast, world electricity will demand 24,000 fast breeders in fifty years' time. To site even 1/100th part of this total in Western Europe would prove difficult. To insure the technical and social control of these breeders and their wastes would overtax man's capacity. Unlike normal reactors, breeders are not inherently safe. Yet normal reactors would require half a million tons of uranium *a year* by the end of the century, as opposed to a total absolute requirement of that magnitude under a fast breeder programme. [5]

These figures raise questions not only as to the price of future energy supplies, but also about their future availability. Energy, however, is a critical and increasingly important input in the expansion of the supplies of *all* commodities. For metals and energy itself, producing and processing lower grade deposits requires more energy, as does transport from unfavourable locations. Recycling, one of the most important contributions to an expanding supply of metals, is highly energy intensive.

However the more serious implications apply to world food production. The four inputs into agricultural production—energy, water, land and fertilizer—are all limited, with energy compounding the limits of the last three. Energy is needed for building and operating irrigation systems that could increase the amount of available land. Half the world's fertilizer use consists of gas- or naphtha-based nitrogen. Yet even if Third World agricultural production, by means of a massive transfer of capital and fertilizers, could be raised to the level existing in the rich countries, the studies made by Mesavoric and Pestel for the Club of Rome show that, in South Asia alone, population growth would in fifty years lead to an import need equal to the present total grain production of the Western world [6]. Western production, however, will no longer be able to increase at historic rates as limits to the genetic improvement of plants are reached, all arable land is now under the plough, and lack of water looms as a serious limitation in the United States.

Here we come, indeed, to the real difference between the resource optimists and pessimists, which lies to a considerable extent in the decoupling of the rich

5. David Fishlock, "Future energy threats that require a fast reaction," *Financial Times*, 1st october 1975.
6. Mihailo Mesavoric und Eduard Pestel, Menschheit am Wendepunkt: *2. Bericht an Club of Rome zur Weltlage*, Stuttgart, 1974, p. 115.

country from the global problem. If such a decoupling were possible, our analysis could limit itself to the points made earlier that Europe is potentially autarchic in food and can afford to pay the higher resource costs of other primary commodities. The problems of the LDCs could be left outside the analysis as a welfare problem. In fact, the scale of potential shortfalls of resources for the LDCs is such that it will directly influence supply availability in industrialized countries.

Firstly, civilized society, however structurally orientated to satisfy domestic demands and to give only marginal consideration to external demands, ultimately will not be able to ignore the likely successive waves of famine. It will have to divert not only long-term financial resources, but, periodically, real (food) resources to LDCs. This may well entail a self-imposed change in consumption patterns, e.g. a reduction of the animal protein intake to release grain for the feeding of people. A crisis allocation of fertilizers to LDCs, where the marginal utility is a multiple of that obtaining in rich countries, could also become necessary. In both cases the sudden diversion of supplies could lead to unrest among farmers and consumers, as well as a general dislocation of economic policy. In 1975, American grain sales to the Soviet Union are expected to give a 2 % boost to United States inflation. Without question, crisis allocation of significant amounts of food and fertilizers would represent a threat to social harmony in Western Europe.

There are, of course, many experts who question this view. Unfortunately, the occurrence of a major famine, a multiple of the Sahel disaster, could well take place, not in twenty but in two years. The United States' grain reserves are depleted and will remain so at least until the autumn of 1976. A catastrophically bad harvest, such as recurs in North America every two or three decades, is overdue. Governments, faced with tight budgets and high grain prices, hesitate to institute an international grain reserve of sufficient size.

A major world famine whether in two or in ten years not only represents a threat to life for millions and a potentially disruptive event for Western societies, it would also touch on the—by comparison trivial—access-to-supplies concerns of the industrialized world. A starving world would be one beset by domestic strife, revolution and civil war, regional wars, and international terrorism. Among other things, the production and expansion of commodities could come to a halt.

A contrary if somewhat cynical view is also possible; growing dependence on Western food exports would make LDCs more amenable to Western demands, just as dependence on development credits did in earlier decades. The use of the food weapon as a carrot (Middle East) or a stick (India), is never entirely absent in postwar United States diplomacy, and is increasingly seen as a central bargaining asset in the North-South confrontation. But when such aid falls short of needs, as it would in a really bad supply-demand imbalance, the utility of food as a diplomatic instrument would be small. There may not be many viable governments on the other side with which to bargain.

This reference to governments brings us to the main problem of scarcity as it touches Western Europe. This is not the—admittedly debatable—shortage of resources as such, but the impact of government policy on the actual availability in the medium term. Before returning to this issue, a more detailed analysis of the import dependence of the Community will be attempted, coupled with an evaluation of producers' ability to manipulate markets, a matter that plays such a prominent role in present international bargaining.

The importance of the Third World

Like generals always fighting the last war, we tend to analyse the supply issue in terms of our experience with OPEC and OAPEC. As will be suggested later, supply interruptions, insufficient production, sudden price changes and high prices for non-oil commodities are quite likely to come from sources other than collective market management by producer associations. But these associations cannot simply be dismissed as hopeless endeavours unable to stem the irresistible tide of the market. References to the historical failures of such endeavours are unconvincing in today's context.

One of the most comforting arguments for the likely ineffectiveness of LDC radicalism, with respect to raw material markets, is their relatively small share of total world production. A survey published in 1975 by the German Federal Institute of Geological Sciences and Raw Materials, Hanover, made headlines by showing that the Western industrialized countries accounted for 40.9 % of world mineral output, the Communist countries for another 30.1 %, leaving 29 % for the developing countries. The conclusion was that LDCs could not hope to manipulate world commodity markets. The following table gives a breakdown for the most important minerals in 1973, ranked in order of the developed countries' share as well as of the changes in percentage shares since 1962. (See Table 10 p. 108.)

The relative importance of LDCs increases somewhat if we look at exports rather than production shares. LDCs account for 88 % of bauxite, 77 % of tin and half of world manganese exports. For most non-energy minerals the shares are as shown in Table 11 p. 109.

The disaggregation of the total 33.7 % share of the LDCs as the bottom of table 11 shows that LDCs account for 40.7 % of exports of ores, i.e. for raw materials proper. How these relative shares will develop in the future (the changes over the last decade are listed in the table) will obviously depend on a number of factors, some of them political. But it is worth noting that although the LDCs produce only one third of the world's minerals, they hold 42 % of known reserves and contain half of the world's land surface, as against one quarter for Western developed countries.

Table 10

Share of different groups of countries in world mineral production 1972 (1962)

Commodity	Group	Share in 1972	% diff. to 1962
Nickel	DCs*	68.1	— 1.9
	LDCs*	12.9	+ 5.9
	CPEs*	19.0	— 4.0
Zinc	DCs	58.2	+ 2.2
	LDCs	19.6	— 1.9
	CPEs	22.2	— 0.3
Lead	DCs	54.3	+ 6.3
	LDCs	19.0	— 6.6
	CPEs	26.7	+ 0.3
Phosphate	DCs	43.0	— 7.3
	LDCs	29.0	+14.4
	CPEs	28.0	— 7.1
Copper	DCs	42.9	+ 0.3
	LDCs	37.4	— 3.7
	CPEs	19.7	+ 3.4
Iron	DCs	41.2	— 5.3
	LDCs	25.7	+ 5.1
	CPEs	33.1	+ 0.2
Fluorspar	DCs	40.5	— 6.3
	LDCs	38.6	+12.6
	CPEs	20.9	— 6.3
Bauxite	DCs	35.3	+14.2
	LDCs	50.8	— 8.5
	CPEs	13.9	— 5.7
Chromium	DCs	32.8	+ 6.9
	LDCs	27.6	—14.7
	CPEs	39.6	+ 7.8
Manganese	DCs	23.2	+ 9.3
	LDCs	33.3	+ 0.3
	CPEs	43.5	— 9.6
Tin	DCs	8.8	+ 4.7
	LDCs	76.5	+ 2.1
	CPEs	14.7	— 6.2

* DCs: (Western) developed countries.
  LDCs: less developed countries.
  CPEs: centrally planned economies.

Source: Bundesanstalt für Gewissenschaften und Rohstoffe: *Regionale Verteilung der Weltbergbauproduktion*, 1975, pp. 13-14.

Table 11

Shares in 1970 exports of the principal minerals and metals

	World export bill $	LDCs %	DCs %	CPEs %
Aluminium bauxite	0.29	88	12	—
metal	2.44	5	84	11
Chromium (ore)	0.10	22	37	41
Copper ore	0.56	42	58	—
metal	5.62	44	54	2
Tin ore	0.05	64	36	—
metal	0.60	77	23	—
Iron (ore)	2.20	42	58	—
Manganese (ore)	0.15	51	34	15
Nickel ore	0.48	24	76	—
metal	1.02	7	93	—
Lead ore	0.12	12	88	—
metal	0.40	11	84	5
Zinc ore	0.25	14	86	—
metal	0.39	12	74	14
Phosphate	0.45	43	22	35
Total	15.12	33.7	61.8	4.5
of which:				
Ore	(4.65)	(40.7)	(54.4)	(4.9)
Metal	(10.47)	(30.6)	(65.0)	(4.4)

Source: Doc. A/9544/Add. 1 Sixth Special Session, UN, April 1974. From *Annales des Mines,* January, 1975, p. 27.

Table 12

Comparative import dependence for ferrous (f) and nonferrous (nf) metals, by importing and exporting regions

Importer	% import depen- dence		LDCs*		Africa		of which Latin America		Asia		DC*		CPEs*	
	nf	f	nf	f	nf	f	nf	f	nf	f	nf	f	nf	f
EEC-9	58	70	65	54	34.3	31	27.5	22	3	1	31	43.5	4	2.5
Japan	74	98	62	54	20	5	18	25	24	24	34	45	4	1
US	35	32	74	45	1.5	4	66.8	41	6	—	25.5	55	0.2	—

* Customs statistics corrected to show the real origin of raw materials processed in third countries.
Source: Annales des Mines, January 1975, pp. 37-38.

Table 13

Western European raw material imports - Major suppliers

(Share of Total, 1972)

	United States	Canada Australia So. Africa & Rhodesia	Developing Countries Africa except So. Africa & Rhodesia	Latin America Caribbean	Asia [a]	Communist Countries	Yugoslavia
Aluminium	14	26	13	5	2	27	8
Bauxite/Alumina	—	51	15	12	1	4	17
Chromium ore & conc.	—	33	12	☆	9	42	2
Copper ores & conc.	2	48	6	23	10	2	9
Copper	7	41	21	21	1	7	3
Iron ore & conc.	—	20	39	37	—	4	☆
Lead ores & conc.	4	27	34	28	—	2	5
Lead	1	65	6	12	1	10	5
Manganese ore & conc.	3	39	38	15	1	4	☆
Nickel ores & conc.	—	89	☆	1	10	—	☆
Nickel	8	67	2	4	1	17	
Phosphate rock [b]	22	—	53	—	—	11	☆
Tin	—	1	18	4	66	11	☆
Tungsten ore & conc.	11	16	4	26	25	18	☆
Zinc ores & conc.	1	65	9	21	2	1	1
Zinc	1	43	15	—	—	36	4

☆ Less han 0.5 %.
a) Includes Middle East and Oceania.
b) Percentage figures do not account for all imports.

Source: Council on International Economic Policy, *Special Report, Critical Imported Materials,* December 1974, p. 45.

Table 12 allows a comparison between the EEC, the United States and Japan as regards their import dependence for nonferrous metals and iron ore; it further gives a regional breakdown for LDC-supplied metals. The shares of the Western and Socialist countries are also listed.

The margin of comfort has thus successively been reduced by passing from the LDC share in world production, one-third, to world trade and reserves, two-fifths, to their share in the total imports of the core-OECD countries, namely two-thirds.

The safe suppliers

Comfort is further reduced by taking a closer look at those Western industrialized countries, the fellow capitalists whose weight, in the view of the optimists, will thwart any attempt by LDCs to manipulate the market. There are, *grosso modo,* only four regions where Western developed countries produce non-fuel minerals: the United States, Australia, Canada, and South Africa/Rhodesia. The United States is a substantial importer. Canada and Australia are becoming advocates or at least practitioners of resource nationalism. The future of southern Africa is uncertain. Table 13 p.110 gives the share of non-fuel mineral imports from this last group of countries in the total import figures for Western Europe.

Since 1972, Australia's importance has grown substantially as regards bauxite (80 % of Germany's imports are derived from its huge new deposits) and like Canada, it will become crucial as regards uranium in the near future.

Consumer countries looking for a haven from LDC economic revisionism will be disappointed by both Australia and Canada. The familiar demands of the developing countries—national ownership of resources, control over the rate of exploitation, the extraction of a maximum economic rent from the possession of raw materials, and insistence on domestic processing—are all being successfully advanced by both Canada and Australia. The Petroleum and Minerals Authority Act, adopted by Australia in August 1974, has the purpose of ensuring maximum national ownership and control over mineral resources and related industries. The Australian Industry Development Corporation, like its Canadian counterpart, the Canada Development Corporation, has been set up to obtain majority shares in foreign-owned resource companies. The Minister for Minerals and Energy, Mr. R.F.X. Connor was especially active in the pursuit of nationally oriented policy. Before his resignation in October 1975, he had announced that the 1976 elections would be fought on the issue of "Who owns Australia?"

Australia's fiscal policies in 1975 were such that on average mining companies would have to receive 30-40 % more for their products from comparable fields to attain the profitability of American operations. As a result of low profitability and the threat of being forced to divest themselves of majority control

111

(not necessarily through nationalization, but through forced sales of stock to the Australian public), companies significantly reduced exploratory activity in 1974-1975 to its lowest level since 1968. Important new discoveries, like the Agnew nickel deposits in Western Australia, are not being developed [7]. The unilateral imposition of a stiff export tax on coal developed by Japanese capital under supposedly long-term contractual agreements, has also undermined Australia's image as a partner playing by the classic rules of the liberal world economy. In its negotiations with the European Community, Australia has made the export of its badly needed uranium (without which present plans to expand European nuclear electricity production would simply have to be abandoned) conditional on enrichment in Australia, which would require a transfer of technology by one of the European enrichment consortia. During a recent visit to Europe, former Australian Prime Minister Whitlam linked the issue of uranium supplies to securing an assured market for Australian beef [8].

Australia not only acted like a developing country, it was also moving diplomatically closer to the Third World. When announcing its decision to join the Association of Iron Ore Exporting Countries in July 1975, the Minister for Overseas Trade said that the decision was influenced by a commitment to closer relations with developing countries [9]. Like Canada, Australia has applied for associate membership in the copper exporters' association, CIPEC [10]. During an official visit to Yugoslavia, Prime Minister Whitlam sought Tito's help to be accorded observer status at the nonaligned summit conference in Sri Lanka in 1976. The joint communique issued after the visit also stressed the need for substantial changes in the world economy, the establishment of a new economic order, and the introduction of more just terms of trade in the exchange of primary and industrial products [11]. Resource nationalism of the rather ideological kind was associated with the former Labour government. By mid-1975 some of the new policies were beginning to be watered down. It is too early to say whether the election of a conservative government in December 1975 will lead to a complete reversal of policy.

Canadian policy shows many parallels with that of Australia. But Canadian resource nationalism is less narrowly based on a particular party and its leadership. The issue of national ownership of resources is linked to the more general resistance against American domination of the Canadian economy. As in Australia, resource conservation, particularly in the field of energy, plays a large role. Like Australia, only much more forcibly, resource nationalism is compounded by the federal structure of the country. Resource-rich provinces like Alberta defend their interest against consuming provinces in the east. The issues

7. "Lessons from the Agnew Postponement," *Financial Times,* 23rd June 1975.
8. "Whitlam kritisiert die Agrarpolitik der Europäer: Junktim zwischen Uran-Lieferungen und stärkerem Export?" *Frankfurter Allgemeine Zeitung,* 18-I-1975.
9. "Australia to join the iron ore association," *Financial Times,* 4th July 1975.
10. *Financial Times,* 31st October 1974.
11. *Australian Foreign Affairs Record,* January 1975, pp. 23-24.

are those familiar from the international context: conservation, local processing and, above all, keeping the economic rent in the provinces.

The legally-contested sovereignty of the federal governments of both Canada and Australia over the natural resources of the provinces and states respectively, introduces an element of instability and unpredictability in their international and domestic resource policies that is likely to last indefinitely into the future. In Canada's case, this dispute has had particularly disruptive results in the field of taxation. In their struggle over the benefits derived from natural resources, both the provincial and federal governments have taxed the companies, often without the kind of elementary double taxation agreement common between different countries. One copper company in British Columbia, for example, had to pay out 136 % of earnings during the first half of 1975 to satisfy the combined royalty and tax demands of the provincial and federal government [12]. The Newfoundland government deprived another company of the right to develop further an important iron ore deposit, paying it compensation which was a third of the $ 3.4 million already invested in the project [13]. Not surprisingly, exploration activity in Canada is sharply down; hard-rock mineral exploration is 60 % below the 1972 level in British Columbia. The federal government responded to the fall in exploration activity by raising taxes further while at the same time allowing for tax reduction for exploration activities [14]. Both the provinces and the federal government increasingly insist on local processing of raw materials (including timber) as a condition for granting future development rights.

Trade unions constitute another element making for uncertainty as regards both costs and the assurance of steady suppiles from the industrialized countries. Like governments, and often in competition with them, unions try to obtain the economic rent for their members which a given international market situation may provide. This can be observed with respect to coal miners in all low-cost producing countries as well as in Great Britain, and to uranium miners in Australia and elsewhere. As a result, international cost patterns become harmonized at the highest level, and temporary price fluctuations are permanently locked into the cost structure of the industry. (Royalty and other financial demands by governments now increasingly work in the same fashion.)

Secondly, trade unions may interrupt the supply of raw materials. Since for most materials, five countries hold over half the market, interruption in any single one may cause worldwide shortages and high prices. Such interruptions may occur at the production stage, or involve railwaymen or dockers. Strikes may occur for straight wage related purposes, but also for political purposes. A recent case in point is the refusal by United States longshoremen, under Mr. Meany's guidance, to load grain ships bound for the Soviet Union. Similar

12. *Financial Times,* 26th August 1975.
13. *Financial Times,* 1st July 1975.
14. *Financial Times,* 2nd July 1975.

strikes have occurred in Australia against French shipments in protest against atomic tests in the Pacific.

There is thus cause to question the faith in Western industrialized raw-material producers as safe alternatives to less developed countries. Nor should this conclusion be surprising to Western Europeans. National control over and direct ownership of natural resources are practised by the three European energy exporters or potential exporters, Holland, Norway and Britain. Uncertainty over national policy has already led to a decline of exploration and development in the North Sea, and thus directly jeopardized the economic security of Western Europe. In the wake of the OPEC-imported oil-price rises, Holland has as a matter of course raised the export price of its very low-cost natural gas fourfold, and no one has suggested the application of a cost-plus formula, which the Western countries as a group suggest as fair and reasonable to the developing countries. The same phenomenon can be observed with regard to coal exports from the United States and South Africa; a price which is denounced as unjust and untenable when charged by developing countries exercising market power in defiance of liberal trade practices, in this instance oil, is charged as a matter of course as the world market price by developed countries selling similar or substitute products. This suggests that the developed raw material producers will not be allies of the consumers against an attempt of LDCs to manipulate the prices of other raw materials. On the contrary, the industrialized raw material producers—East and West—may use the LDCs as pacemakers in setting prices. They may reap the economic benefits through increased investment, higher wages, or export and other taxes. In other words, where these countries do not join formally in producer cartels, they may well, in their own interest, practise tacit collusion.

South Africa, the third of the great mineral exporters, differs considerably from its former Commonwealth partners. Exploration and development of mining activities are being encouraged and new investment is booming. Like most mining investment, lead times are such that much of this production will become available only in the 1980s. Whether at that time the conditions for orderly production will still exist is, however, not entirely certain. For some years, strikes among black mine workers have troubled the industry. Some of the new investment now being undertaken is for new, labour-saving technology. Nevertheless, South African production will continue to depend on workers who potentially form a large and effective fifth column in the historic black-white confrontation in Africa. Neighbouring countries, provided they received some financial compensation from, say, oil-rich Nigeria, could stop the flow of labour to the South. Indeed, such a cutoff has already been imposed by Malawi, leading to a reduction of Malawians in South African mines from 130,000 in 1974 to 12,000 in 1975 [15].

15. "Flow of Malawi labour to Mines may resume," *Financial Times,* 6th October 1975.

In other words, the question is not only whether South Africa would be militarily able to withstand attack or guerrilla warfare from the north, but whether mining production could be maintained in a period of sustained conflict. Prime Minister Vorster has for some years pursued a *détente* policy towards Black Africa. Although initial successes, measured by the magnitude of the task, are impressive, they are based on personal relationships with a few leaders in a continent with notoriously uncertain governments. Objectively, the independence of the former Portuguese provinces Angola and Mozambique, and the reduced degree of white control in any future settlement in Rhodesia and for Namibia, have greatly impaired the strategic position of South Africa.

The large amounts of Western mining capital pouring into South Africa in search of a haven from the fiscal and ownership uncertainties of the rest of the world, represent a dangerous hostage. This may persuade future Western governments to support the *status quo* in South Africa, in the interest of the security of raw material supply. Such a course, however, would jeopardize good relations with the much more important black African and other Third World commodity producers. This reinforces the conclusion that there is no safe country alternative, to building stable relations with the Third World, if imports of commodities are to be assured.

The real threat: insufficient investment

In the early seventies a combination of factors—both economic and political—produced a potentially grave threat to the availability of minerals by the end of the decade: insufficient investment in the exploration and development of new deposits with which to satisfy future demand.

Generally speaking, the problem arises from the fact that virtually no raw-material-producing country, developed or underdeveloped, can generate sufficient capital to develop its own deposits. Hence outside capital and outside technology must be brought in.

In the past this presented few problems, at least not in the non-Communist world. Direct private investment from consumer to producer countries made up for the deficiency. In the last decade, however, the world's entire minerals sector has been taken out of the rules of the game summed up in the term "liberal world economy." Instead, governments have been, or are now, taking over a large part of the economic decision-making and even the managerial tasks formerly left to private enterprise. Yet private companies remain essential. The result is a systematic clash that is highly dysfunctional to the orderly development of future supplies.

To start with the simplest consequence, it now takes much longer to negotiate exploration and production contracts. This causes delays of several years. Such contracts now cover such items as production obligations; the ratio of reinvested and repatriated profits; state participation; and the degree of processing to be done locally in addition the tax and royalty provisions that have always been part of such agreements. Furthermore, there is an increasingly wide gap in the perception between a government and a company of the profitability of a given deposit. This gap is not only due to the capacity of the companies, for, in order to maintain overall profitability, a company makes superprofits on some deposits to balance out its marginal operations. A government, understandably, looks at the domestic-cost picture and tries to pocket the possible economic rent in the form of taxes and royalties. Perversely, however, given the greater contacts among producer governments, on the one hand, and the public nature of the contracts (because of their importance to domestic politics), on the other, the most favourable contract quickly becomes the norm for all new contracts concluded. It also becomes the basis for the renegotiation of old contracts, even where economic conditions are less favourable.

At the same time, in order to be attracted by new investment opportunities, companies now require a much higher level of profitability than in the past. This is primarily due to the uncertainty regarding future ownership and/or the degree of autonomy in the exploitation of deposits. Whereas companies used to assess profitability against the total lifetime of a deposit, e.g. fifteen or twenty years, they now want to see their money back within five years of starting full-scale production (which means at least ten years after the first outlay). Even that period is long compared to the speed with which political change takes place in most countries.

Furthermore, the scale of new investment projects is rising steeply. As mining companies are forced into increasingly distant and inhospitable parts of the globe, only very large projects justify the extensive infrastructure development (transport, electricity generation, etc.) required. Lower-grade deposits require more expensive machinery. These larger investments also extend the period between the initial investment and the first commercial delivery of ore. In the past, investment by mining companies was largely self-financed. Now companies are increasingly forced to go to a sceptical capital market for new funds. Uncertainty over future market prices adds further to uncertainty.

In 1972-1973, the consequences of these difficulties became apparent. While in earlier boom periods investment had always increased, it now was failing to do so, in spite of raw material prices which were a multiple of normal prices [16]. We have already sketched the situation in Canada. In Australia, exploration expenditures fell by 33 % in dollar terms between 1970-71 and 1973-74 [17]. The development of huge new copper deposits in Panama [18] and Bougainville (Papua, New Guinea) has been delayed for years, due to protracted negotiations. Yet if the future world demand of copper is to be met, two new "Bougainvilles" a year are required [19]. Furthermore, the productivity

16. According to findings by the Commodity Research Unit, London.
17. *Neue Zürcher Zeitung*, 19-IX-1975, p. 21.
18. The Cerro Colorado deposits may be the largest in the world. On the negotiations with the Panama government see *Financial Times*, 11th March 1975, p. 23.
19. Personal communication by Robert Perlman.

of existing operations, notably in Zambia, has fallen with the takeover of management responsibilities by a local govermental agency.

Nothing could be more unfashionable in today's political context than to argue for more freedom for multinational companies to operate in foreign lands. But a stabilization of the contractual environment is urgently needed if future supplies for consumer countries, and hence the health of the world economy, are to be assured. Joint ventures between governments and companies provide only a partial answer since most of the capital still has to come from outside. A greater role for the World Bank in providing resource investment capital, such as was proposed by Secretary Kissinger at the UN Special Session in September 1975, would de useful. To quote the relevant passage: "The World Bank and its affiliates, in concert with private sources, should play a fundamental role. They can supply limited amounts of capital directly: more importantly, they can use their technical, managerial and financial expertise to bring together funds from private and public sources. They can act as intermediary between private investors and host governments, and link private and public efforts by providing cross guarantees on performance. World Bank loans could fund government projects, particularly for needed infrastructure, while the international finance corporation could join private enterprise in providing loans and equity capital. The World Bank Group should aim to mobilise two billion dollars in private and public capital annually." [20]

Yet even if and when such schemes come into operation on a large scale, private risk capital will need more assurance than the World Bank will be able to provide in the future. With most of its new borrowing coming from the oil producers, the Bank will gradually shed its role as guardian of capitalist orthodoxy. In September 1975, thirteen European mining companies, worried by the fact that Europe will suffer shortages in eight to ten years, if the drop in worldwide investment is not halted, petitioned the European Commission to pledge itself both financially and politically to providing greater security of investment: financially, through providing insurance against political risk (which would ease the companies' efforts to tap the capital markets). A similar service is provided for the Japanese through the Ex-Im-Bank and by American companies through the Overseas Private Investment Corporation. Politically, they want the Commission to exert pressure on producer countries to provide a more liberal investment climate. [21]

Perhaps more promising may be producer-consumer fora on the governmental level for key commodities, proposed by Secretary Kissinger [22]. These could engage in a sort of elementary indicative planning, but also in bargaining between a stable investment climate on the one hand, and stable markets on the other. This raises the issue of commodity agreements.

20. *Wireless Bulletin from Washington,* No. 154, September 1975, p. 25.
21. Cf. *The Economist,* 13th September 1975.
22. In his speech to the Seventh Special Session of the UN General Assembly, 1-IX-1975.

117

The dangers of instability

One of the greatest threats—directly and indirectly—to investments for an expanding raw material supply is the chronic instability of markets. The direct impact is twofold. During recurrent periods of low prices the cash flow of companies deteriorates dramatically (especially now that high fixed fiscal charges by governments are becoming the rule), thus reducing their capacity to invest. Secondly, forecasting profitability of new deposits becomes mere guess work when prices can fluctuate by a factor of three or four within the space of two years.

Price instability also works indirectly by influencing host-government policy towards companies and consumers. When prices are high, governments step up their fiscal and parafiscal demands, thus reducing super-profits to a "reasonable level." These fiscal charges then become permanently locked into the cost structure, severely depressing profitability in bad years. The case of a company paying 136 % tax on profits was mentioned earlier. On the other hand, LDC resentment, understandable in countries earning up to 90 % of their foreign exchange through raw material exports, becomes explosive when prices decline for a year or two, leading to an increase in radicalism towards the industrialized countries in general and the companies in particular.

The likelihood of greater price fluctuations in the future—barring some move towards commodity agreements—is very high indeed. First, because the synchronised world business cycle discussed in Part II leads to tremendous fluctuations in demand. At the same time, given the scarcity of specialized equipment in boom periods, the normal inelasticity of supply characteristic of raw materials is enhanced.

Furthermore, the dangers of speculation are now far greater than in the past. Speculation has always played a large and often perverse role in commodity markets. Since most supplies are under intracompany, commercial, or inter-governmental contract, the physical quantities traded on commodity exchanges are usually quite small. Yet they have to bear the full weight of total supply-demand imbalances. Furthermore, speculators (including user industries) amplify rather than reduce market imbalances: they buy when prices rise (in anticipation of further rises) and sell when prices fall, thus depressing the market still further [23].

In recent years, a further element has increased speculative activity. Monetary instability, the weak stock markets, and inflation have given commodities a quasi-monetary role. In 1973 alone, forward trading in the United States increased by almost $ 100 billion to $ 135 billion. Between 1963 and 1973, London trading increased from $ 8 billion to $ 70 billion [24]. Increasingly, funds move in and out of commodity markets, not because of intrinsic market

23. Cf. *Annales des Mines,* January 1975, p. 43.
24. "The raw material prices time bomb," *Financial Times,* 26th March 1975.

trends, but in response to exchange rate expectations, interest rates on commercial paper, and the ups and downs of the stock market.

A particularly worrisome question is the role of the surplus oil countries in a future boom. These countries will continue to command vast liquid funds for years to come. They see themselves as leaders of an alliance of raw material producers. Economic and political interest could lead to an aggressive purchasing policy during the next upswing of the world economy. Already in 1973 there were rumours that OPEC money was driving up copper prices. At the October, 1974, CIPEC conference, new rumours of a $ 4 billion support operation by OPEC sent copper prices soaring. In July, 1975, Chile's state copper corporation, Codeco, again raised the prospect of OPEC aid to support copper prices. While nothing seems to have come from these moves, better speculative prospects may revive OPEC's interest. The Special Fund for the support of raw material prices decided on by the nonaligned countries in Lima in August, 1975, for which Kuwait has already earmarked $ 1 billion, also points in this direction [25]. Venezuela, in December 1974, agreed to supply up to eighty million dollars to a coffee-stockpiling scheme for Central America—certainly a helpful move, but one that shows the oil-raw material alliance at work.

Finally a word on the impact of price instability on the economies of the consumer countries. Given their relatively low share in total GNP, a long-term increase in raw material prices is easily manageable. An inflationary impact of significant proportions is more likely to arise from sudden price rises. This is not only because these tend to be larger than any conceivable increase in long-term prices, but also because they occur at precisely the worst possible moment, during a general upswing. They are thus pro-cyclical, reinforcing inflationary trends. At the extreme, witness the experience of Britain in 1973: inflationary pressures and a suddenly deteriorating balance of payments may force governments to apply deflationary measures while the economy is still working below capacity. The pro-cyclical effect can also be observed during downswings: as receipts of raw materials producers fall, the demand for the exports of industrialized countries falls when it is most needed to stabilize the economy.

Producer Associations

Since the success of OPEC, associations of commodity exporting governments have proliferated, and those that already existed have tried to expand their scope. Some of these deserve the name of cartels more than OPEC, because they not only try to set prices, but do so with the help of *agreed* production cuts. The professed intentions of some associations to change the terms of trade in their favour has provoked some unease among Western consumers.

25. *Neue Zürcher Zeitung,* 1-IX-1975.

Such fears need to be put into perspective. To a large extent, associations of mineral producers are the logical consequence of a gradual shift of resource control from private companies to governments. Once production, exploration, investment and marketing decisions are handled by governments, there is a functional need to develop an equivalent to the global planning and market rationalisation role, which in the past was discharged by private oligopolies. From the point of view of efficiency, governments may well be inferior to companies. While companies have extensive global information on reserves, production costs, and marketing opportunities, producer governments mainly know about production within their own geographical area.

Yet given this new role of governments in the raw materials sector, which seems irreversible, it may be better for consumers, if producing countries exchange information, to compare notes on investment, and co-ordinate marketing strategies up to and including the keeping of buffer stocks and production and export controls. In a sense, producer cartels are not necessarily part of the problem, but also part of the solution.

A case in point is the Association of Natural Rubber Producing countries. Although natural rubber is technically superior to synthetic rubber, the latter product, because of its more stable market conditions, has taken two-thirds of the total market. Any price gouging would increase this trend. The maximum aim of rubber producers is therefore to stabilize market conditions. They thus hope to gain a greater market share, to avoid the periodic situations of over-supply; and to reap the price opportunities offered by higher (oil) costs for synthetic rubber. None of this is contrary to market efficiency. But the tools for achieving this policy are highly interventionist: production cut-backs, export controls, and the setting up of buffer stocks. Thus, although three member states, Malaysia, Indonesia and Thailand (Sri Lanka and Singapore are also members), account for 85 % of world rubber exports, there is little danger to consumer interests. The danger comes rather from the insufficient financial means at the disposal of the participating developing countries.

The threat of synthetic substitutes also limits the possibilities of fibre producers for receiving significantly increased prices, although more stable market conditions would, by themselves, raise their income. Coffee, cocoa, and tea could probably find a market at higher prices; although a doubling of cocoa prices in the United States in 1974 led to a reduction of consumption by 18 %. If it were sustainable, this would constitute an attractive tradeoff for producers. With a combined trade value of about $ 5 billion, even a 50 % rise in the price of the three beverages would represent a not insignificant transfer of resources from industrialized and developing countries. Yet an attempt by coffee producers to form a cartel in 1974 had failed by early 1975, forcing the producers to seek a renewal of the International Coffee Agreement; Brazil, Colombia, Ivory Coast and Angola, which account for 60 % of world trade, had formed a joint company, strategically buying and stockpiling coffee to drive up the price. The Central American coffee producers, with the help of Venezuelan money, set up a similar firm. Yet even a producer decision to hold back 20 % of the 1974-75 crop could not prevent a fall in prices [26]. Through consumer resistance, cartelisation had increased instability.

A somewhat different cartel is the Union of Banana Exporting Countries, UPEB, formed in September 1974 by five Central and South American countries accounting for 60 % of world trade. Their main quarrel is not with the consumer countries, but with the three international banana companies which have a joint monopsonistic hold over trade. An attempt to levy a 10 % export tax was promptly countered by successful bribery of cabinet members of the Honduras government [27].

As regards non-fuel minerals, a successful cartel is operated in the field of phosphates by a group of North African countries, Morocco being chief among them. In 1973, prices were tripled, and a further 50 % rise was pushed through in 1974. Although the United States is the world's largest producer, American demand is expected to exceed supply by 1977 [28]. Alternative sources of supply, for example in Australia, are costly and the possibility for further price gouging exists. The Moroccan takeover of Spanish Sahara serves to consolidate the hold of the cartel over the phosphate market.

The second-oldest producer association (after OPEC) is CIPEC (Comité International des Pays Exportateurs de Cuivre), founded in 1967. Its founding members—Chile, Peru, Zambia, and Zaire—control about 40 % of world production and 70 % of primary copper exports. In its first phase, CIPEC co-operation was instrumental in bringing about a policy of gradual national ization or majority ownership, and the formation of national marketing companies. Yet it was not until the slump of copper price in 1974-75 that the more ambitious plans of CIPEC to control prices through export cutbacks were tested. That year, world consumption fell by 5.2 %, Japan's consumption by 33 %. More importantly, Chile's production picked up sharply under the military regime (by about 22 %) in 1974, and sales from the United States strategic stockpile further depressed the market [29]. The CIPEC-imposed export cutbacks of 10 % in the autumn of 1974, and a further 5 % in the spring of 1975 could not prevent a fall of prices to around £ 600 by August 1975 (down from £ 1,300 in May 1974). Western observers have noted with satisfaction that the market proved stronger than the cartel. Yet the evidence is not conclusive: a number of extreme conditions (fall in demand, rise in production, United States' stockpile sales) combined to give producers an exceptionally weak market power. The real testing time will come during the next boom. Even then, however, the CIPEC pricing policy will be relatively moderate. Substitution by other minerals is a major fear. For the low-cost producers, notably Chile, which

26. *International Herald Tribune,* 24th March 1975.
27. *Financial Times,* 16th April 1975.
28. *Special Report on Critical Imported Materials,* Council on International Economic Policy, Washington, December 1974, p. A-60.
29. *Financial Times,* 6th February 1975.

has reserves for 100 years of current production, the fear of market loss through excessive prices is especially worrying [30].

This being said, some increases in long-term prices would seem to be inevitable. With a world trade volume of between five and ten billion dollars, such increases would have some economic impact on consumer economies. The scope for increases would be enlarged, if the threat of substitution from other metals could be reduced. It was therefore interesting to note the presence of observers from the bauxite exporters (IBA) and the iron ore producers at the 1974 session of CIPEC in Lusaka. As a UN report notes ,these producers were conscious of the need for parallel action [31]. Furthermore, as regards copper itself, extension of membership in CIPEC to Indonesia, as well as to Australia and Papua New Guinea (Associates), could possibly add strength to the association.

The International Bauxite Association (IBA) is of much more recent origin. Formally established in March 1974, its membership consists of Australia, Guinea, Guyana, Jamaica, and Sierra Leone, and accounts for about 80 % of the world's bauxite-alumina trade [32]. Jamaica made headlines in 1974 by increasing the government's take sevenfold, thus doubling the price of ore but adding only 10 % to the price of aluminium. Other Third World producers followed suit. With such a small final market effect, the risk of market loss for producers as a group would seem well worth taking. So far, efforts by IBA to impose a floor price have failed. Much more significant for consumers than the 10 % ore cost are the 90 % of the cost derived from the capital- and energy-intensive processing sector. Here the low profits due to the recession and the need for expensive but nonproductive environmental investment (25 % of the total in the United States in 1974) have held back the expansion of capacity, raising the prospect of shortages following the present glut [33]. No doubt the ore producers will take a share of the profits to be derived from such future market conditions.

The most recent addition to the growing family of producer associations is the OIEC, the Organization of Iron Ore Exporting Countries. Among its members are developed countries, Australia, and Sweden, as well as such leading LDCs as Algeria, Brazil, India and Venezuela. Like bauxite, iron ore accounts for a small proportion (9 %) in the final price of steel. Thus a price rise of, say, 50 % would not lead to a significant market loss. World iron ore trade amounted to about £ 2.5 billion in 1972. The Organization has set itself the goal of improving prices, although its developed members deny any similarity to OPEC. With ore production well below capacity [34], market pressures will make concerted action difficult for some years.

30. *Financial Times,* 31st October 1974.
31. *Souveraineté permanente sur les ressources naturelles,* Rapport du Secrétaire Général, A/9716, p. 14.
32. Special Report on Critical Imported Materials, *op. cit.*
33. "When a glut can lead to shortages," *Financial Times,* 19th September 1975, p. 28.
34. Special Report, *op. cit.* p. A-19.

The Organization's goal of influencing long-term investment policy [35] could, however, change this state of affairs. With most low-cost reserves in the hands of the OPEC countries, it can be of little comfort for consumers to know that iron is one of the most abundant materials, with reserves amounting to 200 years at current rates of consumption [36].

It is far too early to judge the future effectiveness of cartels. As it happened, the general enthusiasm for cartels coincided with the biggest drop in demand from the consumer countries since World War II. To a considerable extent, the loss of revenue suffered by the LDCs has caused bitterness and a renewed determination to do something about the conditions of a market which puts such a disproportionate burden of adjustment on them. With time, the conditions for successful collective action will improve. Effective control over production by governments will increase, as will experience in working together. Lastly, every economic upswing will see new efforts to exploit and consolidate market advantages.

If one's bias is towards the assurance of adequate supplies as being more important than price, and if the stability of the price level is viewed as more important than its absolute amount, then the statement holds that producer associations are part of the solution. But even then they are clearly a second-best solution. Unilateral moves, based on a sense of grievance, are unlikely to lead to optimum solutions for either producers or consumers. No doubt producers associations as bargaining bodies are with us to stay. The question is the form which such bargaining will take. An active participation by consumers in the efforts to create more orderly commodity markets would clearly be preferable.

Commodity market stabilization

Schemes for bringing greater stability to world commodity markets can range from completely voluntary to totally co-operative and centrally controlled means of intervention. A certain amount of stabilization always takes place through national stockpiling and production cutbacks by individual producers when prices are low and supplies overplentiful (Brazilian coffee, Australian wool, Malaysian rubber); and through intervention buying by companies or other producers' agents on commodity exchanges, such as the London Metal Exchange (LME), which may involve stockpiling in the warehouses of the LME. The shortcomings of these methods are (a) the insufficient financial means of poorer countries to undertake stockpiling, plus the temptation by other producers to reap the benefits of the tighter market conditions by selling and, (b) that LME interventions are usually too small to offset huge imbalances in supply at the

35. *Financial Times,* 1st April 1975.
36. Special Report, *op. cit.,* p. A-18.

123

production stage. The limited size of the supply overhang thus created is also ineffective in preventing high prices during periods of strong demand.

On the consumer side, individual attempts at market stabilization are much more limited. With the exception of stockpiles of oil and coal (which are largely held for reasons other than market stabilization), European industry generally lives from hand to mouth as regards its raw materials. Sweden and Switzerland have strategic stockpiles as part of their policy on neutrality. France has begun to constitute state-financed strategic stockpiles. None of these helps to stabilize markets. The position of the United States' strategic stockpile is more ambiguous. Established after World War II to give the defense industry safe supplies of some 90 materials for five years in case of war, their purpose had become less strictly defined in the sixties. On several occasions, they had been used by government to stem price gouging by mining companies. In the late sixties, a large proportion of these stockpiles were formally declared in excess of strategic needs and slowly sold off (sales of copper in 1975 helped to drive world copper prices below some producers' costs). Basically, the existence of the huge American stockpiles served as a deterrent to excessive speculation in the past, and their disappearance would be a loss to world price stability. The events of October 1973 have caused some rethinking in the United States government about the wisdom of reducing stockpiles further. The following table lists American stockpiles levels as of June 1974.

Table 14

United States national stockpile levels for selected materials
(As of June 30, 1974)

	Strategic Stockpile Objectives *	Amounts in Excess of Strategic Stockpile Objectives *
Aluminum/Bauxite	2 1/2	7 1/2
Chromium	4	36
Tin	9	35
Manganese	5	13
Nickel	0	0
Platinum group metals	3	5
Zinc	2	2 1/2
Cobalt	7	28
Tungsten	6	85
Vanadium	0	1
Copper	0	0
Lead	3/4	8
Natural rubber	0	2 1/2
Columbium	3 1/2	18
Flourspar	1	8

* In months of peacetime consumption of new material (excludes usage of scrap and reprocessed material).

Source: Council on International Economic Policy, Washington, *Critical Imported Materials, Special Report*, December 1974, p. 22.

Equally unfortunate for world price and supply stability was the adoption by the United States of the Agriculture and Consumer Protection Act of 1973, which sharply reduced the financial resources and targets for stockpile purchases by the American government. The risk of evaluating future market development thus falls on the farmer, who may therefore underproduce. In that case, only low stocks would be available to meet supply shortfalls elsewhere. However, the attempt by the United States to get nations to agree to the establishment of an international grain reserve of perhaps 30 million tons [37] (cf. estimated Soviet import needs of an extra 25 million tons in 1975) may help to offset the change in American policy. This would also be distributing the financial costs of maintaining a world food reserve more evenly among countries.

One general consequence of the shift in American policy on stockpiling, in both the industrial and food commodity sectors, is that the failure by the rest of the world to increase their efforts at stabilization would not leave us in a situation of status quo. Rather, the world would be decidedly worse off than it was in the sixties.

The next higher level of commodity stabilization involves co-operation among either producers or consumers acting unilaterally. Efforts among producers have been discussed above. Among consumers, we have a co-ordinated stockpile policy in the field of oil—both on the European and the OECD (IEA) level—but not for stabilization purposes. Richard Cooper is sceptical of any formal commodity agreements because the price range around which commodities are to be stabilized is so difficult to agree upon. Producers want prices near historic highs; consumers are arguing for historic lows as floor prices. He therefore suggests that Europe, Japan, and the United States buy commodities for stockpiling when prices are low, agreeing on target amounts, on financing, and on the price at which purchases would be made. The circumstances under which the stocks would be used to relieve a particular market pressure or to deter an incipient producer cartel would not need to be specified in advance. Such stockpiles would have a deterrent effect on both speculation and market manipulation [38].

A more sophisticated version of commodity stabilization with a minimum of formal regulation, but which involves consumer-producer co-operation, has been suggested by the Director of the London Commodities Research Unit, Robert Perlman [39]. It is also designed to overcome the drawbacks of formal commodity agreements, i.e. that they are cumbersome and difficult to negotiate, and inflexible once negotiated. Unlike Cooper, Perlman would seek to avoid

37. A United States proposal made to the International Wheat Council in London on September 29, 1975, calls for 25 metric tons of wheat and 5 metric tons of rice to be held by participating countries. *USIS Wireless Report, Bonn*, No. 175.

38. Cooper, Richard, "Trade and Monetary Relations between the United States and Western Europe," unpublished manuscript, June 1975, p. 26.

39. Verbal communication at a working meeting of the Trilateral Commission task-force meeting on access to supplies, Shimoda, Japan, September 1975.

the need for agreement even on broad principles among consumers and producers. Instead, he suggests that a given consumer country negotiate with a producer country the purchase of raw materials for stockpiling purposes at a concessionary price (perhaps half the market price) which covers the variable (labour, etc.) costs of the producers. The low purchasing price would offset the financial burden involved in stockpiling. During a boom supplies would be sold out of the stockpile, with the producer country receiving a portion of the profits negotiated in advance. If several major consumers had such schemes, the effect on market stabilization would be considerable. The proposal is virtually the only one which could be instituted in time to make a difference if world reflation fails to materialize in 1976 and commodity markets collapse further. The scheme, however, is not an adequate answer to LDC demands for stable export receipts, and therefore would have to be complemented by other measures. Stocks constituted under bilateral agreements could, however, become part of international buffer stocks if and when these are negotiated.

In 1975 the Japanese government, under pressure from traditional suppliers of raw materials, instituted a scheme of subsidized stockpiling by firms, aided by the EX-IM bank.

The stabilization of export earnings by raw material producers—an important aim of Third World countries—is not necessarily identical with the stability of prices for their products. While for most mineral and agricultural industrial raw materials, variations in price are due to a conjunctural shift in demand in developed countries, for many tropical food products the variations are due to changes on the *supply* side. A stable price during periods of oversupply would leave countries with huge unsold stocks which could otherwise be disposed of in the market at lower prices. Greater quantities, at a lower price, can mean constant or increased export earnings.

In the past, the only means available for stabilizing export earnings was a special IMF compensatory finance facility, which provided low-interest swing credits in bad years, to be repaid in good years. At the September 1975 Special Session of the UN, Secretary of State Kissinger proposed a much more ambitious version of this scheme, a development security facility to be established by the IMF. Its purpose would be to stabilize *all* export earnings of LDCs by annual loans up to £ 2.5 billion, with a provision that loans be converted to grants under certain conditions.

A less ambitious scheme, covering fewer countries and fewer products (commodities only), and with a stabilization fund whose size is one-twenty-fifth of Kissinger's proposals, is the export earnings stabilization scheme concluded between the European Community and its African Lomé associates.

Stabex

The Lomé Convention was concluded in February 1975 [40] between the European Community and 46 developing countries. It includes all the Black African states that were sovereign at that time, some formerly British Caribbean states (Guiana, Jamaica, Trinidad, Barbados, the Bahamas, etc.), and some Pacific islands (Fiji and Western Samoa). It has a duration of five years.

Apart from a non-reciprocal free trade argreement (the Community receives only guaranteed MFN treatment), and a substantial aid agreement (3.39 billion u.c., or pre-Smithsonian dollars, of which 2.1 billion are straight grants), the most notable feature of the agreement is its export earning stabilization scheme, or Stabex.

The scheme covers cocoa, coffee, cotton, copra, coconut and cake, groundnuts and oil, palm products, hides and skins, timber and wood products, bananas, tea, sisal—and as a last-minute concession, iron ore (but not copper, which the ACP countries also wanted included). A different scheme was applied to sugar.

The ACP countries will receive compensation if their annual export earnings from any commodity fall by more than 7.5 % below a rolling average of the previous four years (2.5 % for the twenty-four poorest countries). The compensation is in the form of an interest-free loan (grant for the twenty-four poorest). It has to be repaid when receipts are higher than the moving average, *provided* these higher receipts are due to higher prices, not just to higher quantities.

A fund of 375 million u.c. is available in yearly tranches of 75 million u.c., although a twenty percent claim on the following year's portion is permitted. Half-yearly advance payments are envisaged to sustain earning power when it is most needed. Note that Stabex finance represents only one-ninth of total aid under the Lomé Convention.

The regulation for sugar exports to the Community is much more far-reaching. The Community guarantees the purchase of 1,222 million tons annually at a price determined annually on the basis of the intra-Community intervention price for sugar. Prices are thus indexed to domestic European prices. The quotas granted to each participating ACP state also imply an obligation to supply. If a country fails to fulfill this obligation (barring *force majeure*), the quota is reduced and distributed to other countries. Unlike the Convention, the Sugar Protocol is not limited to five yeears.

The Stabex scheme and the Agreement in general have been hailed as the most far-reaching, progressive scheme ever negotiated between industrialized and developing countries. There can be no question that, under pressure from the unified negotiating position of the Forty-Six, the Nine went much further in the direction of managed trade than the more market-oriented among them

40. The agreement will not formally come into force until early 1976, as ratification of national parliaments is needed. However, upon ratification it will be backdated to February 1975.

would have wished. Of course, the scheme has some unfortunate similarities with the *caisses de stabilisation* which characterized the late-colonial French regime in Africa. However, that scheme was essentially designed to support French colons, not the local population. It is too early to say whether Stabex will lead to a perpetuation of colonial patterns of production. The fact that substantial financial aid is given (and was demanded) for the purpose of industrialization—hence diversification away from the monocultures—allows considerable hope. A more serious limitation of Stabex is the modest financing: about $ 2 million per country per year.

As a contribution to the security of supplies for Europe the Agreement is probably marginal. Most products covered by Stabex, with the possible exception of sugar, timber and skins, are usually in ample supply. Its true significance is as a model for global action.

Full commodity agreements

A full commodity agreement is one incorporating buffer stocks and export and/or production limitations with the aim of stabilizing prices within a narrow range. The purposes of such arrangements are (a) income stabilization for producers; (b) stable supplies under predictable conditions in both the short and the long term for consumers. Unlike schemes that only stabilize earnings, commodity agreements give greater security not only to countries, but also to private firms engaged in the production and consumption (processing) of raw materials. Commodity agreements, especially those for industrial, nonperishable raw materials, are therefore of particular interest to industrialized countries. The disadvantages are, as mentioned above, the difficulty of negotiating such agreements, especially as regards the price range that is to be the basis for stabilization, and the difficulty of amending such agreements once they are concluded. Much opposition comes from consumer governments that fear the high cost of purchasing the initial buffer stock. Finance ministers in all developed countries, using the somewhat narrow time perspective of the annual budget, see expenditure on buffer stocks as a net outflow, not as an investment.

Although technically and politically more difficult, the stabilization of prices rather than incomes through full commodity agreements has certain advantages over compensatory financing schemes. These advantages accrue especially to consumers of raw materials. Full commodity agreements include buffer stocks and export and production restrictions with which to keep prices around an agreed reference level. Only two commodity agreements at present fulfill these criteria: the International Tin Agreement and the International Cocoa Agreement [41]. Other commodity agreements, now more or less defunct but in the

41. In fact, no buffer stock exists for the Cocoa agreement, as prices remained above intervention levels. Yet prices have deteriorated sharply in real terms in 1975, suggesting the need for indexing intervention levels (see below).

128

process of renegotiation, are the International Wheat Agreement, the International Coffee Agreement, and the International Sugar Agreement. All lack buffer-stock provisions (though this may change). It is therefore quite misleading to argue that the historical experience of commodity agreements is negative. The only true commodity agreement, the Tin Agreement, was reasonably effective. The floor price prevented the collapse of the industry in bad times, although ceiling prices were often broken due to insufficient buffer stocks.

The Corea Plan

In December 1974 the Secretary General of UNCTAD, Gamani Corea, startled the industrialized world with an "Integrated Programme for Commodities," which proposed full commodity agreements for 18 major commodities of interest to developing countries. A list of these commodities, their value and the trade shares of different groups of countries, is given in Table 15 p.130.

Wheat is included because developing countries want stable conditions for *supplies* of this commodity; if excluded, the share of LDCs in the export of these commodities is about twice that of the industrialized countries. In spite of this, Western spokesmen have rejected the proposal on the grounds that commodity agreements mainly favour the rich countries (making the implicit assumption that commodity agreements involve a transfer of benefits from consumers to producers).

One important element of the Corea Plan is the "integrated" approach to commodity management. This in fact means a single agency responsible for managing stocks, etc. In theory, important advantages can be claimed for such an approach. Many commodities are mutual substitutes (e.g. feed grains and oil cake). The financing requirements could be reduced, as different commodities, except during long and deep business cycles, do not fluctuate all in the same direction (cf. high wheat and coffee prices, low metals prices in mid-1975). World macroeconomic (anticyclical) measures could be combined with stock management. International agreement on commodity agreements would be facilitated because "the scope for mutual concessions and reciprocity would be much greater than in dealing with single commodity schemes" [42].

As it turned out, the prospect of a single international bureaucracy "taking over" the bulk of world trade in primary commodities was particularly frightening to Western governments. Indeed, the suspicion that such an agency, perhaps under the UNCTAD auspices, would become a pressure group under the domination of the developing countries seems justified. The precise balancing of consumer and producer interests which in the Tin Agreement is guaranteed

42. "An Integrated Programme for Commodities: The role of commodity stocks." *UNCTAD* TD/B/C.1/166/Supp. 1, p. 19.

Table 15

Major stockable commodities: Trade values, 1972 [a]

(Millions of United States dollars)

	Exports f.o.b.				Imports c.i.f.			
	World	Developed market-economy countries	Socialist countries	Developing countries	World	Developed market-economy countries	Socialist countries	Developing countries
Wheat [b]	4,366	3,818	388	160	4,609	1,540	1,291	1,778
Maize	2,298	1,914	53	331	2,444	1,905	324	215
Rice	1,120	537	143	440	1,232	175	82	974
Sugar	3,334	921	178	2,235	3,379	2,304	460	614
Coffee (raw)	3,049	—	—	3,049	3,368	3,101	126	141
Cocoa beans	723	—	—	723	729	572	131	26
Tea	745	79	57	609	784	470	72	242
Cotton	2,828	587	484	1,757	3,055	1,714	792	549
Jute and manufactures	762	71	21	670	840	520	120	200
Wool	1,346	1,143	42	161	1,722	1,361	257	105
Hard fibres	87	3	—	84 [c]	106	92	7	7
Rubber	904	—	—	904	1,095	689	305	101
Copper	4,113	1,364	354	2,395	4,226	3,635	377	214
Lead	418	257	45	116	470	379	60	31
Zinc	862	558	110	194	938	736	77	125
Tin	730	70	28	632	758	613	53	92
Bauxite	305	82	5	218	363	325	36	2
Alumina	609	265	46	298	685	532	91	62
Iron ore	2,608	1,213	403	992	3,484	3,039	425	21
Total	31,207	12,882	2,357	15,968	34,287	23,702	5,086	5,499

a) The figures are preliminary. In sugar, cocoa and copper, import values appear understated in relation to exports. In metals and ores, EEC intra-trade is excluded.
b) Including flour.
c) In addition, $ 49 million exports of hard fibres manufactures.

Source: United Nations Conference on Trade and Development, TD/B/C.1/166, p. 7.

130

through an equal number of Council votes for both groups, irrespective of the number of countries involved, would be difficult to achieve. Indeed, a kind of trade union loyalty among producers could lead to automatic support for high-price decisions, while the single financial pool would remove the discipline which limited finances impose on stockmanagers.

All Western governments therefore insist on a commodity-by-commodity approach, and individual commodity agreements suited to each particular case. Some of the advantages of an integrated programme could, however, be achieved even under a piecemeal approach. In the area of financing buffer stocks, broader use of loans from the IMF, already an established if limited practice under the Tin Agreement, is under active consideration. A greater use of IMF-finance for buffer stocks would have considerable advantages over other kinds. It would represent a constructive use of world monetary reserves. It could allow for some macroeconomic management that would take account of the growing para-monetary role of commodities; and it would separate the issue of commodity stocks from short-term budgetary consideration of governments.

As regards co-ordination, both for short-term market management and long-term development and price forecasting, an international agency with no oper-ational responsibilities but as a source of global expertise should be considered. For food, by far the most complex area of forecasting, this function (among others) is already being performed by the FAO. A much smaller agency for industrial commodities could be a useful addition.

The cost of buffer stocks—of their initial purchase and capital cost, and the storage costs—represents an important barrier to the conclusion of com-modity agreements. UNCTAD estimated the cost of setting up an 18-commodity scheme at 10.7 billion dollars. Later revisions which left out cereals put the figure at 6 billion. This amount represents about 2.7 % of total world monetary reserves of SDR 183 billion (April 1975), and less than 5 % of the reserves of the industrialized countries. Since most countries now need smaller reserves than before, because floating exchange rates minimize the amounts needed for central bank intervention, a subscription by the industrialized countries and the oil producers (whose reserves stand at SDR 43 billion) [43] of about 3 % of their reserves to the IMF would raise enough capital to finance substantial buffer stocks [44].

But the figure of 6 billion is a "worst case" figure, since it assumes simul-taneously intervention buying to the limit of the buffer stock for each com-modity. The annual storage cost is about 3 % for the "core commodities" selected by UNCTAD, e.g. excluding grain and iron ore, while the interest rate

43. All reserve figures taken from *IMF Survey*, No. 13, July 1975.
44. This would get around the legal constraints that may prevent Central Banks from engaging in commodity purchases directly, as has been proposed by the German deputy Dr. Ehrenberg in Germany. In practice, the sums required will be much smaller, since the producer countries, which at present carry the full burden of stockpiling, will wish to contribute in the future, if only to enjoy a greater say over the operation of the fund.

of the present limited buffer stock facility of the IMF is 5 %. If the margin between buying and selling is 10 %, and stocks are held no longer than 18 months, the buffer stock would make a profit if prices were indexed. These profits would increase the shorter the periods of price swings.

Indexation

Few aspects of the "New Economic Order" have roused as much passionate opposition as the demand for an indexing of raw material prices to a measure of inflation of developed country exports. Article 28 of the Charter on the Economic Rights and Duties of States makes the achievement of this goal a duty of all states. The Corea Plan more generally states that commodity prices should be at levels that take due account of world inflation [45].

The relevance of this demand for Western European security is at least twofold. If indexing requires worldwide administration of all commodity prices, a large proportion of world trade would cease to be governed by market forces. Administered prices could lead either to underproduction, which would threaten supplies, or overproduction, which would require costly support operations. Most broadly, the opposition to indexing stems from a conviction that bureaucratic intervention in a free market leads to an inefficient allocation of world resources, and thus a net welfare loss.

But the contrary argument can also be made, namely that indexing would be an asset to economic security. It starts from the proposition that radicalism and unilateral actions threaten the development of resources, and that such radicalism is unavoidable if the rich countries not only fail to respond to demands for a redistribution of income, but refuse to consider means of maintaining the status quo.

There is considerable argument among specialists as to whether, historically, the terms of trade of LDCs have deteriorated. There are difficulties in choosing the right base year for comparison, and even greater difficulties in comparing unit prices for manufactures which have qualitatively changed over the decades. If the terms of trade have not changed, indexing is a non-issue. More to the point, since the real costs of producing almost all materials are bound to increase in future (higher land, fuel, and fertilizer prices for agricultural materials, higher capital costs and government levies for minerals), the maintenance of steady terms of trade (not annually, but as a trend) should represent no problem.

In the heated discussion on principle, furthermore, a number of subtle points were missed. There are several kinds of terms of trade, and many different kinds of indexation. One objection to the stabilization of the "barter terms of trade" (commodity/manufacture unit prices) was the fear that productivity gains, such

45. UNCTAD, "*An Integrated Programme for Commodities.*" TD/B/C.1/166, p. 5.

as occurred for bauxite, would no longer be reflected in falling prices and increased consumption. There is, however, another measure, the double factoral terms of trade, which takes account of the real resource cost in producing a unit and compares it to the prices of imported manufactures. Preliminary studies show, incidentally, that these terms of trade have fallen even more than the barter terms of trade, which according to UNCTAD and the World Bank [46], fell by 1.6 % annually between 1952 and 1972.

Opposition to indexing also stemmed from the conviction that achievement of this goal would require an extensive bureaucratic apparatus for price fixing, and that this apparatus could subsequently be abused to push through an *increase* in real price. The same critics, however, affirm with equal conviction that commodity agreements could never work. Yet the only means of achieving direct indexing would be through commodity agreements, including buffer stocks and export controls. Surely, such agreements would be already hard pushed to fulfill their role of stabilizing prices within a broad range. Buffer stock managers would not have unlimited funds with which to buy unwanted high-price production—unlike the European Community agricultural support mechanism, an often used but thoroughly misleading analogy. Low-cost producers would not wish to forego the chance to expand the market for their products through artificially high prices.

Two qualifications have to be made. Stable prices could mean slightly higher prices on average, since the periodic dumping of surplus production below real cost would be avoided. Stable prices would also increase the market for the product, e.g. rubber, because it becomes more attractive to users (i.e., the periodic, often irreversible substitution of the commodity during periods of high prices is avoided). Even if direct indexing would lead to an improvement of the terms of trade of, say, 1 % annually, the effect on industrialized countries would be infinitesimal. If we assume the share of LDC-relevant non-oil commodities imports in European GNP is around 3 %, probably a high estimate, a 1 % improvement would add 0.03 % to inflation.

To oppose indexing of the double-factor terms of trade (which would allow prices to fall where a commodity benefits from productivity gains) is to have learned nothing from the long debate with the LDCs. There can be little doubt that terms of trade have deteriorated because of unequal market power. Trade unions in the developed world are better organized to claim a share of productivity increases than workers in developing countries. Firms exporting manufactures to developing countries almost never are in a position that forces them to dump huge surpluses below real costs. Formal and informal export cartels are the rule rather than the exception. This may be a fact of life. But it has nothing to do with the virtues of the free market in whose name this state of affairs is to be perpetuated [47].

46. *"Terms of Trade of Developing countries"*, UNCTAD/CD/Misc. 60, p. 3 and 13.
47. Cf. *"Restrictive Business practices,"* Report by the UNCTAD Secretariat, TD/122/Supp. 1 January 1972.

If one wants to enter into commodity agreements at all, it would be absurd, dishonest and counterproductive to fix floor and ceiling prices in nominal terms at a time when a 5-10 % inflation will remain the world norm. Absurd, because it is difficult to accept the logic that an equilibrium price range, once negotiated, should fall by perhaps 10 % annually in real terms. Dishonest, because the commitment to stabilize entered into by the industrial countries would be quickly eroded to the point of irrelevancy. Counterproductive, in a literal sense, because one of the functions of commodity agreements, i.e. to stabilize expectations of investors and therefore to contribute to an orderly expansion of production, would be undermined.

But direct indexing, i.e. through commodity agreements, is not the only way in which real earnings of LDCs can be maintained. "The other way in which indexing could be made effective is by compensating individual countries for declines in real prices for their commodity exports by means of financial transfers," to quote from an UNCTAD document [48].

The document makes clear that a restitution of the transfer is envisaged, i.e. that indirect indexing is synonymous with an effective scheme of compensatory finance. Both the Community's Stabex scheme and the development security facility proposed by Kissinger (although his scheme covers all LDC exports, not just commodities) are in fact measures to achieve indexing. Since both proposals contain a grant element for the poorest countries, they go far towards meeting the objectives of the Third World.

A number of further measures would contribute towards improving LDC terms of trade, thus reducing the financial efforts required for both direct and indirect indexing schemes. The untying of aid, still practised by only a few countries, could reduce the prices for goods paid out of credit by perhaps 25 %. The breakup of monopolistic purchasers of commodities, particularly in the field of tropical agricultural products (bananas, etc.), could do much to improve the terms of trade. Most of all, the transfer of processing industries to the developing countries, which is the declared aim of the Community, the United States and Japan, would automatically index product prices to those of industrialized countries. A failure to meet the LDCs' demands for maintaining real incomes would be the surest way to provoke unilateral cartels.

48. "Indexation," Report by the Secretary General, TD/B/563, July 1975.

Conclusion

While there is no absolute physical risk to the supplies of raw materials, a number of political developments threaten the actual availability of supplies in the medium term. Insufficient investment in the expansion of supplies is the greatest single danger for Western Europe. A modest contribution towards achieving stability in raw material markets would significantly improve both the political and economic conditions for new investment. For welfare and political reasons, as well for purposes of maintaining stable export markets, agricultural commodities that pose no threat to supplies should also benefit from stabilization.

Most international commodity agreements in the past have failed because of insufficient financial resources. As regards the former, a small proportion of world monetary reserves, freed from the constraints of domestic legislation by being placed in the IMF, could be used to finance the initial purchase of buffer stocks. In a real sense, reserves would fulfill their main function when used in this way, i.e. to insure the availability of imports.

To be realistic, the outlook for timely measures of this sort is extremely poor. The next economic upswing, however modest, will quickly lead to high commodity prices, making it financially impossible and indeed counter-productive to constitute stocks. In a strong market situation, the producing countries, disappointed by the likely slow response of the consuming countries, and with replenished war chests, will look to unilateral measures to improve their trading conditions.

A tight supply situation would quickly worsen worldwide inflationary pressures. Since further deflationary measures would be politically impossible, direct incomes policies will become inevitable. To be politically acceptable, these will have to be matched by price controls. These in turn would quickly lead to export restrictions for raw materials in their first stages of transformation, and then for finished products containing the scarce material. The Japanese export stops on petrochemicals and fertilisers, the United States ban on scrap and the licensed trade in special steel during the last crisis show the consequences of price controls during a tight market situation.

The choice is thus not between intervention and non-intervention in the market. Rather, it is between intervening in the international context, where it corresponds to the preferences of most trading partners, and in the domestic context where it threatens not only the internal free market system, but also the part of the trading system that is still relatively liberal.

135

Summary

Economic security is threatened when external economic parameter changes put the domestic sociopolitical system at risk. It is thus also a function of the strength of society. The gradual breakdown of the liberal world order in the 1970s has coincided with an increase of mutual dependence of nations.

Growth, stable employment and price stability can be adversely affected by Western Europe's dependence on both export markets and uncertain sources of supply. Export markets are potentially dangerous to Western European security in the long term, if they fail to provide the dynamic growth element as they did in the postwar period. Of the two policy responses, keeping export markets buoyant through credits and other subsidies is economically wasteful and only postpones adjustment. The deliberate decision to look for internal sources for a growth in demand would lead to both greater welfare and stability. An exception is that third of Western European export markets represented by the developing countries, where a continuation of subsidized exports and subsidized earning capacity would both provide a growing market and correspond to global welfare objectives.

Reliance on export markets may not only jeopardize growth in the medium term, but may also impinge on the ability of governments to carry out their central task of managing the economy. This is particularly true for Western Europe with its high ratio of trade relative to the total national product. In the 1970s, the synchronization of world business cycles led to very large fluctuations in global demand and with it inflationary and deflationary pressures which can not be offset by domestic demand management. Crucial to any European effort to regain conjunctural autonomy is a shift both in attitude and economic structure by the Federal Republic of Germany as Western Europe's key economy.

The security of commodity products other than oil is relevant in the medium-term to prospects for growth. A moderate shift in the terms of trade between raw materials and manufactured products seems both probable, and, in the interest of long-term supply security, desirable. While in purely economic terms there is little likelihood of physical scarcities, relative scarcity of crucial energy and food supplies to developing countries may indirectly jeopardize European supplies: partly because resources would have to be diverted for welfare purposes, partly because a severe supply crisis in developing countries would destroy the internal and external political conditions for stable supplies.

136

The disproportional burden suffered by LDCs from the operation of partially free commodity markets has led them to question the very principles of free trade. The continued possibility of maintaining free commodity markets has been further undermined by the universal shift towards direct government control over resources, dictated by the bargaining possibilities offered by this sector as well as by the perceived need for long-term resource planning. The industrialized raw material producers are, if anything, leaders in this process, increasing the need for a response by consumers on the governmental level.

Possibilities for unilateral management of markets by producers are greater than commonly realized, even if these cannot approach in scope and importance the actions of the oil producers. Consumers have a considerable interest in stable commodity markets. Violent fluctuations in commodity prices, which have increased in recent years due to monetary instability and the synchronized world business cycle, are pro-cyclical both as regards industrial costs and the propensity to import by raw material exporters. Perhaps most important from the standpoint of consumers, these fluctuations contribute to the generally poor prospects for investment in the expansion of the world resource base by increasing the risk element in investments, and by contributing to periodic radicalism in raw material producing countries.

Insufficient investment is the most important danger to future supplies. Unilateral changes in the terms of operation and property rights of private corporations have added to the risk element at a time when the scale of new projects surpasses the financing capacity of companies. While multilateral sources of financing can make a contribution, the establishment of broad forms of co-operation with manifest benefits to both sides seems indispensable to adequate resource investment. Full commodity agreements would offer the economic conditions and provide the institutional framework for such co-operation.

Employee Participation and Company Reform

A Report on the Participating Members
and Young Leaders Meetings

Edited by Fabio Basagni and François Sauzey

With a Commentary by Benjamin C. Roberts

Preface

by John W. Tuthill

In November, 1975, the Atlantic Institute for International Affairs held meetings of 1) participating members in London and 2) young leaders outside of Paris on the subject of the role of labour and management in the modern corporation.

This subject, commonly referred to as "industrial democracy", has very broad implications on a number of crucial elements in the enterprise and in society, such as profits, productivity, new investments, wages, working conditions, the creation of new jobs, etc. All these aspects warrant careful attention. However, as will be seen in this report, the emphasis of the Institute's meetings lay primarily on one facet of industrial relations, namely, the role of employees in management decisions.

West Germany has taken the lead in this area with its postwar provisions for *Mitbestimmung* (or co-determination) in the coal, iron and steel industries. Provisions for labour participation on supervisory boards have now been in effect for more than two decades. Different people will react in quite different ways as to just what lessons can be learned from the German experience. In any event, the issue continues to be very much alive in Germany. The governmental coalition parties (SPD, FDP) have now agreed on a workers' participation plan, which will be put before the Parliament. This bill provides for an equal number of seats for representatives of the shareholders and of the entire work force on the supervisory board of every company with more than two thousand employees. Provision has been made for the capital side to have the ultimate power to choose the chairman of the board, who would hold a casting vote if there is a deadlock. Foreign subsidiaries operating in Germany may well expect to have to comply with such provisions in the future. In addition to the German experience, there has been considerable experience of workers' participation in other European countries such as the Netherlands and, for the past two years, Sweden. In France, at the request of President Valéry Giscard d'Estaing, a special committee chaired by former Minister Pierre Sudreau, with François Lagrange as rapporteur, has prepared a widely discussed report on company reform. As to the United Kingdom, it has established a commission of inquiry to look into the matter.

Perhaps most dramatically, Mr. Finn Gundelach, the European Commissioner responsible for this area, has made wide-ranging proposals for a European

Company Law. Companies operating in the nine countries could choose either to operate under the nine national laws or to register under a new European Company Law. According to Mr. Gundelach's proposals, the European Company Law would require that all companies have supervisory boards with one-third of the members selected by the shareholders, one-third by the employees and one-third co-opted by the other two groups to represent "general interests." These plans stand high on the agenda of the Commission and are being considered by member governments.

The Atlantic Institute for International Affairs has been concerned with this problem for some time and believes that a study analysing the experiences and the types of proposals being made in each of the national situations would be useful for the European governments as well as management and labour in private firms. It could also be helpful for the governments, labour and industry in North America, Japan, Australia and other highly industrialized countries.

As a step in this direction, the Institute held the two meetings mentioned before. A considerable amount of the discussion was built around Mr. Gundelach's proposals. Careful attention was also given to the Sudreau report in France. Officials from the European Commission, representatives from management and labour throughout Europe, and some representatives from governments were invited to attend and to participate. A list of speakers, panelists and participants is given in Appendix A.

These meetings, which were considered among the most successful ever organized by the Institute, could not have been held without the advice and assistance of Benjamin Roberts, Professor of Industrial Relations at the London School of Economics. Professor Roberts gave his time freely in defining the programme, in the selection of the speakers and panelists and, in addition, not only made an initial presentation but also participated actively throughout the entire discussion in both meetings. Furthermore, he has written the concluding summary and commentary to this Atlantic Paper. The Institute is most appreciative of the contribution that he has made and the expertise that he has provided on this issue. This Atlantic Paper has been put together and edited by Fabio Basagni and François Sauzey, both Research Associates at the Institute.

This paper is intended only as a first step in a comprehensive study of this crucial issue. It will be noted in the following pages that the debates did not focus on the North American and Japanese experiences. The Japanese system of consensus decision-making is obviously quite different from that of Europe. Nevertheless, there is much to learn from both sides and it is expected that within the Institute's future, study project, an analysis will be made of Japanese practices which associate labour with the aims and directions of the enterprise.

In North America, the bulk of labour and management remain rather surprisingly complacent concerning this issue. The overall position is that neither labour nor management is interested in the type of labour participation on supervisory boards as inaugurated in West Germany. Nevertheless, the problem will come to North America, Japan and the other industrialized countries. It will arise in the first instance in terms of the role of labour in subsidiaries operating in Europe. Later, regardless of the success or failure of the various experiences in Europe, the issue will also come to North America in a direct manner in terms of the effort to convince workers that they have a stake in the success of the enterprise. For this surely is the basic issue: can the industrialized democracies provide an economic and social system that convinces labour as well as management that its participation is desired and that ways and means will be designed to achieve this?

Employee Participation : Trends and Issues

by Benjamin C. Roberts[1]

All over the industrial world there has been a rising demand that unfettered managerial authority should yield to an extension of trade union bargaining rights and the development of a system of industrial democracy. This demand is clearly an aspect of fundamental changes that have been taking place within both the wider society and the enterprise itself.

The maintenance of high levels of employment, the advance of modern technology and unsurpassed rates of economic growth leading to great improvements in the general standard of life have been accompanied by immense social changes which have had a powerful liberalising effect on societies. There has been a radical transformation of the traditional authority of the *pater familias,* of the school teacher, of the priest, of the police and courts. The democratic process is no longer confined to the electoral procedure. All those who have traditionally enjoyed the trappings of authority, from presidents to prime ministers, are now subject daily to the humbling pressures of exposure, public protest and a clamour for an instant response.

Class structures have been eroded and society has become more open to the ambitious and the insistent. In industry, there are fewer obstacles in the way of the able and the talented to reach the top. In this context, it is not surprising that it should be widely felt that authority in the enterprise should rest not on a legal right to manage derived from those who happen to own the capital of the enterprise, but on the consent of the managed. The diffusion of stock holdings and the growth of institutional investment have divorced management from ownership. Management is now a professional function exercising the authority necessary to achieve the competent administration of an enterprise.

There is, however, no escape from management in some form or another, since there has to be a process of decision making and a means of ensuring that when decisions are made, they are effectively carried out. What is at issue today throughout the world is not only the appropriateness of the traditional patterns of management, but also the alternatives that have been proposed and in particular the role of employee participation.

1. Head of Industrial Relations Department, London School of Economics.

During the past twenty years the debate on the issue of participation in management has centred on the different forms that participation might take and the implications for all those concerned in the success of the enterprise, for workers and unions, managers and shareholders, customers, governments and the public at large. Throughout the discussion and at the core of the present debate have been a number of key questions. These have focused on the level and type of decisions to be made , on the role of individual employees and trade unions in the managerial processes , and on the role of legal regulation.

The rise of trade unionism provided the first challenge to managerial authority. In Britain, the United States and the Scandinavian countries, the unions have developed an extensive bargaining role within the enterprise as well as within the wider society. Although the formal limits of negotiation are the subjects of continuing conflict, there is initially no limit to the range of managerial decisions that might be the subject of union bargaining pressure. There may, however, be important restrictions on the ability of the unions to bargain effectively in many areas of managerial responsibility imposed by traditional procedures and sustained by the bargaining power of employers and the law.

The situation has been somewhat different in Austria, Germany, France, Italy, and Holland, where traditionally the unions have concentrated on negotiating industry-wide agreements on pay and basic conditions of employment with employers and in bringing pressure to bear on governments to regulate industrial practices by law. Throughout Europe, the State has compelled employers to establish Works Councils through which the interests of employees could be protected in the enterprise irrespective of the strength of trade union organisation.

Everywhere throughout Europe there has been a change in the situation, with a marked trend towards the growth of collective bargaining within the enterprise. The extent to which unions are able to impose their influence on management within the enterprise varies greatly, but as the AKZO and LIP cases have shown, when the concern is great enough there are no limits to the lengths to which unions may be willing to go to protect the interests of their members. Such cases, however, indicate a breakdown of the system of participation through works councils and the organs of management, rather than confirmation of a basic shift to the Anglo-Saxon model of conflictual industrial relations based on power bargaining within the enterprise.

Development of the German Model

It was against a background of trade union reconstruction, and an absence of a collective bargaining tradition within the enterprise, that the German unions were led to seek the legal imposition of a system of co-determination, which gave employees and unions rights to participate in the management of the enterprise at the lower levels through works councils, and at the highest level through representation on the supervisory boards. In the coal, iron and steel industries, parity of employee representation and the right of veto over the appointment of the personnel director, permitting an extra degree of employee and union control, was conceded by agreement with the allied occupying powers for political reasons.

The German system of co-determination has provided an important model of employer and trade union participation which has been given the greatest social significance by its undoubted contribution to the German economic miracle. Although there has always been some element of doubt voiced in Germany by the extreme left on the workers' side and by the extreme right on the employers' side, *Mitbestimmung* is generally regarded as a successful social development. This view was endorsed by the Biedeinkopf Commission of Inquiry, which reported in 1970. It agreed to recommend an increase in the number of employee representatives but not to end their minority position. The proposals of the Commission were not acceptable to the D.G.B. which sought to extend the principle of parity co-determination with its implicit right of veto to the private as well as the public sector of the economy.

The Social Democrats, who had come into office in 1969, decided to ignore the Commission's proposals and support the demand of the unions. The other two parties eventually decided to accept parity, but only if management was separately represented as a section of the employee group on the *Aufsichtsrat*. The present Social Democratic government hoped to secure parliamentary approval for an agreed bill which would concede parity, but satisfy the desire of management for at least one representative elected in a separate constituency. In the face of opposition from the D.G.B. to this compromise, the parity proposals have been shelved until the next session of parliament.

In spite of this conflict it is extremely unlikely that there will be any retreat from the general principles of parity co-determination; most experts on the German scene believe that acceptable compromise will soon be reached. It is clear that co-determination has its roots in both the history of German social democracy and in the contemporary roles and attitudes of workers and unions and the managers and owners of German industry. Although the system of co-determination has grown out of the German system of industrial relations, it has inspired emulation in other countries. This is not the first time that Germany has developed and exported a social process; it did so when it invented, in Bismarck's time, the method of contributory social insurance.

It may well be difficult, as it is often argued, for a nation to import an institution developed in a different social and political environment; nevertheless, there is much evidence from the past that a successful social idea will be borrowed and adapted to meet the needs of another country. In the process of transfer it might well be radically changed to meet the needs of the new environment.

The influence of Germany on Holland, Luxemburg, Sweden, Norway and Denmark is obvious in their introduction of two-tier boards and employee directors and on the British T.U.C. and Labour Party which have adopted proposals based upon the parity co-determination objectives of the D.G.B.

E.E.C. Proposals

The most important influence exercised by the German system has been on the European Commission. The decision of the Commission to incorporate in its draft European Company Statute a requirement that it should have employee directors on the supervisory board, and that it should also have to establish works councils at both national and European Community levels, was of great significance. Perhaps even more so was adoption of similar requirements as necessary elements in the relevant draft directive to achieve the harmonisation of the company laws in member states.

The European Company Statute, after exhaustive discussion and debate at all levels, will now go to the Council of Ministers in an agreed proposal for a supervisory board consisting of one-third shareholder representatives, one-third employee representatives and one-third public representatives jointly agreed by the shareholders and employees. It would seem to be the opinion in Brussels that final approval by the Council of Ministers is not far off.

Directive V is still a long way from agreement and approval by the Council. This situation reflects the sharp differences of opinion that exist in the member states of the Community on the issue of participation.

Divisions of opinion on the issue of participation reflect differences in employer, union and government attitudes, and differences between countries.

British Developments

In Britain there is a major cleavage between the Confederation of British Industry and the Trades Union Congress. The C.B.I. is completely opposed to introducing into Britain the concept of two-tier boards and union-appointed worker directors. It prefers to maintain the traditional British company structure of a unified board of directors, though it would be prepared to see a wider appointment of non-executive directors. The C.B.I. is also strongly in favour of the development, though on a voluntary basis, of works councils. The Trades Union Congress on the other hand has come down in favour of adopting a two-tier board system with fifty per cent of the directors appointed by the trade unions. The T.U.C. rejects out of hand the idea of setting up works councils as unnecessary and divisive bodies. It prefers to maintain the traditional British system of shop stewards' committees.

The government has given an undertaking that it will introduce legislation in 1976 after limited inquiry into proposals that have been made by the T.U.C.

There is by no means unanimous support among the unions for the T.U.C. policy as the debate at the 1974 Congress showed. On this occasion, a number of delegates voiced a reservation about the appointment of worker-directors. A resolution was passed "recognizing that the best way to strengthen industrial democracy is to strengthen and extend the area of collective bargaining giving union representatives increasing control over elements of management including dismissals, discipline, introduction of new techniques, forward planning of manpower, rationalisation, etc.." The resolution went on to reject "the mandatory imposition of supervisory boards with worker directors and calls for a more flexible approach giving statutory backing to the right to negotiate on these major issues, but relating control more directly to collective bargaining machinery."

Although it was possible for the General Secretary of the T.U.C. to argue that there was nothing in this resolution that conflicted with the official policy of the Congress in favour of the introduction of two-tier boards and parity co-determination, it was clear from the debate that left-wing trade unionists believed that there was a danger, as one delegate said, "of falling for theories that in my opinion will tie the movement lock, stock and barrel, with the interests of capital and to the detriment of our movement."

France, Italy and the United States

It is the same fear that has led the C.G.T. in France and the C.I. G.L. in Italy to regard proposals for workers' participation on German lines with hostility. The C.F.D.T. on the other hand has, since the events of 1968, supported *autogestion* — workers' self-management — as a main aim but one that can be realized only when capitalism is overthrown and socialism achieved. The C.F.D.T. makes common cause with the C.G.T. in opposing management introduced *ad hoc* participative methods.

In France and Italy there have been important advances in collective bargaining that have strengthened the role of shop organisation. At this level, there has been a growing demand that management should be prepared to negotiate on issues rising out of the organisation of work. A similar trend has become strongly evident in Italy.

Unions in Italy have shunned the idea of worker-directors but they have been ready to negotiate agreements that provide for job enrichment, control of assembly line speeds, job training, manning levels and other aspects of the way work is actually carried out.

Although the French and Italian systems of industrial relations are very different from the United States' system of industrial relations, the unions in all three countries wish to preserve their oppositional role but for different reasons. In the United States, the unions have no wish to see the basic system of private enterprise changed; they accept capitalism but demand the right to share in its advantages. The objective of American unions was classically defined by Samuel Gompers, the founding father of the American Federation of Labour, as *MORE*. Socialism, the goal of most European unions, was rejected as a utopian red herring. Nevertheless, the most socialist unions in Europe, those of France and Italy, would appear ready to be satisfied with *more* now rather than endanger the parity of their socialist goals.

The Sudreau Report

Faced by the fundamental changes of opinion on the concept of participation and the makings of a considerable political battle, but recognizing the necessity to bring about reforms in the enterprise so as to make it more viable, more dynamic and more responsive to the needs of its employees and the public as well as to its shareholders, the French government appointed a Commission under Mr. Sudreau to investigate and to make proposals.

The report of the Sudreau Commission sees the enterprise as the vital instrument of technical and economic progress in modern society. It recognizes the role of the trade union as a partner in the reform of the enterprise and thinks that collective bargaining should cover the widest possible range. There is nevertheless a fundamental role for the Comité d'Entreprise, which is a crucial element in the constitution of the enterprise. The Commission believes there is a need to deepen and make more effective the work of the *Comité d'Entreprise,* and it makes a number of proposals to bring this about. It ought to be made more representative, given a more active role, receive more information; and in multi-plant firms, it is necessary to have a *Comité d'Entreprise* at every level of the enterprise. The central committee will be entitled to receive full information concerning every aspect of the company's economic situation.

The report points out that an enterprise must satisfy a variety of ends. Its main objective can no longer simply be profit. It must satisfy the shareholders if it is to retain capital within the business; but it must also satisfy its employees if it is to retain their willing and active services; it must satisfy its customers if it is to survive and prosper, and it must satisfy the wider community with regard to its use of resources, its effect on the environment, its contribution to the welfare of society as a whole.

To achieve these different and sometimes conflicting goals it is essential that management decisions should have the full support of those who will be affected by them. They should not, however, compromise the freedom of the trade unions to challenge and oppose decisions when made. What then is required is the maximum degree of consultation and supply of information between managers and employees in the period when the making of a decision is being prepared. The decision itself, however, ought not to be shared. It must be made in the interests of the enterprise as a whole and therefore ought to be *made by the manager,* who is accountable to the enterprise as a whole.

The carrying out of the decision will, however, require the full co-operation of the employees. At this stage the report offers a new idea as an alternative to co-determination, namely *co-surveillance.*

Co-surveillance should be exercised through councils of administration in which employees would have up to one-third of the membership. Alternative methods of electing the members of the council of administration are discussed.

The aim of the Commission is to separate the function of direction from that of control. It is not clear, however, how the function of co-surveillance differs from the role of the supervisory board in the private German company. The Commission is far from precise in defining the function of control, but they are emphatic that the extension of the rights of employees should neither undermine the authority and role of managers, nor be a substitute for the trade unions and collective bargaining.

The report refers to the fact that France is the only country to grant employees a legal right to share in the net profits of companies. It recommends that profit sharing and capital accumulation should be further developed for the benefit of employees and suggests a number of ways in which this might be achieved.

It also calls for a reform of the law that would permit the establishment of new forms of enterprise in which capital is held in part by shareholders and in part collectively by the wage earners. The report also recommends that it should be possible to establish companies which pay only a fixed rate of interest and companies which are not profit-making and provide no return on the capital employed.

The Sudreau Report has much to say on many other aspects of the enterprise in modern society. In the reforms which it proposes, it constantly emphasises that they must be seen as part of a total industrial relations system. The report is a political compromise based upon a realistic social analysis. It offers no panacea but suggests the direction that reform of the enterprise could take on the basis of a consensus in contemporary French society.

Scandinavian Developments

In Scandinavia there has been a limited acceptance of the idea that employees should have the right to nominate a small number of representatives on supervisory boards. Since the early 1970s, in Denmark, Norway, and Sweden, employees have had a legal right to appoint two representatives to the boards of private companies. Whilst accepting the idea of participation in principle, the employers and trade unions have been cautious and practical in their approach to its realization.

Employers and unions in Scandinavia have given powerful support to the concepts of both economic and workplace democracy.

In all three countries the central organisations of unions have insisted on a right to be consulted and informed about national economic policy, but they have also insisted on retaining their independence and freedom to negotiate with the central employers' federations on the making and administrating of national policies.

There has also been a considerable emphasis on workplace democracy in all these countries. Only recently, the Swedish Employers' Confederation published in English an analysis of organisational innovations in some 500 companies made in the period from 1969 to 1974.

The focus of this development has been on the encouragement of the idea that there should be increased participation between managers and workers, that the aim of work reform should be expressed in both increased productivity and efficiency and increased job satisfaction. This has meant that when monotonous, boring work was eliminated it could not be at the cost of lower output. Considerable attention has been given to the redesign of systems of work, the most famous case being that of the elimination of assembly lines at Volvo. Reorganisation of the production system is based on small work groups which are responsible for a whole section of car assembly. The groups are largely self-governing, controlling their own pace of work and task allocations.

It is important to emphasize that the approach to job reform in Sweden has been in close consultation with the unions through the established system of collective bargaining and works councils.

Not long ago a group of American automobile workers were invited to spend three weeks in the new Volvo plant at Kalmar. They left dissatisfied, believing that the Swedish workers had been tricked into working harder by the new methods of work organisation. They preferred the assembly line system with the union negotiating on the speed of the track and seeking shorter hours as a means of ameliorating the effects of repetitive assembly line work. This reaction points up some of the basic cultural differences in the approach of the American and Swedish unions. In Sweden, the workers did get satisfaction out of directly controlling their own pace of work even if this meant—as the Americans believed—that they actually worked harder. The workers at Volvo could not accept the attitude of the American workers that only managers should be responsible for management decisions and the only function of the union should be to protest after the decision. The Swedish workers were not afraid, as were the Americans, that participation would weaken the ability of their unions to bargain effectively on their behalf at national and enterprise levels to secure improvements in pay that could only be achieved through a stable and efficient economy and prosperous industry and enterprise.

The Swedes are not convinced that parity co-determination would be a wise policy to adopt. They feel that management ought to be responsible to employees, as well as to shareholders and the public, for every decision it makes

151

but they also want to retain independent trade unions and free collective bargaining.

The great debate which is now taking place in Sweden over clause 32 of the general agreement between the Swedish Employers' Federation and the Swedish Trade Unions Federation demonstrates the crucial importance of the collective bargaining process in the Swedish system of industrial relations. Clause 32 has maintained the right of Swedish managers to manage: that is, to make decisions that employees must obey unless they fall specifically within an agreed area of collective bargaining. Now it is proposed, by a committee on labour legislation which was divided on the issue that a new law should be introduced next year which would in effect abrogate clause 32. Under the new law—if it is passed—any group of workers through their union will be free to challenge *any* managerial decision, no matter what it is concerned with, and that on such a challenge the management will have to negotiate on its proposal, before the decision is carried out.

The development is likely to have immense repercussions, since at a stroke it enables employees to participate in all managerial decisions. There is a danger that the veto which the employees will be able to exercise could lead to serious delays in decision making. Swedish employers are especially concerned that the peace obligation, which has been a main feature of the Swedish system of collective bargaining, will no longer be insisted upon when joint influence on a decision is not accepted. In other words, the trade unions will be free to take strike action on any issue, even if it merely involves the interpretation of an agreement if the employer refuses to agree to joint determination.

The Committee also considered whether there ought to be established special representative bodies within the firm, through which joint determination could be agreed. The Committee was divided as to whether the decision to establish such bodies should be jointly determined or a right reserved for the employees.

The new Swedish proposal is likely to attract attention in England, France and Italy, since it would clearly satisfy those who have doubts about the wisdom of proceeding on German lines. The Swedish proposal will greatly strengthen the power and influence of shop floor leaders, since they will have a statutory right to insist that any decision shall be jointly determined. Unofficial strikes have grown considerably in Sweden during the past few years as power has shifted to the shop floor. It is not unlikely that the new law, if passed, will lead to a much greater increase in lawful wildcat strikes.

The Swedish proposal raises quite sharply the problem of a conflict between militants on the shop floor and employee representatives on supervisory boards who are party to decisions which are not accepted. This problem inevitably exists in any system of employee representation on boards, but it would seem to be enhanced when the right of the shop floor to participate is extended to every managerial decision and is made effective by strike action.

In Norway, where there has been a good deal of experimentation in participation in the enterprise with the official support of the trade unions and the employers' organisations, it has been suggested that the community ought to have representatives on the board of directors in addition to representatives of shareholders and employees. Since there is an important national interest in the conduct of business firms which cannot necessarily be safeguarded by a board composed solely of employer and employee representatives, this proposal has attracted support. The proposal is not in itself new, since governments that have lent large sums of money to private firms have often insisted on nominating a director. However, a director elected to represent a general interest would be a rather different matter and the procedure of appointment might well give rise to some difficulty.

Conclusion

That there is a powerful current flowing in the direction of increased participation in the management of enterprises can not be denied. It may well be asked, however, whether this development will lead to greater employee satisfaction, to a lower level of conflict in society, to greater efficiency, and to the prevention of inflation through more responsible management and union behaviour.

There is evidence from the experiments in shop-floor democracy that a greater degree of self-management, more consultation and more information can improve employee morale and bring about a greater satisfaction in work. This is not an automatic result. The most utopian system of employee participation will not overcome the effects of poor pay, bad conditions of employment and technological situations which overwhelm the human spirit.

Participation on the board of directors of a company through representatives is looked upon by employees with favour, but it will bring little satisfaction if it is not associated with improvements in conditions of employment and the achievement of tangible benefits which can be achieved only by well-managed and efficient enterprises.

There it little evidence that participation will of itself lead to greater efficiency. It may in fact lead to the opposite result, to a slowing down of decisions, to a less positive response to production requirements if the greatest care is not taken.

Nor does a greater degree of participation necessarily lead to the end of industrial conflict. Conflict is inevitable in any organisation in which there are different interests and there is freedom to express these interests. Conflict cannot be altogether eliminated but participation offers a means of avoiding unnecessary conflict and of reconciling differences of interest and opinion without recourse to damaging strife. Participation is not a panacea, but if it is working effectively it provides an opportunity to arrive at decisions that are more acceptable than would have been the case without it.

Participation, whether at national, intermediate, or shop-floor levels can go wrong. Participation cannot simply be introduced and then be left to look after itself. It is a continuous process that must be maintained and carried on through appropriately tailored institutions.

Participation cannot provide a substitute for management, but it will not succeed if it is no more than window dressing; it will fail if it is bypassed by powerful individuals or groups who refuse to accept its imperatives. Nor can it exist in isolation. If it is to be effective, it must be integrated into the existing processes of consultation and collective bargaining. Nevertheless, new institutions and new processes have to be developed and these may well pose threats to existing institutions and patterns of behaviour. This is the challenge that now confronts every advanced industrial society in one form or another.

It is a challenge that goes far beyond the issue of extending the rights of the employee. It is, as the Sudreau Committee recognize, a challenge that is concerned with the fundamental role of the enterprise in modern society. This role is one that must give satisfaction to workers and managers in the performance of their tasks, to trade unions, professional associations and other bodies closely concerned, and to society as a whole, which is ultimately the final tribunal responsible for, but also dependent upon, the economic and social achievement of the enterprise. Each country is evolving its own solutions; each will be different in important respects, but in the long run it may turn out that the similarities in democratic societies prove greater than at present might be expected.

August 1975.

A German Experience

by Gunter Geisseler[1]

We all know that the terms of a law and its practical application are two different things. Only in its implementation in day-to-day business does an industrial law prove whether or not it is a good one. The purpose of this brief presentation is to appreciate to what extent the German law on parity co-determination in the coal and steel industry has passed this examination. To do so, an analysis of the case of Mannesmann AG provides some particularly interesting insights.

Mannesmann originally had the vertical structure typical of the Ruhr area, that is, mining, iron and steel production, and steel processing. Because of this structure, after the Second World War, Mannesmann was subject to the decartelization directed by the Allies. Already in 1947 in the course of such decartelization, parity co-determination had been introduced in three subsidiary companies of Mannesmann. May I here point out that it was the British administration that introduced parity co-determination on German territory. The reasons for this were not economic but purely political. The Allies were hoping that the imposition of co-determination might hamper the recovery of the economic and consequent political strength of German heavy industry. Their political intention coincided with the interest of German trade unions in participating in the supervision of German heavy industry.

In 1947, the newly founded German iron and steel enterprises got a supervisory board based on the principle of parity. To this board the capital owners and the employees delegated equal numbers of representatives. The board additionally comprised two representatives of the public interest. A steel trustee appointed by the Allied Steel Control Group took the chair. The executive board, on the other hand, was to comprise one technical director, one commercial director and—as the third man—the so-called *Arbeitsdirektor*, in charge of personnel and social affairs, who was nominated by the trade unions. Threatening to call a general strike, in 1951 the trade unions made the German Bundestag pass the so-called *Montanmitbestimmungsgesetz*. By this law, the parity co-determination in the iron and steel industry was confirmed and extended to the coal and ore mining industry. For Mannesmann, this also meant that Mannesmann AG, the holding company, and all its subsidiaries in

1. Former Chief Legal Adviser, Mannesmann AG.

155

the iron and steel industry as well as in coal and ore mining, fell under the new law.

The regulations of 1947 and 1951 had one thing in common—and this I want to say with special reference to the Draft of a European Company Statute —i.e. the attempt to moderate the strict parity in the supervisory board by a neutral element. Under the 1947 model, there were the two representatives of public interest and the steel trustee whereas the co-determination law of 1951 provided for a neutral or 11th, 15th or 21st man and for two further members to be appointed to the supervisory board each by one of the two parties from which, to a certain degree, they had to be independent. Practical experience proved, however, that these three men did not constitute the really neutral element intended by the law. In reality, the two additional members were much more inclined to consider themselves as members of that group which had appointed them, than as members of an independent and objective part of the board.

Parity co-determination finally led to a situation in which the supervisory board no longer regarded itself as a body consisting of independent personalities but much more as an entity of two factions with opposing interests. This development was supported by the fact that usually the employees' representatives met before sessions and agreed on the position they wanted to take in the sessions. In other words, confrontation became usual. And the neutral man was in constant danger of becoming a mere object of the opposing parties instead of an equal partner. The trade unions tried to establish the principle that the one party nominated the neutral man and the other party the chairman of the supervisory board, who under German corporate practice enjoys a prominent position. In fact, this principle was commonly practised between Rhine and Ruhr.

The neutral man was generally confronted with the interests of the representatives of the capital owners and the employees. In some cases, he would encourage the groups to come to an agreement. In other cases, where agreement could not be reached, the established principle of parity made him vote alternately for one or the other side. More and more supervisory board decisions were made according to the so-called horse-trading principle: "if you agree with me on this point, I will agree with you on the next one." This principle was applied even if there were no connection between two such points. In many cases the capital-owners had to make very far-reaching concessions. The expansion of the parity co-determination over and beyond the law can be explained only by this fact. In many cases, the employees' side was ready to give its consent only to important corporate policy decisions, especially on structural changes of the enterprise, on the condition that the parity co-determination was to be extended to companies that by virtue of their structure were not subject to the law.

Another disadvantage of the principle of parity was the difficulty of decision making. I remember a variety of cases when urgent and important resolutions could not be made at all, or sometimes only with intolerable delay. In all cases the results were damaging to the company. To be fair, it should be noted that the trade unions in most cases restricted their influence on the appointment of the management board to the position of *Arbeitsdirektor* without interfering in the choice and nomination of its other members. On the other hand, the representatives of the capital-owners did not try to influence the appointment of the director for personnel and social affairs. The director for personnel and social affairs was thus unanimously considered as the trade unions' man. The employees' representatives in the supervisory board as well as in the works councils expected him to keep in line with the official trade unions' policy, and in many cases he was unable to resist such pressure.

What will be the position of the trade unions if parity co-determination is introduced in the entire German industry? There are sound reasons to believe that the trade unions will give up their restriction as soon as parity co-determination is no longer an exception but the rule. As an argument for the anticipated extension of co-determination to other than the mining, iron and steel industries, the trade unions argue that, in these industries, the parity co-determination has proved practicable and successful. In my opinion this is by no means true! Constant repetition does not make the argument more convincing. An unbiassed consideration of the scenery reveals that this is one-sided reasoning.

For years nobody on the side of the capital-owners and management has been prepared to agree with the trade unions' view of the success of co-determination. Only recently the opinion expressed by the trade unions was backed in public by two high-ranking representatives of German management: Ernst Wolf Mommsen, chief of the Krupp group, a personal friend of Chancellor Helmut Schmidt, formerly state secretary in the Social-Liberal coalition, and Hans Birnbaum, Chairman of the board of the Salzgitter group, the share capital of which is entirely held by the government of the Federal Republic of Germany. On the other hand, three leading businessmen expressed their serious objections to parity co-determination in their capacity as speakers for the whole German economy on the occasion of the hearings arranged by the German Bundestag: Dr. Hans-Günther Sohl, president of the Confederation of German Industries (Bundesverband der Deutschen Industrie), Dr. Hanns-Martin Schleyer, president of the Confederation of German Employers' Associations (Bundesvereinigung der Deutschen Arbeitgeberverbände), and Dr. Egon Overbeck, president of Mannesmann AG.

In his very interesting speech, Professor Roberts raised the point that parity co-determination has significantly contributed to the so-called German economic miracle. I am afraid I cannot support this view. The German economic miracle was achieved not only by the German coal and steel industry, but by the German economy at large, the decisive factor being the overwhelming desire of all groups of the population to rebuild a destroyed country and its economy. In 1970, the Biedenkopf Commission—a committee of independent

157

experts set up by the Federal Government—although admitting certain positive aspects of co-determination, was not prepared to support the request that the system of parity co-determination be extended to the entire industry. Instead, it recommended a slight predominance of the capital owners' representation. Indeed, as we put it in German, this is *des Pudels Kern* or—as you say—the crucial point.

Co-determination in the supervisory board must be seen in its context not only with co-determination in the works but also with co-determination in the entire social constitution of a country. Wherever the principle applies that two equal partners have to bargain for the conditions of work, the interference of one partner in the decision making of the other partner will substantially disturb or even destroy the balance of power . In the German company system, the members of the managing board are appointed by the supervisory board for a maximum term of five years. And the members of the management board cannot feel independent because they are conscious, on the one hand, of having to represent the employers' side, but depend—on the other hand—on their appointment and reappointment by the representatives of the employees on the supervisory board as well.

The very reasons for which I object to the parity co-determination in the German coal and steel industry are also at the root of my objections to the draft under discussion at this meeting. I think the proposal of the European Commission for the regulation of co-determination in the European Company will in practice amount to very much the same thing as the parity model of the German co-determination law for the coal and steel industry. As to the appointment of the last third of the members of the supervisory board by the employees and capital-owners it will come down to a struggle for the last man of the last third who is supposed to be really neutral. It is quite understandable that the draft statute is meeting with so little approval and so much criticism. Those who are aiming at European integration should prepare and offer to European companies a statute that these companies can accept without running the risk of losing their effectiveness.

Industrial Democracy in Germany

by Rudolf J. Vollmer[1]

Worker participation has a long tradition in Germany. The first Works Council Act was passed in 1920, and at the same time also the first workers' representatives appeared on German company boards. As a political demand, co-determination (*Mitbestimmung*) goes back even to the March Revolution of 1848. During the Nazi period every form of industrial democracy was suppressed, but after the war, the Federal Republic went back to the best Weimar traditions and re-established an improved system.

In private industry, worker participation today operates at two distinct levels—on the shop floor and at board level. The purpose is to give workers at all levels of their company a share in the making of economic, social and industrial decisions and thus to establish a democratic control and management of the economy.

I. Works councils

Under the Works Constitution Act 1972 (which recently replaced the 1952 Act), a works council has to be elected in every establishment in private industry employing more than five persons.

Membership and Rights

The works council is not a joint body, but represents exclusively the workers. Nor is it—at least not in law—a trade union body like Shop Steward Committees in Britain. Candidates for membership do not have to be union members, although in practice the great majority of the 200,000 German Works Councillors belong to one of the 16 industrial unions affiliated with the DGB, the counterpart of the British TUC. They are elected in a secret ballot by all employees of the firm, independant of trade union membership. This means that on the shop floor and, in particular, in plant bargaining, German unions can exercise influence and power only if they manage to get elected to the Works Council.

---

1. Labour Attaché, German Embassy, London.

However, German unions are not afraid of and do not object to facing free elections of all workers including non-union members. In fact, the rule "one man—one vote" (whether or not he is in a union) is based on a bill proposed by the German trade unions themselves. Works Council elections are held nationwide every three years between March and May. The last elections took place in spring 1975. About 90 per cent of the total work force took part in the poll. In many industries there was a 100 per cent turnout. And although on average only a third of German workers are organised, 80 per cent of the candidates returned were members of a DGB industrial union. This means that whatever a man's reason for not joining a trade union, in the case of works council elections, he votes for the union man. This is an achievement of which the German unions are naturally very proud.

Works council members are elected for three years. According to the size of the work force in the plant, their number may vary between one and (under the new law) over 35. Companies with several divisions must establish a central company council for the whole company. Young employees under 18 years of age elect their own youth delegation. The youth delegation may send one of its members to attend any works council meeting. Where a matter concerns mainly young employees, the full youth delegation is entitled to participate in the discussion and to take part in the vote of the works council. The members of a works council enjoy special protection and certain privileges to make them independent and efficient in their job. They cannot be dismissed by the employer while holding office nor for one year thereafter. In larger companies, the chairman and other members of the works council have to be free from production work so that they can devote all their time to works council matters:
— In plants with more than 300 employees at least one member of the works council has to be released.
— In establishments employing more than 10,000 persons, at least 12 works council members must be excused from work completely.

The employer must provide appropriate facilities for the works council, including offices and secretaries, and he has to defray all costs arising out of the council's activities. Each member of the works council is entitled during his first term of office to four weeks' paid leave to attend a course of further education or training—in any subsequent term, the period is three weeks.

General Tasks

The basic aim of the Works Constitution Act is to bring about a co-operation in mutual trust between works council and employer. Employer and works council have to avoid any action which could disturb industrial peace on the shop floor. They have a common duty to ensure that all employees are treated equally and equitably and that nobody is discriminated against for reasons of race, nationality, religion, political convictions, or sex. Furthermore, they must promote by positive action the personal advancement of all employees within the plant.

The works council has the following general tasks:

1. To see that all Acts of Parliament, statutory instruments, regulations, safety rules, collective agreements and works agreements are enforced for the benefit of the employees.
2. To make recommendations to the employer for action promoting the interest of the company and its workers.
3. To receive suggestions from employees and the youth delegations and, if they are found to be reasonable, to negotiate with the employer for their implementation.
4. To promote the rehabilitation of the disabled and other persons in particular need of assistance.
5. To organize the election of a youth delegation and to co-operate closely with that delegation in promoting the interests of young employees.
6. To promote the employment of elderly workers in the company.
7. To promote the integration of foreign workers in the company and to further understanding between them and their German colleagues.

The employer has to supply comprehensive information to the works council in good time in order to enable its members to carry out properly their duties under the Works Constitution Act.

Areas of Co-determination

The works council has an equal say with management in such matters as the following:
— Job evaluation, piece rates and wage structures.
— Working times, overtime arrangements, breaks, and holiday schedules.
— Manpower policies, including guidelines for the recruitment, promotion and deployment of workers.
— "Social plans" in the case of redundancies.
— Training, accident prevention, and welfare schemes.
— Allocation of housing provided by the employer.
— Workers' conduct on the shop floor.

In personnel matters and grievance disputes, under the new law management can no longer act alone. Hiring, firing and promotion, allocation of work, and transfers all require the advance consent of the works council. For example, if an employer wants to hire a man from outside to fill a certain post, the works council could claim that a man should be promoted from within the company. When the employer wants to dismiss a worker, he has to consult the works council first and to explain the reasons for the dismissal. Any dismissal without such consultation would be void in law. The works council even has the right to object to a dismissal, for instance, on the ground of "social hardship" for the worker concerned. Conflicts go to the labour courts and, during the two or three years that the case may take to go through the system, the man cannot be dismissed.

Economic Committee

In matters affecting the actual conduct of the business, the powers of the works councils are more limited. In companies employing more than a hundred workers, the works council must appoint an economic committee of between four and eight members. This committee is entitled to information on all important matters such as manufacturing methods, automation, production programmes, and the financial situation of the company.

Shutdowns, staff cuts, works moves, and reductions or alterations in the scale of production require the prior consent of the works council. In the case of major redundancies the employer has to set up, jointly with the works council, a "social plan" providing employment elsewhere in the firm, retraining, or—if this is not possible—severance pay for the affected worker.

Arbitration and Works Assembly

If there is a deadlock between employer and works council on matters in which the works council is entitled to co-determination, either side can bring the case before a joint arbitration committee under an independent chairman for compulsory arbitration. Where statutory rights are involved the final decision lies with the labour courts.

The works council in turn is responsible to the works assembly, which is a meeting (at least quarterly) of all the workers and employees of the firm. At this meeting, which takes place during paid working time, the works council has to submit a progress report of its activities. The employer is always invited to the meeting and is entitled to address it. If the works assembly is dissatisfied with a member of the works council, or indeed the whole works council, it can apply to the Labour Court for his or their removal. The unions represented in the plant can do the same.

Merits of the Works Council System

Summing up, it would appear that the works council system has three great advantages beneficial to industrial relations in Germany:

1. Though not perfect, it tends to create or at least favours a democratic balance of power between employer, works council and workers.
2. It secures friendly co-operation between management and works council, as representative of all workers and employees of the enterprise.
3. It promotes industrial peace on the shop floor.

In short, through their works councils, workers in Germany have achieved such influence and power that, today, they have an equal say with management in all decisions that are vital for their employment. This also gives the unions a tremendous influence on the shop floor, especially in plant bargaining. The only snag is that their members must be able to get democratically elected to the works council, in a secret ballot by a majority of all employees of the firm. In Germany, the unions have achieved this aim. They are practically running the works councils and, therefore, regard them as a pillar of industrial democracy.

II. Public Sector

Similar co-determination rights have recently been achieved in the public sector by the reform of the Personnel Representation Act 1955, which came into effect on 1st April 1974. Elected Personnel Councils representing civil servants, salaried staff and manual workers in all public services and enterprises including government, courts and German embassies, will in future have an equal say with their employers in all important matters affecting their employment and the organization of their work.

III. Workers on the Boards

In addition to the works councils, there is a system of co-determination at board level in joint stock companies and all other limited companies with more than 500 workers. Unlike the single-board Anglo-American system, German companies have two boards: a supervisory board (*Aufsichtsrat*) and an executive or management board (*Vorstand*).

The supervisory board meets generally about four or five times a year, appoints the management board, scrutinizes the annual accounts of the company and is responsible for all major policy decisions such as mergers, takeovers and overall manpower planning. The management board conducts the day-to-day business of the company. Its members are full time. They are not allowed to sit on the supervisory board and vice versa.

In all joint stock and limited companies outside the coal and steel industries, one third of the supervisory board have to be elected labour representatives. Usually one of them will be the chairman of the works council, but trade union officials from outside the company may also be elected, so that there is a permanent communication between works council and unions. By law, the workers' representatives on the board have a direct control over the firm's activities and enjoy the same rights and obligations as all other board members. In practice, the inherent minority on the workers' side leads to a situation whereby in the event of a conflict it is usually the interests of the shareholders that prevail.

Parity Co-determination in Coal and Steel Industries

The unions therefore prefer the so-called "parity" co-determination system existing in the coal and steel industries. Here the Co-determination Act 1951 stipulates equal representation of shareholders and workers on the supervisory board. All boards contain an uneven number of members: eleven, fifteen or twenty-one. Thus, in a supervisory board of eleven members, five are appointed by the shareholders and five by the workers. The eleventh member — known as the "neutral man" — is co-opted by the two sides of the supervisory board. He represents the public interest and has a casting vote in the event of a deadlock between the two sides.

The workers' side on the Board consists of three sections. Where there are five labour representatives:

— Two are proposed by the works council. As a general rule these two are the chairman of the works council and his deputy. They must be workers or employees of the company.

— Two are delegated (from outside the company) by the trade unions represented in the undertaking, after consultation with the works council.

— The fifth or so-called "further" member is nominated by the German Trade Union Federation. He must not be a direct union representative, but he would, of course, have a bias towards the workers' side, and, like the "neutral man," he represents the public interest.

In the coal and steel industries, the workers are also represented on the board of management by an elected "Labour Director." He has the same responsibilities as the other executive directors and is usually entrusted with wage, personnel and welfare questions.

IV. Extension of Parity Co-Determination

For more than 20 years the German trade unions have been demanding that this level of "parity" co-determination as practised in the coal and steel industries should be extended to all major companies complying with two out of three of the following criteria:

— More than 2,000 employees.

— Annual turnover of DM 150 million (about £ 27 million at the current exchange rate).

— A balance sheet of DM 75 million.

Up to the November 1972 elections the distribution of power in successive Federal Parliaments did not provide the necessary majority. But it now seems likely that the present Parliament will do so.

Reform Bill

In fact, after five years of negotiations, the two partners in the Government coalition, the Social Democrats and the Free Democrats, agreed upon a comprehensive plan to give workers an equal voice in industry. The Federal Government has proposed a bill which will—when passed by Parliament—apply to all firms with more than 2,000 employees. This will affect about six

RESERVATION SLIP

Author .Mash..et..al......

Title ..European..Economic.
.................(Lives)............

Reader's name .R..Evans.....

Date .....17/8.................

million workers in West Germany's 650 biggest companies. The new scheme is based on the following principles:

— The policy-making supervisory board in every major company will be made up equally of workers' and shareholders' representatives, usually ten from each side.

— Of the ten workers' representatives, seven are chosen from the shop floor and from the staff of the company, and three must be union officials from outside.

— The workers' side on the supervisory boards must represent all employees in the company, whether union members or not, and they must include at least one senior executive.

Though in law non-union members may be elected, in practice the supervisory boards will draw membership largely from the unions.

Careful Compromise

The new proposals are a compromise between the unions' demands, advocated by the Social Democrats, and the proposals of the Free Democrats. The Liberals wanted separate representation of management in addition to that of the workers on the shop floor and at board level, and they suggested the so-called six-four-two principle for the supervisory board: six shareholders' representatives, four from the trade unions and two from among senior executives.

Under the proposals now agreed, all ten workers' representatives on the supervisory board, including the three from outside, are chosen by an "electoral college," which is in its turn elected by the entire work force by secret ballot. The electoral procedure is so devised that the supervisory board represents all the different groups in the work force (manual workers, the white-collar staff and senior executives), and includes at least one senior executive as part of the workers' side. Voting is secret. The selection of candidates on the workers' side is largely influenced by the unions; the shareholders' representatives are elected at the annual general meeting of the shareholders.

Unlike the supervisory boards in the coal and steel industry, where the two sides select an independent chairman from outside, the chairman and his deputy are chosen from the board members and cannot both belong to the same side; if the chairman comes from the workers' side his deputy must be from the shareholders' side, and vice versa. If the chairman and his deputy are elected by a two-thirds majority, they remain in office for the full electoral term of the supervisory board, three to five years depending on the company articles. If the election is by simple majority, the chairman and his deputy will alternate every two years.

When there is a deadlock in the supervisory board's discussions, the chairman has a casting vote if both sides agree on this in advance. If they cannot agree that the chairman has a casting vote, both sides have to go on discussing the matter at issue until they can agree. The example of the coal and steel industry, where the chairman is co-opted from outside, was deliberately avoided as it was felt essential that the board should seek agreement among its own members. The supervisory board appoints the management board. As under previous legislation, members of the management board cannot sit on the supervisory board and vice versa.

The management board elects from among its members a chairman who is regarded as *primus inter pares* and has no casting vote. One member of the management board must be entrusted solely with personnel and social matters. The set-up in the coal and steel industries remains in effect unaltered. In firms with fewer than 2,000 employees, the principle of one-third participation by workers in the supervisory boards continues as well.

Opposition to the Bill

The Government believed that the new bill would in the end be accepted by both sides of industry. But as it turned out, the bill ran into considerable opposition from both unions and management. In public hearings during the committee stage of the bill, the long standing controversy about fifty-fifty representation and its benefit for the workers flared up again. For the employers the bill goes too far. For the unions it does not go far enough. The unions want the coal and steel model extended to the rest of German industry and commerce, no more, no less.

It is now doubtful whether the bill will be passed by parliament in its present form. However, the government remains committed to the principle of parity co-determination and will try to fin an acceptable solution. [1]

V. Social Partnership in Public Administration

Beside their role as industrial partners, German trade unions and employers play an important part in Government and public administration. In Parliament, more than half of all deputies are union members, and in Helmut Schmidt's cabinet twelve ministers belong to a trade union including the Chancellor himself.

German unions regard the Federal Republic and its Constitution as friendly soil and the law as a useful ally. In fact, they have developed considerable skill in pushing demands through Parliament which otherwise they could not have hoped to achieve by collective bargaining. On the other hand, both unions and employers in Germany are prepared to accept the responsibilities that come with power.

Health insurance, old age pensions, industrial injuries and unemployment insurance, employment services, occupational training, retraining, and rehabilitation are in practice run and financed by both sides of industry.

1. Since this paper was written, a compromise has been reached (on December 9, 1975) by the SPD and the FDP, and the passage of the amended bill during the life of the present parliament appears as a realistic possibility. (Editors' note.)

This means that public funds representing more than one quarter of Germany's total gross national product are to a large extent run jointly by both sides of industry. Last year Germany spent more than £ 50,000 million on social services, education not included. By 1978, social expenditure will have risen to almost £ 78,000 million. The purpose of these social investments is not merely to enable people to retain their status and living standard in the case of illness, unemployment, disability, or old age, but to keep labour mobile and fit, and to encourage them to develop their full potential in the economy.

Joint responsibility for social security, employment services, training and rehabilitation has helped to create an atmosphere of "social partnership" which no doubt is one of the main reasons for industrial peace in Germany. Employers and trade unions may in collective negotiations quarrel about how to divide the cake. But they basically agree that it is their joint task to make the cake big. Not only through productive co-operation in industry, but also through massive investment into the social and economic vitality of man.

It is accepted, today, in Germany that human skill and mobility have become the most important factors for economic growth, more important even than capital. We believe, therefore, that our technical, economic and thence social progress depends more than ever before on what we are ready to spend on health, education, training and social security. Government, trade unions, and employers in Germany agree that social policy has become a "pacemaker of economic progress".

Company Reform in France: the Sudreau Report

by François Lagrange[1]

One of the first decisions made by the President of the French Republic and his government shortly after the presidential election of May 1974 was to investigate ways and means for company reform. He assigned the task of forming a Research Committee for drawing up company reform proposals to a political figure, M. Pierre Sudreau, a former minister and Deputy and mayor of the city of Blois.

This Committee was comprised of ten *independent* members:

— Three industrialists, including a director of one of France's major firms (a multinational), the head of a medium-sized company and one woman who was the founder, owner and manager of a small company.

— Three labour leaders, holding (or who had held) major union posts.

— Four experts, including three university professors and one Counsellor of State.

The Committee carried out its investigations over a seven-month period. It consulted with all union and professional organizations, as well as with a number of well-known figures. It also drew from the ideas evolved by the twelve working groups that it formed, made up of company directors, trade unionists and academics. Each of these groups was given the task of examining a particular theme. All in all, at least three hundred individuals were involved in this study.

After difficult but full discussions, the Research Committee submitted its report to the President of the Republic and the Prime Minister on 7 February 1975. Immediately after, this report was published in the *Documentation Française* series. And, an event unusual for the French Government, it was also published in a paperback edition.

This report was widely discussed following its publication. In particular, it was submitted to the Economic and Social Committees * of the various regions of France. Last July, it was submitted to the Economic and Social

---

1. Member of the French Conseil d'Etat; Rapporteur General of the Sudreau Committee.

* These Committees are consultative bodies bringing together representatives of a region's professional and trade union organisations.

Council, which gave a favourable overall opinion. The government, however, has not yet indicated how, or when, it plans to apply this report. One thing is certain: the Government looks upon this question as a fundamental one. In point of fact, it already has two Committees of limited numbers under the chairmanship of the President of the Republic to consider company reform. Other such Committees are to be set up between now and the end of the year. The most likely hypothesis is that, by next spring, the government will submit one or more draft laws on this subject.

The fact should be emphasized that the report is directed as much to French companies and to the various trade unions as to the government. Its implementation is substantially dependent upon negotiation at management and union levels. The emphasis on negotiation is in effect one of this report's fundamental principles, as we shall see in an examination of its content.

Briefly, I shall summarize the Sudreau Report on the basis of three questions which are invariably asked when the problem of company reform is raised.
— Why company reform today?
— What were the major difficulties encountered by the Research Committee?
— What are the Report's main proposals and recommendations?

What considerations led to raising the question of Company Reform?

At a first glance, the wish for company reform is paradoxical. In a market economy, it would seem that companies unceasingly evolve and adapt themselves without the need for any government intervention. In fact, a lot of ground has been covered since the Industrial Revolution: be it working conditions, management methods or organisational structures, there are few aspects held in common between the company at the turn of the century and that of 1975. Especially striking, if one looks at the past 30 years, are the company's remarkable economic and technical achievements. To cite only the case of France, productivity was doubled, while wages and consumption increased in real values by 80% between 1959 and 1973. Throughout the entire Western World, the company thus proves itself to be an instrument of expansion and innovation, which disseminates progress throughout the entire social fabric and offers a field for individual initiative and advancement.

But it is precisely this company economic achievement which generates new aspirations, now making company reform a necessity, an imperative. It is undeniable that the company is undergoing increasingly intensive criticism in the majority of the developed nations. If the company is not to lag behind the advance of ideas and realities, consideration must be given to these new expectations. In a very rough outline, I would suggest that there are three major contradictions between the company and present-day society.

The rejection of the "productivity principle"

The first contradiction involves working conditions, and might be summarized under the heading of an exaggerated orientation toward productivity. In this regard, our society is based upon a dual paradox. Thanks to economic advance, young people are receiving an increasingly high level of education. In most countries, education is compulsory up to 16 years of age, and many young people continue their studies beyong this level. In 1920, only 3% of the French population had schooling beyond the age of 18, while today this figure is nearly 25%. Attitudes are completely transformed by an evolution of this sort. On the other hand, while the educational level rises, companies continue to offer a large volume of unprofitable, nonskilled jobs, involving tasks which are fragmented, repetitive and sometimes degrading or physically trying. Moreover, this is true in both the industrial and service sectors: many bank, insurance company or department store employees hold down jobs no more enriching than that of the workman paid to perform the same motion hundreds of times each hour on his car assembly line.

Contrary to what might be believed, the number of nonskilled or low-skilled jobs has not diminished in the past ten years. On the contrary, the proportion is tending to increase. Even if working times are steadily diminished, work remains at the centre of human existence. It cannot be looked upon as lost time, devoid of any responsibility or any share of initiative for the worker. The development of a demand for self determination of working conditions might logically be expected.

The second paradox involving the worker's situation is the increasingly sharp contrast between the conditions prevailing at places of work and the general standard of living. In other words, we have on the one hand a consumer attracted by a superabundance of goods and services, who sees companies capable of mastering increasingly sophisticated technologies, who is submerged in mass media characterised by omnipresent advertising which continually sings the praise of ever more attractive consumer goods; and, on the other hand, a man whose work, whose factory, whose office represents an environment more often than not dominated by ugliness, an absence of aesthetic values, heat, noise, lack of air-conditioning, a grindingly uniform rhythm of work and sometimes even overcrowding and safety hazards. Obviously, this involves a contrast which is felt to be unacceptable. * This explains the increasing alienation of the younger generation from certain jobs, the signs of which are well known: absenteeism, turnover, necessity of immigrant labour, unfilled vacancies during periods of increasing unemployment. This is a set of contradictions calling for a far-reaching renovation of working conditions, in the private as well as the public sector. In this regard, there is no boundary between the

* To this is added another split involving interpersonal relations: young workers who have grown accustomed to simple and direct interpersonal relationships at school, at the university and within their family, have a hard time accepting the weight of the rigid company command structure.

private company and the public company, or even the governmental administrative services themselves.

An essential characteristic of our pattern of growth has been its striving for intensive development of consumption, production and investment. Within the constant and more or less conscious balancing off between improvement of working conditions and expansion of productive investment and consumption, the second of these goals has tended in France to assume priority. This explains the constant pressure for increased productivity and the maintenance of a high degree of rigidity in work patterns and the physical environment of shops or offices.

The re-examination of the principles of company organisation and its traditional juridical structure

The second major contradiction involves the organisational structure of the company itself. The very heavy concentration undergone by industrial companies during the past twenty or thirty years—and particularly during the last decade— has led to the formation of increasingly large companies characterised by complex, constraining, hierarchical and anonymous organisations within which the individual is unhappy. This unease affects the workers and executives alike. The individual is less and less able to identify himself with the company's interests. He feels submerged within an organisation over which he has neither control nor influence.

And this new organisation, in its entirety, is developing on the basis of a completely obsolete juridical structure. From a given standpoint, it may be true to say that the company has no legal existence; what does exist is the company, backed by capital. And what shape has the company today? That consists of general meetings of shareholders, who in principle own the firm and theoretically control its activities. But everyone knows that the majority of shareholders, particularly in the largest companies, have absolutely no wish to exercise or involve themselves in the management of the company. The average stockholder buys a share to put money aside and make an investment: he awaits his dividend or appreciation of his shares without the slightest desire or possibility to participate in company management; the board of directors, elected by the shareholders, is quite often only a "rubber stamp" organisation, substantially dominated by the Chairman and General Manager.

In point of fact, the real power is held by the team of managers who have at their disposal the technological structure under the leadership of the Chairman and General Manager. This management team customarily co-opts itself. This constitutional outline of the company, conceived over a century ago, leads to two sets of criticisms that are, moreover, in part self-contradictory.

In many situations, on the one hand, there is inadequate control over the real holders of company power. Of course, the managers know that, if they fail, they will end up without jobs. But a prolonged evolution may take place before such failure becomes evident and, afterwards, control is meaningless.

171

On the other hand, capital comes into its own at strategic moments within the life of the company. It might be called upon to play a fundamental role in certain decisive circumstances: merger, concentration, shake-up of the management team. Now, many of our contemporaries no longer accept the proposition that managerial power is justified by ownership of capital alone, or through appointment by this capital ownership. There is a widespread aspiration to participation, information and control among workers. Even if the trade unions often assert, as in France, that they do not wish to share power and assume a managerial role within the firm, this nevertheless does not keep them from contesting that power can be based upon capital. In any case, regardless of the trade unions' complex ideological positions, there is no evading the problem of a re-establishment of balance between the respective roles of the workers and all categories interested in the company's activities—other than the capital shareholders.

Criticism of the excesses of the profit economy

There is increasing denunciation of the split between company objectives and the interests of society as a whole. Within the logic of the market economy, a company naturally seeks its own development, expansion and maximum profitability, and does not take into immediate consideration certain goals in the public interest, of which our society is becoming more and more aware—protection of the environment, an end to waste of natural resources, public nuisances, artificial obsolescence of products. Consequently, the company is seen as a sort of tool for blind and selfish expansion, leading to an endless race between production and creation of new consumer needs: a race in which the individual is more alienated than liberated, and which engenders more inequalities than it eliminates. The company is thus subjected to a trial which should in fact be directed against the economy as a whole and against a certain process of industrialisation. As is quite natural, however, public opinion can hardly distinguish the boundary between the economy as a whole and its basic cell, the company.

Company reform must therefore be situated within this overall context, summarily outlined. While this problem is raised with an acuteness that varies from country to country, we believe that it involves the entire body of industrial companies, and is not a specifically French one. *

Difficulties of company reform

I believe it useful to recall the three major difficulties encountered by the Research Committee on company reform in the drafting of its report. While one is relatively specific to France, two are general in scope.

* The Atlantic Institute's initiative for this colloquium is an indication of this, as are the draft reforms drawn up and proposed by the EEC.

Company diversity

A modern economy involves an extraordinary variety of companies. There are such differences between situations that one might even say that "the company" does not exist; what does exist are "companies." Is there anything in common between a given multinational industrial company employing over 100,000 people, and a given service company whose dozen members are on first-name terms? Beyond the criterion of size, companies are differentiated by their activities, their layout, their financing, their outlets, their age, etc. For example, should the question of power within a company be raised in the same way for an enterprise founded generations ago as for a company still managed by its founder? The first requirement for reform is therefore to take this company diversity into account, and one can imagine that this is not easily reconcilable with an approach at the central level, at the governmental level of company reform.

The nature of company reality: more sociological than juridical

A company is not simply a legal structure, nor even an economic organisation matching an exact diagram. Above all else, it is a living community, made up of traditions, of customs. It is a complex grouping of human relationships. It is a network of communications and information. As a consequence, the real nature of the operation transcends the institutional and juridical plane.

Thus the workings of the company substantially elude the confines of the law. Any action decreed by the public authorities, can have only a limited effect. The trade unions themselves are quite aware of this: leadership decisions are often overruled by reactions from the rank and file.

The difficulties of social dialogue in France

In France, the company bears the imprint of the history of all our social and ideological struggles. It may be seen that, within a profoundly divided society where each partner has a differing concept of the company and the economic system, it is difficult to outline the paths of reform. At the same time, there is no chance for reform to succeed without a minimum level of mutual agreement and confidence between the interested parties.

Without describing the entire system of professional relationships in France, which is primarily based on the existence of five trade union organisations—considered as representative on the national level—it is necessary to briefly summarixe the ideological and political poles separating the social partners in order to become aware of the difficulty facing company reform.

On the trade union side, two of the major organisations are imbued with socialist ideology, and place their hopes in a change of the economic system. The consequences for their positions vis-à-vis the company are twofold.

For these organisations, no true company reform is possible within the framework of the capitalist system. Transformation of the political and economic system is a prerequisite to any company reform. Regardless of the situation, sharing of power and co-management proper are not possible under a capitalist system. The French trade unions tend to present their claims within the concepts, or in support of an overall review of society, and not solely of the owner-management of the company within which they are active.

The shop steward or union section almost always goes beyond the mere transmission of an individual grievance; each action is viewed as a particular aspect of a class conflict. Hence the introduction of political considerations in local negotiations, or at least the presentation of demands and goals which frequently go beyond the individual company. In other words, French trade unionism does not acknowledge any *a priori* limitations upon its disputes; it does not consider itself bound to the application of the law as it stands or to the execution of the contract as it has been negotiated. Within a given company, moreover, the trade unions quite frequently maintain a stand against the company's own interests, as evaluated by management, even if this evaluation is based upon objective and competitive data.

While the so-called "reformist" trade unions are more willing to accept negotiation and contractual settlement, one of them (the C.G.T.-F.O.) rejects the principle of co-management. For their part, the employers stand behind economic liberalism and free enterprise. While they now acknowledge the fact of trade unionism, they rebel against intervention by trade unions, which they consider systematically hostile to private enterprise and steeped in a revolutionary ideology whose aim is the destruction of the free enterprise system. For many employers, trade union demands are suspect from the start, as they originate within organisations whose aim is a change in the economic and social system.

This virtually ceaseless struggle against an alleged intent to destroy the social fabric is, of course, incompatible with the minimum requirement of trust between partners who must take seats around the same bargaining table.

Hence the difficulty of pursuing negotiation in France, a process which by itself is incapable of leading to company reform. It is necessary, then, to turn to the legislator.

The main proposals of the Report

The proposals of the Sudreau report, in the very midst of all of these difficulties—"difficulties" akin to attempting the impossible—are derived from three basic principles.
— Company diversity must be respected. The report thus clearly indicates that it does not deserve its name: it is not a report on company reform, but a report proposing a set of reforms for companies.
— The company must be viewed as a global entity, with as complete and pragmatic an approach as possible. Today's company is not beset by a

174

single problem, but by multiple problems calling for a multiplicity of solutions.

It is not a matter of applying a miraculous solution, but of gradually introducing numerous changes involving all company levels, from the shop floor to the Board of Directors, and all its components: shareholders, employees, managers, consumers.

— A priority role should be assigned to negotiations as an instrument of change. Negotiation respects the autonomy of all groups. It involves each individual in the collective future. It permits the application of solutions adapted to concrete situations. It is the path by which the freedom to create Law is manifested, and it facilitates the birth of consensus at the very moment in which the new convention is being drafted.

This also makes it clear that application of company reform must not be judged solely in relation to any individual major law which might be passed by the government during forthcoming months or years. This reform should thus be evaluated by observing the events within the collective bargaining life of each branch and within individual companies.

The report, divided into ten chapters, puts forward some seventy proposals. We shall outline here only a few of the most significant ones.

1. The first chapter is entitled "*For transformation of daily life within the company*". It is in fact within the area of working conditions that the most urgent problems are posed, as well as those for which agreement between social partners is the least difficult to achieve. Four basic operations may be singled out from this chapter:

The first of these operations consists in drawing up a *company report and a social plan* within all companies of a certain size. Each year, the company would draft the most complete possible report of all operations implemented during the preceding year under the heading of improvement of working conditions. Moreover, a programme for forthcoming years would be drawn up, at given intervals, which might vary within the individual company. Short-range plans would be extracted from this medium-range plan (covering a five year period, for example); these short-range plans might have the value of a commitment for the first year and contain guideline goals for subsequent years. The major priority operations for improvement of working conditions and the overall social situation would be programmed in this manner. This report and social plan would have to be discussed with the works council or, as applicable, with the company's trade union organisation. Such methods should have a significant educational value. It would seem absolutely normal to employ methods for the company's human and social management which are at least equivalent in value and weight to those proven methods customarily employed for economic and financial management. Naturally, the social and human problems are fundamentally qualitative in nature, while finances and economics are quantitative. But it should not be impossible to refer to concrete social indicators, varying by company and by branch and giving a more or less planned base and greater objectivity to the company's social policy. Here are a few examples: wages, the discrepancy between company wage levels, a comparison between wages of male and female workers, weekly or annual working hours, the proportion of night work, the number and seriousness of industrial accidents, the rate of employment of handicapped persons and of immigrants, the number of internal promotions, training expenditures turnover, absenteeism, etc.

The study of social indicators should be developed, and there is no apparent reason why they should be of less importance than financial ratios.

The second basic operation is the revaluation of manual work. * A number of measures can bring this about: enrichment and expansion of tasks; definition of special benefits awarded to persons performing the most onerous jobs, such as lowering of the retirement age or shortening of weekly or yearly working hours; increased rights to training which would permit a change of jobs after several years, etc.

The third proposal under the heading of working conditions, one of the most difficult to implement and to understand, is the acknowledgement of each worker's right to self-expression concerning the nature of his work. This right to free speech is based upon a dual justification.

The daily working existence is comprised of numerous constraints which, without forming actual grievances of a sort to be brought forward by the shop steward or union section, are no less irritating for the individual thus placed at a disadvantage: poor arrangement of facilities, inconvenient layout, useless formalities, inconvenient schedules. Why not organise a regular dialogue at the rank-and-file level, between workers and their direct superiors in the chain of command, on all of these subjects concerning concrete job aspects? These could be shop, office or department meetings, which can vary from company to company. Besides providing an opportunity for airing minor grievances, these meetings and this dialogue would present an opportunity to offer suggestions of great value to the company. There are reserves of inventiveness and creativity at all levels of a company. They are insufficiently known and exploited. Wage-earners often feel that they possess knowledge and experience which the company fails to use.

Naturally, this right of self-expression, which introduces an amount of direct democracy, should in no way diminish the role of union representatives and shop stewards. It exists upon a different plane. There is no doubt that this right to self-expression, acknowledged for each individual, enhances the worker's dignity. It goes without saying that such a reform cannot succeed without meti-

---

* In France, the life expectancy of a 35-year old labourer is 33 years, while that of an executive of the same age is close to 40 years. The labourer's average working week is nearly two hours longer than that of the white-collar worker. Obviously manual labourers are the ones who most suffer from industrial accidents and illness, while they have the lowest rate of wage increase due to seniority.

culous preparation, and in particular suitable training of foremen and executives.

The fourth operation involving working conditions concerns the government, which must develop its entire policy on the working environment: this might involve expansion of the role of the national agency responsible for working conditions, of the responsibilities of the factory inspectors who supervise the enforcement of regulations, of the position held by industrial medicine as applied to industry in companies, of general training in working conditions and ergonomy for all executives holding positions of responsibility within the company. In this regard, the curricula of all engineering and technical schools must certainly be revised in order to make graduates aware of the problems of working conditions and relationships. For example, there is no question that the working layout should be taken into consideration at the beginning of the construction phase of factories or offices.

2. The second chapter is entitled: *"To establish the role of workers within the company"*. It deals with the role of the trade union and the works council and with joint management-labour supervision.

The report clearly indicates that the trade union should be an essential partner of the company director. Such a proposal might seem odd to British observers. In present day France, however, it is far from irrelevant to recall that companies must deal concretely with the consequences of trade unionism: provide trade unions with honest information, as exhaustive as possible; agree to regular negotiations; grant the facilities required for unions to function.

The Works Committees, established in France in 1945, have had variable success. Company leaders are unhappy to see them transformed into arenas of dispute and confrontation. The trade unions complain that the Committees fail to provide what they should: solid, continuing information on the company's economic and social situation and future prospects.

In spite of these criticisms, the trade unions are very much bound to the Works Committees. The Sudreau report therefore recommends various measures to make these committees the venue of concrete and precise discussion, particularly with regard to working conditions and training programmes. Above all, the report suggests that, within large companies, the Committee designate an economic sub-committee, i.e. a sort of semi-permanent working group, to study in depth the common approach to economic questions and prepare background papers to be submitted to the Committee. This sub-committee should meet at least once monthly, while the main committee should meet quarterly.

On the other hand, observing that large companies nowadays often take the form of groups divided into parent companies and subsidiaries managed by a holding company, the Sudreau Report suggests that group and holding-company committees be established, thus providing employee representation at the highest level. Naturally, the Report does not conceal the difficulty of defining the concept of the "group," given the extreme diversity of specific

177

situations. In the case of multinational firms, the Report suggests that a representative of the holding company be sent to explain and justify the group's strategy to the personnel of its French subsidiaries at least once yearly, and prior to certain decisions which would have substantial repercussions upon the body of employees.

Finally, in connection with the company's labour force, the Report suggests the introduction of joint management-labour supervision in France, i.e. to allocate one-third of the voting membership of a company's Board of Directors or Supervisory Board to representatives of the firm's employees.

Nonetheless, it should be noted that the members of the Research Committee are divided on this proposal, a very controversial one in France. Some members indicated their wish that this measure be made optional; others, in contrast, were of the opinion that this reform should become compulsory within three to five years from now, at least in the case of companies of a given size. Likewise, the Research Committee was unable to resolve the difficult question of the system of appointment: appointment by the trade unions or by the Works Committee, or one man one vote, by all employees, or with the union alone putting forward candidates.

Generally speaking, the employers prefer the one man one vote system with free candidacy; the trade unions prefer direct appointment by themselves or by the Works Committee. In any case, the Research Committee on Company Reform was of the opinion that this major question of joint supervision can no longer be evaded: it is a reform capable of contributing effectively to better communication to wage earners, and of giving them an additional instrument of control. In so far as company boards of directors or supervisory boards are in fact not merely management bodies but the body which determines the company's major guidelines and monitors its activities, the presence of employees at this level is not equivalent to a sharing of managerial power: the principle of managerial authority remains unimpaired; at the same time, trade unions in no way lose their autonomy and their potential for challenging management. Joint supervision also has the advantage of marking the shift from the company of shareholders to the company conceived as an association of three basic partners: contributors of capital, wage earners and management. As is natural, however, joint supervision is incapable of assuming its true meaning unless associated with other reforms, and is not offered as a panacea or with too much glamour.

I shall touch upon the other chapters of the report more briefly.

The fourth chapter is devoted to the revision of Company Law. It contains two basic recommendations. The majority of French companies, having the legal form of the limited company, are currently headed by a chairman-general manager, an individual whose position in fact consolidates the functions of company management and supervision. The report recommends that the functions of management and supervision henceforth be separated, particularly in the case of companies of a certain size. To this end, it suggests that companies be encouraged to adopt the article, derived from a 1966 law, providing for a supervisory board and a managerial board. In this case, there is a separate chairman for each of the two bodies. Moreover, the Report stipulates that, within the context of this statute, there should be a free choice between a collegiate board of management and a single manager. In the case of companies maintaining their Board of Directors, a separation should be established between the functions of the Chairman of the Board and the Administrator-General Manager.

The second recommendation involving company law is aimed at facilitating the replacement of the executives within the company. Thus, Board members would be prevented from exercising more than three *consecutive* three-year tenures. This rule would not apply to chairmen and general managers, but they would be prevented from exercising more than three-year tenures after the age of 60. In effect, this amounts to the establishment of an age limit of around 70 for holding such offices.

Merely as a reminder, I shall mention the chapter which proposes measures to revaluate the status of shareholders, by improving both their lines of communication and increasing their influence (particularly in the case of minority shareholders), as well as the chapter aimed at expansion of wage-earner's financial participation.

I shall end this general review of the Report by summarizing two chapters that are somewhat complementary, one of which is entitled "Encouragement for the Establishment of Companies," while the other tackles a question of great current interest: the prevention of difficulties, and assistance to companies in overcoming them. No dynamic, job-creating economy exists without renovation of the structure of companies. The Report proposes a set of fiscal and financial measures designed to bring this about.

In particular, it suggests the financing agencies specialized in raising capital for new company ventures be established, and that institutional investors be compelled to put a percentage of their annual asset appreciation into the operating capital of small and medium-sized companies. It also recommends that regional development companies—semi-public financing bodies which already exist in France—provide practical advice for any individual desirous of launching a new business venture. Workers and shareholders, subcontractors and the community at large all suffer from the collapse of a company, which can sometimes assume dramatic proportions.

It is a fact that the majority of the major conflicts in France during the past two or three years stem from mass layoffs caused by the shutdown—or liquidation—of individual companies. The notorious "Lip affair" has had extensive repercussions. Since that time, other conflicts of the same type have flared up; even if less spectacular, they nonetheless illustrate the fact that workers no longer accept their fate as victims of poor management, or even resign themselves to the vicissitudes of the general economic situation. Under these circumstances, every step must be taken to prevent a catastrophic outcome.

Of course, the solution does not lie in a completely rigid economy which prevents internal rephasing. A dynamic economy, capable of increasing the worker's living standard and encouraging full employment, implies some liberation of capital and, in extreme cases, one has to accept the phasing out of some companies. But this latter course must be the exception to the rule, and a policy of simultaneous prevention and cure must be established.

The Report recommends two measures to facilitate the prevention of difficulties. First, data on companies should be centralized within the Commercial Court system, "Tribunaux de Commerce" so that timely information concerning possible company difficulties is available to banks, to the government or to any other interested party. Secondly—and this is one of the Sudreau Report's major reforms—a sort of legal emergency procedure should be set up for the benefit of all parties involved in the company's existence: the Works Committee representing the labour force, minority shareholders, the auditors and, if applicable, subcontractors.

This emergency procedure would work in the following manner: upon the appearance of certain danger signals, the interested parties could address a formal request to the management and board of directors for information concerning measures planned to remedy the situation. The reply must be made within a fixed period of time. To prevent an excess of litigation, the criteria authorizing the setting in motion of this procedure would be defined in advance, and might embrace only certain objective points such as: a deficit of a certain volume and duration; loss of a certain amount of capital; announcement of massive lay-offs; delay in payment of taxes or social contributions, etc. Obviously it is desirable for this investigation to remain within the company. If the management's reply is unsatisfactory, however, or if there is no response at all, the interested parties must be entitled to notify the presiding judge of one of the ten major French Commercial Courts, who would have the authority to order an expert appraisal.

In the opinion of the authors of the Sudreau Report, this emergency procedure offers a number of advantages: it strengthens the role of both the Works Committee and the minority shareholders; it clearly defines the limits of management's authority. As long as management is successful, this authority is not disputed. On the other hand, management must account for itself when failure threatens.

Finally, in order to assist companies involved in serious difficulties threatening their survival, the Report calls for the establishment of an agency geared to assist redeployment. This agency, set up in the form of a public body, would have a threefold mission:
— Determine the nature of the financial difficulties of the company in order to judge its viability and the conditions under which it might return to normal activity or be reconverted.
— To assign some of its experts to the company for temporary assistance recovery.

180

— To bring in a temporary management, within the context of the recovery plan resulting from a legal "bankruptcy" * procedure. In this case, the agency's role would be to seek out new shareholders or partners to replace their predecessors. Naturally, intervention by this agency should be *quite exceptional,* remaining above all an instrument available to the Commercial Courts called upon to pass judgment on bankrupt firms, so that an *economic* as well as a legal solution is available for problems raised by ailing companies. This agency's success depends upon its ability to recruit a body of skilled experts.

Briefly summarized, these are the major guidelines of the Sudreau Report, which is concluded by a few recommendations designed to strengthen the influence of consumer organisations.

I should like to end this discussion of company reform with two questions:

1. At a moment in which the world economy is entering a difficult era, is it realistic to believe that the problem of company reform and working conditions will still be regarded as an essential question in the coming years? If it turns out that expansion is profoundly curtailed, will not protection of employment have the upper hand over demands for improvement in working conditions? In this regard, it is significant to observe that, in most countries, the new awareness of the quality of work took place between 1968 and 1972, i.e. during a phase of strong growth.

This frequently advanced objection should be bluntly dismissed: economic efficiency is conditioned by social equilibrium, and this will increasingly be the case. The risk of the GNP growth rate dropping a few points is no reason to envisage a static society and a rigid company structure in the future. On the contrary, reforms of labour management relationship will have to be intensified as the rate of production becomes more uncertain.

A democratic society cannot allow itself to be Malthusian and restrictive in allowing access to knowledge and education. It will thus be necessary to rethink both the working environment and the company structure, to adapt them to the potential and aspirations of modern man. A democratic society can no longer accept a working community which is divided between those who participate in creative activity, with its opportunity for fulfilment and progress, and those who are no more than a cog in a wheel.

2. Is it possible to imagine company reform on a national scale alone? The reply is surely negative.

In a market without economic boundaries, forming a huge field of competition, no government can allow itself to saddle its companies with new restrictive measures likely to hinder its competitive potential. If it is desired that companies offer completely new working conditions, then improvement in this direction must be able to take place at a more-or-less even rate of progress

* This term is employed here for purposes of simplification, and no longer corresponds to current procedures of French Law.

181

in all the major industrialised nations. In this regard, the European nations participating in a single community must certainly commit themselves to a resolute joint action to change the face of their companies, even if it means finding different solutions for specific national situations.

If there is a meaning to "Europe," it is to offer individual governments something which they cannot accomplish alone. Company reform comes up against so many obstacles and raises so many ideological controversies in each country that it would be absurd not to use "Europe" to encourage—or force—us to transcend and overcome our national difficulties.

The Reform of European Company Laws

by Finn Gundelach[1]

The Commission of the European Economic Communities has for some time, as you are probably aware, been making proposals for Community legislation relating to industrial and commercial companies. I would like to take this opportunity to explain briefly to you what the Commission has been doing, and why.

What is being proposed?

Two broad categories of measures are contemplated. The first category is a series of directives to the member states which will have the effect of ensuring that the laws which they apply to *sociétés anonymes* or public companies do not differ by too great a margin.

Uniformity is not the goal. Rather, the Commission seeks to create a framework which will ensure an appropriate degree of convergence, while leaving member states free, within the parameters laid down, to adopt solutions which take proper account of national conditions and traditions, economic, social and legal.

Five such proposals have been made, the first of which, relating to disclosure, authority to represent the company and nullity, was adopted by the Council of Ministers in 1968. The second proposed directive, relating to the formation and capital of public companies, is currently being actively considered by a working group in the Council, as is the fourth proposed directive on accounts. The latter will give full significance to the requirements of the first directive as to the annual disclosure of accounts by companies. It will regulate the minimum contents of the accounts which must be published.

The proposed third directive on mergers within a single member state will shortly be submitted to the Council in an amended form which, in the Commission's view, achieves a proper balance of the interests of shareholders, creditors and employees in merger situations.

The proposed fifth directive on the structure of public companies raises issues relating to employee participation which are of greater political significance than any other of the proposed directives.

1. European Commissioner for the Internal Market.

Further proposals are likely to be made in the future for directives relating to groups of companies and to consolidated accounts, which will be of particular significance in that they will have an impact on the operations of multinational enterprises, an issue of almost universal interest and concern.

The second category consists of proposals for the creation of wholly new Community company law, the principal example [1] being the proposal for a European Companies Statute, which the Council of Ministers will begin to consider in the near future. When enacted, the Statute will constitute a complete company law, existing independently of the national legal orders, which will give enterprises wishing to operate in more than one Member State the option, but no obligation, to adopt a modern, legal form appropriate to the scale and requirements of the European market in which they wish to operate. For the first time, multinational enterprises can be governed by a company law designed with them in mind, a law which being a Community regulation is itself multinational in character.

Why Has the Commission Made These Proposals?

The first reason is that a common market for companies is an essential part of the basic structure which must be constructed if progress is to be made towards a European Community in the real sense of the words.

Public companies are institutions of strategic importance in the economic and social systems of the Community. They are the principal buyers and sellers of goods, the major borrowers and lenders of capital, the most significant developers and users of new technology, the main producers of wealth, and, as employers, they have an immediate impact on the lives of large numbers of the Community's citizens. At present, the decisions of these industrial and commercial enterprises, and of those responsible for the channeling of investment, have to be made in a Community in which nine different legal systems, with complex and, sometimes, widely divergent provisions, exist side by side.

This situation operates as a considerable barrier to transnational industrial and commercial activity in the Community. Only when enterprises and individuals can pursue their affairs throughout the Community with a facility similar to that enjoyed within the boundaries of a single member state will industrial and commercial activity develop fully across the boundaries of the member states. Only then will a free trade area mature into a robust commercial, industrial and social Community.

The importance of such an evolution for all the member states can hardly be denied, both as regards their relationships with each other and their relationships with the rest of the world. For if progress is not made, the member states will find it increasingly difficult to maintain what they have already achieved.

1. Another example would be the draft International Merger Convention (Goldman Convention).

If there is no sound economic and social structure for the Community as a whole, there is a serious danger that, sooner or later, the needs and interests of certain parts of the Community will be so different from those of other parts that the whole edifice will collapse like a house of cards. Similarly, only by developing a common structural foundation can the member states hope to present a common front to the world around us, a matter of vital importance. If the underlying structures are disparate and inconsistent, so will be the policies pursued by the member states.

The situation which arose following the substantial rise in energy prices, and of certain other raw materials, demonstrated the clear reality of both these threats. A radical change in our economic environment, of a kind that we must learn to expect, provoked, within months, serious threats to the existing structures of the Community, and a disheartening pursuit of divergent nationalist policies in relation to the outside world. We cannot say we have not been clearly warned.

The final, and by no means the least important, reason for the Commission's proposals in this field is that the time is ripe in many of the member states for the reform of certain social institutions, companies included, to take account of certain important evolutions which have been gathering momentum for some time.

The first of these evolutions is the increasing recognition being given to the democratic imperative that those who will be substantially affected by decisions made by social and political institutions must be involved in the making of those decisions. In particular, employees are increasingly seen to have interests in the functioning of enterprises which can be as substantial as those of shareholders and sometimes more so. Decisions taken by or in the enterprise can have a substantial effect on their economic circumstances, both in the short and long term; the satisfaction which they derive from work, their health and physical condition; the time and the energy which they can devote to their families and to activities other than work; and even their sense of dignity and autonomy as human beings. Accordingly, increasing consideration is being given throughout the Community to the problem of how and to what extent employees should be able to influence the decisions of the enterprises which employ them.

The second evolution is a growing awareness of the need for institutions which can respond effectively to the need for change. This awareness is based upon the perception that the present era is one characterized by change, and that this feature may well become more pronounced in years to come. As far as economic affairs are concerned, the situation which has arisen relating to supplies of energy and certain other raw materials (to which I have already referred) has dramatically emphasized the trend. The need to pay much higher prices for energy is making increasing demands on the industrial and commercial structures of the member states. Enterprises must produce more efficiently. Exports must be increased to cover deficits in the balance of payments. The economic need for industrial reorganisation to achieve these goals has been

185

markedly increased. And it should not be forgotten that the completion and operation of a genuine European Community will itself involve structural changes of a substantial kind.

In some ways, there is a degree of tension between these two evolutions. Changes that are desirable from a broad economic and social point of view may appear to be more difficult to achieve if those concerned, particularly those with a vested interest in existing systems and structures, are to participate in the decision making. However, for sophisticated, industrial societies of a democratic character, there is no real alternative. Difficult problems will be easier to solve properly, fairly and with a minimum of wasteful confrontation, if there are mechanisms which involve those affected in the process of finding solutions. For while such mechanisms cannot always produce complete agreement, they can at least ensure a reasonable degree of understanding and an adequate level of acceptance. And there is no real doubt that the days of unquestioning acceptance of the decisions of those in administrative and managerial positions are well and truly over.

The laws applying to public companies are inevitably caught up in these evolutions, and it is important that the Community institutions participate fully in the process of reform to ensure that the Community makes its full contribution to economic and social progress in the member states, and also to ensure that the measures taken in the member states are sufficiently convergent, and do not themselves become obstacles to the development of a genuine industrial and commercial Community.

For these reasons, as regards both the proposed European Companies Statute and the proposed fifth directive on company structure, the Commission is currently taking initiatives. As regards the former, for example, following the opinion of the European Parliament, the Commission has amended its proposal to provide that enterprises choosing to adopt the European Company form will have to have a supervisory board one-third of whose members are elected by the shareholders, and one-third by the employees. Together these elected members will co-opt the final third. In view of the Statute's optional character, and taking account of the fact that, when adopted, it will probably be in force for more than twenty-five years, the Commission considers that such an arrangement is a reasonable and pragmatic compromise.

As for the fifth directive, the Commission will shortly publish a Green Paper [1] which will describe and analyse the situations and developments in the member states concerning the decision-making structures of public companies, and suggest certain possible approaches to the problem of constructing a Community framework for national legislation on this matter. There is no doubt that the problem is a difficult one. Community legislation must seek to promote convergent developments in the future while recognizing that the

1. Since this paper was presented, the Green Paper was actually released (on November 12, 1975) under the title *Employee participation and company structure in the European Community.*

divergent developments of the past impose certain limitations, as regards both the definition of Community objectives and the speed with which they can be approached. The ultimate goal is the establishment in all member states of decision-making structures which are broadly equivalent, but not identical.

The green paper will not make detailed formal proposals, but will present certain orientations as a focus for debate and discussion, particularly with those who will be closely affected by the solutions ultimately adopted. It is itself an exercise in participation, and something of a constitutional innovation at the Community level. In this case, at least, the Commission cannot be accused of not practising what it preaches.

Summary of the Discussions

by Benjamin C. Roberts

There was a general recognition among the participants that the growing emphasis on the rights of employees to have a larger role in the making of decisions which affect their working lives raised issues of great political, economic and social concern throughout the advanced industrial world. The achievement of a greater degree of employee participation everywhere presented a challenge to the organisation of the enterprise, to the classic roles of management and trade unions and to the political authorities. Although the demand for more participation was universal, participants stressed that it was greatly influenced by factors which were particular to each nation's pattern of industrial organisation, social structure and political environment. Any discussion had to start from the fact that there were considerable differences between countries within the European Economic Community and even greater ones between the countries of Europe and the United States and Japan.

Nevertheless, the institutional changes affecting employee rights which had taken place in the European countries, or were under discussion, had often been greatly influenced by developments occurring in other countries. The European Economic Community was itself a powerful political factor making for common developments in institutional change, but the basic social forces at work which were changing the relations between managers and workers were not limited by national boundaries, though they were inevitably shaped by national experiences. The international dimension to processes of institutional change could not then be ignored in the field of industrial relations any more than in any other area of social, political, and economic development.

The problem of analysing the significance of the development of the concept of participation was made difficult not only by differences in national experience, but also by the different forms of participation that could occur. What do we mean by the term participation? This was a question raised by a number of discussants who urged that clarification of the meaning of the concept was essential to the achievement of an understanding of the issues, especially across national boundaries, and to a rational debate of their merits.

It was clear that the effective participation of employees could be analysed at different levels of decision making within the enterprise. Of central concern to the participants in these symposia was the extent to which employees had already achieved, or desired to achieve in the future, the right to be directly represented on the board of directors of private and public enterprises. The need to develop more effective participation was not, however, limited to securing representation on the board of directors; it was equally necessary, and strongly believed, to bring about changes in processes of decision making at the shop-floor level. It was also forcibly stressed, in particular by the representatives of United States labour organisations, that participation could be and in fact was achieved as effectively through the procedures of collective bargaining as might be attained through the development of employee representation on the boards of directors of enterprises. The role of the trade unions, both through the collective bargaining process and in relation to the representation of employees on boards of directors, and through the activity of works councils, was recognized as of crucial significance in all countries. However, the emphasis on the role of the unions differed from country to country and was changing under the influence of evolving social and political circumstances.

A major focus of the discussion in the symposia was on the lessons to be learnt from the German model of participation that had developed over the past twenty-five years. There was a sharp clash of views between participants from Germany as to the relative contribution to the success of German industry which had been derived from the system of parity representation in the coal, iron, and steel enterprises; and the one-third proportion of employee representation on supervisory boards of the remainder of the firms in the private sector of industry. There was no disagreement as to advantages that had been gained from the one-third system of employee representation, but the so-called Montans system of parity representation divided employer opinion. There was, however, no disagreement as to the value of the role of the works councils. There was also general agreement that the trade unions in Germany had played an extremely responsible role in making the German system of co-determination work smoothly and effectively in the efficient administration of industrial enterprises. The unions were not, however, satisfied with the minority representation of employee representatives on supervisory boards and were locked in a fierce battle with the political parties to achieve parity representation in all enterprises. This extension of parity co-determination was seen by some employers as a development that would damage the efficiency of Germany industry and bring about social and political instability.

Although it was repeatedly argued by participants that it was not possible to transplant special institutions and processes from one national environment to another and expect them to operate without difficulty, it was accepted that this German model of employee participation had been highly influencial. The two-tier board structure of corporate management, which was an essential element in the German system of participation, though it antedated this development, was being widely adopted in Europe, though employers in Great Britain and the United States, where unitary boards of directors and management predominate, were not in favour of its adoption. The Netherlands, Luxembourg and the Scandinavian countries have made provision for the appointment of employee directors on supervisory boards, though by different means and in different

189

numbers from the German model. The importance of this difference in method of appointment of members of supervisory boards in the Netherlands was stressed by a participant from that country, who pointed out that there was no obligation for a Dutch company to appoint employee directors, but that there was an obligation for the board to secure the confidence of both the employees and the shareholders in appointments to the board, since the law gave the employees and the shareholders a right of veto over all nominations. This mutual right of veto, though it had only been in force for a few years, had so far worked without causing major conflicts between the two constituencies.

Perhaps the most important influence exercised by the German model of co-determination had been that on the European Economic Commission. It had been accepted by the Commission, that under the Treaty of Rome it had a duty to promote the development of a common social policy in respect of the structure of corporate enterprise and the rights of employees. In seeking the advance towards these goals the Commission had made proposals for the establishment of a European Company Statute, through a draft directive for the harmonization of the company laws in the member states. In both cases the Commission had based its proposals, to an important extent, on the German model of participation.

The European company statute would provide for the establishment of supervisory boards and works councils. On the supervisory boards of European companies, employees and shareholders would each be entitled to elect one-third of the members, the other third they would elect jointly from persons who would in some respect represent the public interest. This proposal aroused criticism from certain participants who doubted the wisdom of seeking to secure the representation of what must inevitably be either an ambiguous or controversial constituency. It was agreed that representatives of the "public interest" with any knowledge and experience of industry might be hard to find. It had been suggested in Norway, for example, that local governments might have the right to nominate directly to the boards of campanies, but there was some fear that such a step might lead to political factors, rather than considerations of managerial expertise, determining the appointments of this section of the boards of directors.

Following criticism of an earlier draft directive which proposed the harmonization of the laws of member states so as to establish a common pattern of company organisation, including a system of employee representation, the Commission had published, in November, 1975, a Green Paper discussing the principles of employee representation and alternative methods by which these might be given effect.

The essential difference from earlier drafts was the provision for a greater element of flexibility and a longer time horizon for the accomplishment of participation arrangements within the enterprises of member states. It was now recognized that participation at the board of directors level might be achieved by different methods. Perhaps even more important, in the light of major differences in this ideology and the role of unions in member states, was the concession that representation at the level of the "shop floor" might take different forms.

The Green Paper thus recognized that the concept of harmonization advanced in earlier proposals from the Commission, which had been based on the German model, had to be modified to take account of the marked differences that existed in the systems of industrial relations in member countries. In each of these countries there were powerful sections of the trade union movements that were strongly opposed to the German model of participation. Some unions were in particular opposed to the underlying philosophy of co-determination, as well as to particular aspects of the German model. In the case of Great Britain there was a strong preference for a shop steward system rather than one of works councils.

Nevertheless, in spite of these reservations there has been a broad acceptance by the member state governments that there should be an advance towards a more participative system of industrial relations within the enterprise, even though this might involve accepting that there would be wide differences in the way in which this was brought about.

The papers presented at the symposia and the discussions based upon them brought out a number of areas of major difficulty and controversy. Three of these stood out as of special significance. They were:

1. The relation of participation to the powers of collective bargaining and the role of the unions.
2. The impact of participation on the efficiency of management.
3. The effect of proposals to extend the participation of employees in corporate capital formation.

The fear of the trade unions that the development of a system of employee participation might undermine the bargaining power of the unions was widespread in the United States, and was strong in powerful sections of the trade union movements in Britain, France and Italy.

Participants from the United States in particular insisted that there were virtually no limits to what might be achieved through the collective bargaining process. The development of collective bargaining in the United States had shown, they contended, that if the unions had a strong bargaining position, they could compel management to discuss and negotiate on any issue of concern to union members; ranging from questions of pay and conditions of employment to plant closures and corporate development.

An American participant drew attention to the agreement which had been negotiated in the steel industry, as an example of the ability of trade unions in the United States to act with a high sense of responsibility towards an industry faced with difficult economic problems. The unions had pledged not to strike for a period of five years and to accept third party arbitration where they were unable to agree with management. In exchange for this guarantee of industrial peace, management would ensure a minimum rate of increase in real wages, and would provide the trade union officials with a monthly presentation of financial and technical information, identical to that given to the Board of Directors. The aim was to develop a responsibility of knowledge, an openness of conduct that American unions and management in the steel industry believed could be achieved and which would bring mutual benefit without undermining the independence and responsibility of either management or unions.

In the United States, it was feared that if employees were given the right to be represented outside the unions, this would lead to a dual loyalty, to conflict between the unions and its members and to a weakening of the responsibility and authority of the leadership of the unions.

It was pointed out by discussants, however, that while recognizing the achievements of the American unions, a very large proportion of employees in the United States were not members of labour organisations, and therefore could not rely upon them for protection. American union spokesmen feared, however, that the development of direct systems of employee participation would make this situation even worse, thus depriving even larger numbers of possible union cover.

The Communist influenced unions in France and Italy had been equally reluctant to accept the concept of employee participation, but for different reasons than the unions in the United States. The C.G.T. and the C.G.I.L. were committed to the notion of a continuing class struggle that was primarily expressed through an irreconcilable conflict between workers and management. They did not see this conflict as merely a difference of interest stemming from differences in function but as the outcome of a fundamental clash between opposing social forces, which were manifested through the roles of workers and managers in capitalist societies. Some unions would be willing to see the development of a system of employee management which went beyond the concepts of co-determination to the establishment of a system of *autogestion,* or workers' self-government.

The unions in Britain had shown similar divisions, but not always for the same reasons. There were genuine fears that the support that the British T.U.C. had given for the establishment of a system of employee co-determination would endanger the bargaining power of the unions. These differences had led the Labour Government, which had given a promise that it would introduce legislation that would bring about greater industrial democracy, to announce the setting up of an independent commission of inquiry as a prelude to political action.

Fear of the affects of the appointment of employee directors on the boards of directors of enterprises was by no means confined to trade unions. While accepting that there might be advantages in having representatives of employees on the boards of companies, managers were afraid that the demands of the unions in Germany for "parity co-determination" would lead to the weakening of managerial authority and expose managers to undesirable pressures. It was suggested that parity co-representation could lead to the extension of collective bargaining into the board room, to the development of decision making by "horse trading" and undesirable deals. Parity could result in the slowing down of the process of decision making. It was pointed out that speed was often an essential element in the making of effective decisions in a competitive economic environment. A company burdened by a sluggish management would be unable to satisfy the aspirations of either its workers or shareholders.

The minimum demand of the German managers was the right to be directly represented on the supervisory boards of enterprises. Only if this were conceded by the German unions could the deadlock, which had held up proposals for the extension and reform of the "parity" model of co-determination, be agreed upon.

The Sudreau Commission, established by the President of France, Valéry Giscard d'Estaing, soon after taking office, had sought in its report to provide an analytical foundation for a series of proposals that would achieve a reform of the enterprise without either undermining the ability of management to manage effectively or destroying the bargaining role of the unions.

In developing the concept of co-surveillance, the Report granted that it was the right of the employees and their unions to be informed on every aspect of the activity of the enterprise and to pass judgment on the performance of management. Management must, however, be free to make decisions in the light of the goals of the enterprise which could not be limited simply to satisfying shareholders and employees.

The company must be viewed as a global entity. The interests of customers and suppliers and the wider community had to be taken into account. It was an essential part of the task of management to reconcile these different interests.

In reforming the enterprise so as to make it more responsible to all its constituents, there was no reason why the unions should not have a more extensive bargaining role. The trade union was an essential partner in the enterprise and it must be given full information and facilities to function effectively in this capacity. There had been a shift in France, as in all other European countries, towards a pattern of greater militancy at the shop floor level. It was no longer possible for unions and employers' confederations to negotiate agreements at the industry level and for them to be implemented in the enterprise without conflict and negotiation. To avoid the shop floor becoming an area of dispute and confrontation, it was necessary to extend the role of works' committees, and to make effective the development of participation at the level of the working group. This was a virtually necessary feature of good industrial relations and of fundamental importance to the improvement of the quality of working life.

The Scandinavian countries had shown a special concern for more than a decade in the carrying out of experiments, within the enterprise, to improve relationships between workers and managers. The re-design of the automobile assembly and engine plants of Saab Scania and Volvo were now known all over the world. These experiments had demonstrated that it was possible to modify technological requirements to meet with the needs of production and the needs of workers to have a greater degree of control over their work activities. There were, of course, some tasks which probably will never be satisfying for those who to carry them out; other means, such as shorter hours, longer weekends, sabbatical leave periods and other forms of compensation, would have to be found. It was especially along these lines that American workers were looking for the amelioration of assembly lines and process jobs rather than for alterations in the organisation of work. In many cases, the only solution to unpleasant work would be its complete elimination through automation or the development of entirely new products and processes.

American workers and unions tended to take the view that the development of participative styles of management or working group autonomy could not provide a satisfactory solution to what was inherently nasty and objectionable in the work process. They therefore preferred to seek the solution of higher pay and shorter hours made possible by high productivity, rather than put a much greater emphasis on the radical reform of work arrangements and patterns of managerial control. They believed self-government at work was a poor substitute for higher standards of life outside of the work environment.

The trade unions in Sweden, though, favouring an extension of participation, gave their support to a proposal to encourage a widening of the scope of collective bargaining at the level of the enterprise. A new law would permit union representatives to demand that management should negotiate and enter into an agreement on any issue of company policy they deemed to be of concern to the employees. There would thus not be any area of corporate decision making where management could claim a right to take unilateral decisions. If management refused to provide the union with the information it required, or refused to negotiate and make an agreement, the unions would be freed from any peace obligation and have a legal right to strike. This extension of bargaining rights would greatly extend the participative rights of the union representatives in the decision making processes of management. The exact implications of these proposals on which the government has indicated it will legislate are not yet clear, but some people were of the opinion that this development could lead to a significant growth of militant trade union activity on the shop floor; others held a different view. They saw this change as a recognition of a needed shift in negociations within the enterprise and believed that it would lead to both unions and managers developing a more constructive pattern of collective bargaining at this level. It was a development that could lead to conflicts between employee representatives on supervisory boards and union representatives seeking to achieve different goals. Whatever the outcome of these important proposals, the debate in Sweden which they had aroused highlighted the problem of integrating collective bargaining systems and other systems of employee representation which provide for other types of participation.

The problem of integrating new concepts of negotiation and participation into an existing pattern of enterprise industrial relations, was further examined in the case of Japan. This country had no experience of co-determination, but one enterprise had recently introduced employee representatives on its supervisory boards. There was concern that any development of formal systems of participation should harmonize with existing patterns of collective bargaining and not lead to a situation of conflict that would have destructive consequences in terms of managerial efficiency and the stability of industrial relations.

An issue of long standing in the capitalist countries which could become of considerably greater significance in the future, is the opportunity which was afforded to employees to become shareholders. Employee participation in the capital structure of companies was historically advanced as a method of giving workers a direct interest in the success of the company. It was often resisted by the trade unions who saw this development as a means

1. Of undermining their bargaining powers.
2. Of locking the workers to their jobs with a particular enterprise, and as a way of deferring the payment of higher wages and improving working conditions.

Despite the importance of these points, the trade unions in Scandinavia and elsewhere in Europe were looking at more radical possibilities of providing for employee participation in the profitability of private enterprise. The most far-reaching proposals envisaged, the distribution of shares in the equity of enterprises through the setting aside of a percentage of profit, which could be used as a means of providing a capital fund, which would be available for investment in both private and public sectors of the economy. An important feature of the fund would be the participation of the unions in its management. The establishment of this type of equity participation had ominous implications for the future of private enterprise. It avoided some of the drawbacks to the classic schemes of company profit-sharing plans, but it opened up new areas of concern since it could lead to a type of syndicalist control of the sources of equity capital that might prove embarrassing not only to managements but also to governments and the unions themselves. It might be possible, however, to devise ways in which employees could share beneficially as equity investors without running into the dangers perceived by spokesmen from both sides of industry.

It was abundantly clear from the comments of participants that increasing participation in the directing and managing of enterprises was a desirable, but in many ways, a challenging and disturbing development. It presented in particular a challenge, perhaps even a threat, to managerial efficiency. It presented equally a challenge and perhaps a threat to the unions and to the processes of collective bargaining. The task before the legislators and managers and trade unions was to find ways of reconciling conflicts of interest by the development of new procedures, that would enable the enterprise to satisfy the needs of the community as well as those of employees and shareholders. Participation was not of itself a panacea, but a way by which human aspirations could be more fully developed in the environment of work if it were translated into an effective programme of institutional change.

Closing Remarks

by Louis Camu[1]

Despite the intricacy and interdependance of all the human, technical, legal and social problems complicated by psychological tension which this long day of debate has provoked, have we succeeded in establishing any common ground? Trade unionists, chairmen of multinational companies, diplomats, professors, sociologists and jurists drawn from Great Britain, France, Japan, the United States, Holland, Sweden, Germany and Italy have taken part in our discussion.

Looking back over the day, it seems to me that we have made some progress in clarifying the meaning of some of the most fashionable portmanteau words which have many definitions packed into them.

In "participation" there is an element of involvement, an implication of the meeting of minds, a hint that there should be equal rights for workers and employers to be informed, to be consulted, to take part in decision-making. The degree and range of involvement are disputed, but the principle is agreed. There are two forceful experiences which have helped: the memory of efficient Joint Production Committees in Great Britain during the war and the conviction in Germany that the two-tier board with the presence of employees on the supervisory board has been an important element in their social peace and high productivity. As Mr. Gerd Tacke, former President of Siemens, has reminded us: "Co-determination has been a success in Germany." The influence of the German innovation on Holland, Luxembourg, Sweden and Norway is obvious.

The humanistic approach is inherent in the conception of "productivity." To achieve a higher yield from the capital invested in a company with no loss of respect for the human element, there must be a centre of authority, a place of last resort decision-making. You cannot get the best out of men or machines if the line of command is amorphous. The entire work force, at each level, has its responsibilities. Expansion and prosperity remain the general aim of the enterprise: bake a bigger cake so that everyone can have a bigger slice. But nowadays there is a new worry: what will be the consequences of zero growth? What will happen with massive unemployment?

1. Honorary Chairman, Banque Bruxelles-Lambert; Chairman of the Economic Committee of the Atlantic Institute for International Affairs.

The word "company" no longer means only the traditional unified structure familiar to us all since the Industrial Revolution. Nowadays, we have to take into account the division of managerial duties between direction and control. The two-tier system of managing board and supervisory board is a development which causes anxiety to some capitalists even if participation becomes co-surveillance and joint control. Industry needs investment on an enormous scale, but what will happen if such a division of authority fails to attract risk capital? To succeed in our changing world, we must envisage structures of capital quite different from those of the past. There will have to be more loan capital, more investment from the public sector than at present, but profit will still be important because it is the yardstick of efficiency in any investment.

Whether from the private or public sector, should a third force, an outsider, be introduced into the game? As a "neutral," he has a worth-while part to play. While most people think he should not represent the State, everyone would like him to be on the side of the angels and to speak for the "general interest," whatever that may be. Concern for the overall well-being of the enterprise and much common sense seem to be what is expected of him.

The reform of company law also implies an enormous effort to improve the lot of the worker on the shop floor. Soul-destroying, monotonous work should be avoided and the dignity of manual labour safeguarded. Good human relations between employees and management are as important a preoccupation for the works council as participation in the supervisory board. The Sudreau Commission is convinced that the works council must be an effective and efficient organ of industry.

Another implication from the debate today is that the European company will never see the light of day without a consensus of contemporary opinion. Unfortunately, this is sadly lacking. The trade unionists are as divided as the federations of employers. There will have to be compromise between positions diverging from the parity proposed in Germany and the abrogation of Article 32 in Sweden. Participation at international, national or shop floor levels is a continuing process which must be carefully nurtured. It must never degenerate into mere window-dressing.

At the moment, the Commission of the European Community is a voice crying in the wilderness as far as a European solution to the problem is concerned. The member countries are preoccupied by their own domestic ills for which medicine for internal consumption only is prescribed. The Commission is pursuing three aims: the harmonization of national company law, the introduction of industrial democracy on the shop floor and a Statute for a European international company. The latter would be optional with no element of compulsion. The Commission stresses the importance of such a Statute, which would facilitate the generalization of modern and sophisticated companies whose efficiency and competitiveness vis-à-vis the outside world would improve the chances of European integration and bring closer European monetary and economic union. The trade unionists are unconvinced of the need for a European scale at company level and distrust sophistication. The European Parliament has, to a large extent, approved the proposals made by the Commission. Its amendments have been directed towards increasing the powers of employees on the Works Council and Supervisory Board of the European company.

The wide differences of opinion between employers, trade unionists and governments mean that there is a long way to go before the new company law advocated by the Commission is approved, but the challenge is there. A progressive solution leading gradually in this direction is more than ever necessary.

Appendix A

I. List of speakers and respondents in the Institute's Participating Members meeting, London, November 7, 1975

Speakers:

Professor Benjamin ROBERTS, Director of the Industrial Relations Department at the London School of Economics and Political Science.

François LAGRANGE, Member of the French Conseil d'Etat; Rapporteur general of the SUDREAU Committee.

N.H. PETERSEN, Chef de Cabinet of Finn GUNDELACH, European Commissioner, assisted by Messrs. SCHWARTZ and COLEMAN.

Dr. Gunter GEISSELER, former Legal Adviser of Mannesmann AG.

Respondents:

Prof. Michael FOGARTY, author of the recently released book *Company Responsibility and Participation*.

Sir Reay GEDDES, Chairman Dunlop Holdings Ltd. (UK)

J.M. GOUDSWAARD, Vice Chairman, Unilever (Netherlands).

Roy GRANTHAM, General Secretary, Association of Professional, Executive, Clerical and Computer Staff (APEX) (UK).

Mr. JANURUS, Labour Attaché, Swedish Embassy in London.

Kozo OKABE, Labour Attaché, Japanese Embassy in Bonn.

Taylor OSTRANDER, Special Assistant to the Chairman, AMAX (United States).

Harry POLLAK, Labour Attaché, United States Embassy in London.

Hans SWEDBERG, Vice President, Skandinaviska Enskilda Banken (Sweden).

Pierre URI, Counsellor of Studies, Atlantic Institute for International Affairs (France).

Rudolf VOLLMER, Labour Attaché, German Embassy in London.

II. List of participants in the Institute's Young Leaders Meeting, Paris, November 13-14-15, 1975

Dott. Gianni ARRIGO, International Bureau, CISL, Rome (Italy).

John CONDON, Labour Attaché, American Embassy, Paris.

John DOHERTY, Labour Attaché, United States Mission to the EEC, Brussels.

Eric HAWTHORNE, Research Assistant, London School of Economics (UK).

Mr. IKEGAMI, Director, Administration Department, Mitsubishi, France (Japan).

Arthur F. KANE, Director of Education, American Federation of Government Employees (Affiliated with AFL/CIO) Washington DC (United States).

Dr. Wolfgang KONRAD, Institut für Wirtschaft und Sozialwissenschaften, University of Münster (West Germany).

François LAGRANGE, Conseil d'Etat, Rapporteur général of Sudreau Committee, Paris (France).

Jay MAZUR, Assistant Manager, International Ladies Garment Workers Union, New York (United States).

Itzhak MESSIKA, Secretary General, Haifa Metal Workers Union (Israel).

M. MÜLLER-STEINECK, Head of Working Group No. 4, CDU/CSU Fraktion, Bundeshaus, Bonn (West Germany).

Stanley NOLLEN, Professor at School of Business Administration, Georgetown University, Washington DC (United States).

Riccardo PECCEI, Research Associate, Imperial College London. Oxford University, Doctorate in Social Studies (Italy).

James POOLE, Sunday Times, London (UK).

Prof. Benjamin ROBERTS, London School of Economics (UK) (introduced debates).

Ph. WILLS, Massey Ferguson, Coventry (UK).

Appendix B

EEC Press Communiqué on the European Company Statute

CONTENTS

The Commission at its meeting in Luxembourg, April 30th, approved a proposal for a European Company Statute. Compared to the previous Commission's proposal of 30 June 1970, the proposal has been amended significantly, following, to a large extent, the advice given by the European Parliament in July 1974.

Since the debate of the European Parliament, extensive consultations have taken place with numerous industrial organizations, trade unions, governments and political parties, as well as independent experts in the fields of workers' participation and company law.

The European Company Statute will provide a modern rational structure for the organization of companies in Europe and help to create what does not exist today—a common market for European enterprises beyond the common market for goods and services.

I. The European Company Statute: a new possibility

The purpose of the proposed European Company Statute is to make possible cross-frontier mergers, holdings and common subsidiaries which would then exist and function as European companies. The proposal is meant to help industry to restructure itself by external growth and internal reorganization and by adaptation to the dimension of the Common Market and the requirements of our times.

As yet, European enterprises do not have the opportunity of acting throughout the Community in the same way they can within the single member state in which they are incorporated. They have to contend with serious legal, practical and psychological difficulties if they wish to engage in certain cross-frontier operations.

The European Company Statute does not seek to replace national company laws. It is a complete European Companies Act, that will exist alongside them. It opens up a new possibility for European enterprises that wish to overcome present legal differences and practical difficulties in cross-frontier operations.

The European Company Statute is optional. No enterprise is compelled to use this legal framework. They can choose to do so, if they fulfill the requirements of the Statute, including the provisions for workers' participation in the decision-making process of the enterprise on the supervisory board, in the European Works Council and through collective bargaining.

II. The need for a legal framework

The Community's ability to respond effectively to the political problems which arise today, and will undoubtedly arise in the future, depends to a great extent upon the existence of solid structural foundations. Without such a structure, the Community is like a modern building without its steel frame. When the winds blow it will fall apart. One of the elements in this structural foundation, not perhaps the most central component, but certainly a very important one, is a common legal framework. The looser economic trading arrangements appropriate in the 1950s and the 1960s will not enable the Community to meet the greater challenges of the 1970s and 1980s. The institutions of the Community must move on to construct a common market in the full sense: a solid economic, social and legal foundation for the Community.

The European Company Statute is a significant part of that common legal framework.

Enterprises cannot today adopt legal structures which are appropriate to the scale and requirements of the European market in which they operate or wish to operate. The European Company Statute will provide them with such a structure and, moreover, a structure of a modern sophisticated kind, which offers protection for the legitimate interests of all concerned in the running of the enterprise. In making this structure available, the European Company Statute will provide a real stimulus for economic activity throughout the Community. For enterprises will have the opportunity to choose a modern corporate form which enables them to operate as European enterprises and thereby increase their efficiency, competitiveness and strength, vis-à-vis the outside world in their own interest and, what is more, in the interest of society as a whole.

The purpose of the European Company Statute is not to encourage bigness in industry as such, but to free enterprises from legal, practical and psychological constraints deriving from the existence of nine separate legal systems. These constraints at present inhibit enterprises from arranging their affairs and relationships with other enterprises in the manner which would otherwise be the most efficient and profitable just as a national company does in relation to its domestic market. Small and medium-sized firms can benefit as much as large ones from this opportunity.

The Statute will facilitate the formation of new multinational companies, but of a different type. Multinationals which choose to take advantage of the new European form will have a transparent structure and clear obligations in relation to shareholders, creditors, employees and society as a whole. This will constitute a step towards establishing a modern uniform company law applicable to European multinational companies throughout the Community.

III. The need for employee participation

The interests of society are increasingly related to wider considerations than economic efficiency.

This is nowhere more true than in the field of company law. In recent years there has been an increasing recognition that in order to ensure that companies operate for the benefit of the society as a whole, other interests than those of the investor, entrepreneur and manager should be able to influence the decision making of the company. Employees have interests in the functioning of the enterprises which are as substantial as those of shareholders and sometimes more so. Employees not only derive their income from the enterprises which employ them, but they devote a large proportion of their daily lives to the activities of the enterprise.

Decisions taken by the enterprise have substantial effects on their economic circumstances, their health and physical condition, the satisfaction they derive from work, the time and energy they can devote to their families and to activities other than work, and even their dignity and autonomy as human beings.

It is therefore not surprising that the problem of how and to what extent employees should be able to influence decisions of the enterprises which employ them has become a problem of paramount interest in all member states. The European Communities can and should play an important role in the search for practical means to ensure employee participation.

This is all the more true in the current period of profound economic and social change in the world. The new situation relating to energy and other raw materials has changed the economic environment of the enterprises. The need for industrial reorganization has increased while at the same time the prospects for immediate wage increases have become more limited. Consequently, conflicts of interest between different groups are more acutely felt.

But precisely in such a period of economic and social tension there is even more need for effective mechanisms whereby those involved and employed in industry can respond quickly and sensibly to the requirements of the situation. Difficult problems will be easier to solve properly, fairly and with a minimum of wasteful confrontation if there are mechanisms which involve all those affected in the process of finding solutions. Here, decision-making machinery at enterprise level and within the enterprise undoubtedly has an important part to play. The Community would fail to make its contribution to economic and social progress if it overlooked the problem of reconciling the principal interest groups in our society.

IV. Opinion of the European Parliament

The European Parliament in July, 1974 by a large majority approved the policy, the concept and the principles underlying the Commission's original proposal of June, 1970. However, three kinds of amendments were proposed:
— Numerous amendments of a technical nature.
— Several amendments of some economic, legal and (or) political significance.
— A few amendments of high political significance.

As far as the technical amendments are concerned, most of them were accepted by Mr. Gundelach on behalf of the Commission, during the debate in the Plenary, because they were ameliorations or did not raise problems. The few technical amendments not acceptable are of minor importance.

As to the amendments of some economic, legal and (or) political significance, again the Commission agrees in all but two instances with the European Parliament:

The Commission wishes to maintain:
— the possibility offered to European Companies to opt for several registered offices,

and it does not consider that
— the sanctions for the offences committed against provisions of the European Companies Regulation should be regulated in detail at the Community level.

1. Access

Concerning the problem of access to the European Company the Commission proposes to open access not only to *sociétés anonymes* (as proposed in 1970), but also to companies with limited responsibility and other corporate bodies for the formation of a common subsidiary, and to lower the minimum capital for mergers and holding companies to 250,000 RE and for common subsidiaries to 100,000 RE.

2. Taxation

The European Companies will conform to the same taxation rules as national companies and will benefit on the same basis as national companies from the provisions of the directive on the common tax treatment of parent companies and their subsidiaries of different member states, and the directive on the common system of taxation applicable in the case of mergers, divisions and contribution of assets taking place between companies of different member states, which were proposed by the Commission to the Council in 1969 (O.J. No. C 39 of 22.3.1969).

The Commission supported by the European Parliament therefore now takes the opportunity to draw the attention of the Council to its timetable for the abolition of fiscal barriers to closer relations between undertakings as laid down in the resolution of December, 1973.

V. Amendments of political significance

These concern three issues:
— The representation of employees in the Supervisory Board of a European Company.
— The problem of how to choose the representatives of the employees for the Supervisory Board and the members of the European Works Council.
— The powers of the European Works Council.

The Commission has decided to modify its original proposal in accordance with the opinion of Parliament.

1. Composition of Supervisory Board

The Supervisory Board will consist one third of representatives of the shareholders, one third of representatives of the employees, and one third of members co-opted by these two groups who are to be independent of both shareholders and employees and to represent "general interest".

The proposal to divide the number of seats on the Supervisory Board into three equal parts is intended to avoid some of the organizational, political and psychological difficulties which could result on the European level from a representation ratio of 50:50 between shareholders and employee representatives. In particular, the proposal attempts to prevent deadlock situations arising which might adversely affect the economic efficiency of the undertaking. The additional proposal that the total number of members of the Supervisory Board should be uneven is also intended to reduce this danger. Moreover, the proposed one third-one third-one third formula has the attractive feature of enabling other, broader interests than those of the shareholders and employees to be represented on the Supervisory Board.

On the other hand, if the representation of shareholders is reduced to one third giving another third to the employees and the final third to other defined interests, there is said to be the risk of reducing the incentive companies may have for using the European Company form. However, it should not be overlooked that no member of the final third can be co-opted without the consent of at least some of the shareholders' representatives because each co-opted member needs at least two thirds of the combined votes of the shareholders' and the employees' representatives.

The co-opted members of the final third must represent "*general* interests." This concept is intended to cover all interests affected by the activities of a European Company other than those of the shareholders and employees directly involved. The concept must be seen as one element together with two other requirements, that is that these representatives be "not directly dependent on the shareholders, the employees or their respective organizations" and have "the necessary knowledge and experience." The underlying idea is that the representatives constituting the final third will enable the supervisory board to take decisions which take into consideration all interests affected by the activities of the European Company, in other words to recognize the special responsibility of the enterprise toward those interests.

Since the "general interests" are not defined in a concrete way, the proposed system has some similarity with the system of the "eleventh man" prevailing in the German coal and steel industry since 1951, who is to be co-opted by the representatives of the shareholders and of the employees on the supervisory board. Nevertheless there are substantial differences. Since the final third of members on the supervisory board of an SE will normally consist of at least three members, there will be not just a single member, but a plurality of independent members who are all equally entrusted with preventing a deadlock in the Supervisory Board of the SE.

The proposed system also contains substantial elements of the Dutch system in force since 1973. The candidates eligible for co-option are to be proposed by the General Meeting, the Works Council and the Management Board as under Dutch company law. Accordingly, the General Meeting, the European Works Council and the Management Board are each expected to propose candidates who will have the necessary knowledge and experience, will defend the long-term interests of the enterprise as a whole, and will therefore probably be acceptable to both shareholders' and employees' representatives.

The shareholders' and the employees' representatives on the Supervisory Board will then probably elect those of the candidates nominated by the three organs who they predict will act as mediators and conciliators rather than a substantial third force, at least as far as the last man to be co-opted is concerned, for the total number of the members of the Board must be uneven. As experience with the system in the German coal and steel industry shows, an uneven number tends to favour compromise candidates who subsequently act as mediators and conciliators.

The proviso that the shareholders' and the employees' representatives have to choose among lists of candidates submitted to them by the General Meeting, the Works Council and the Management Board is to some extent a supplementary guarantee against the choice of nonentities. Since the lists of candidates will probably be a matter of public knowledge, the nominatory bodies will feel obliged to put forward candidates with reputation which will not attract undue criticism of the nominating body itself.

It will not be mandatory for employees to be represented on the Supervisory Board. It is left to the employees to decide—with a simple majority—whether they wish to participate in the Supervisory Board of an SE or not. If not, the Supervisory Board will consist of representatives of shareholders only, fulfilling its normal functions. It would not correspond to the normal rules of democracy if a minority of employees in favour of employees representation were able to impose their views on a reluctant majority.

2. Representation of trade unions by persons not employed by the European Company

The ESC gives the statutory right to the trade unions represented in the establishments of the SE to submit lists of candidates for the election of the employees' representatives to the Supervisory Board. The lists can include a minority of trade union candidates from outside the enterprise, leaving the electors to express their preferences.

It is thus left to the electors and not to the law to decide whether persons not employed by the SE become employees' representatives on the Supervisory Board. The legitimation of all of the representatives of the employees on the board depends on their election, that is, on the will of the majority of the employees of the European Company.

206

3. Election of employees' representatives to the Supervisory Board

Under the election rules the choice of employees' representatives takes place normally in two stages.

First stage: all employees elect in the establishments of the SE a number of electoral delegates by secret direct ballot. The election is subject to the principle of proportional representation. Lists of candidates may be submitted by trade unions represented in the establishment and by groups of employees entitled to vote.

Ten percent or 100 employees in an establishment is the minimum requirement for putting up a list of candidates.

Second stage: the electoral delegates elect the employees' representatives to the Supervisory Board jointly by means of a secret ballot. They must exercise their voting rights freely and must not be bound by any instructions. The election is subject to the principle of proportional representation.

Lists of candidates may be submitted by the European Works Council, by trade unions represented in the establishments of the SE, by 1/20 of the electoral delegates or by at least 1/10 of the employees of the SE.

4. Election of employees' representatives to the European Works Council

The members of the European Works Council are elected by all employees of the SE by secret direct ballot. Lists of candidates may be submitted by trade unions represented in the establishment and by groups of employees (10 % or 100 employees). The election is subject to the principle of proportional representation.

The European Works Council is thought to be the representative body of *all* employees employed in establishments of the SE, irrespective of whether they are organized in trade unions or not. Hence, there must be direct and secret elections in which all employees of the respective establishment can participate. This is of particular significance in the case of undertakings which have establishments in several member states, and it is only then that a European Works Council is created. The degree of organization of workers in a trade union varies as much from one member state to another as it does from one branch of industry to another.

But the degree of the legitimation of the members of the European Works Council should not differ and depend upon the degree to which labour is organized in each establishment.

All employees of the SE, moreover, should enjoy the same rights relating to information, consultation and co-decision. These are intended to be statutory rights and therefore not reserved to organized groups, but available to all employees in accordance with democratic principles.

This does not mean that trade unions are in any way excluded from having members on European Works Councils. Where an election takes place, they have an equal right to submit lists of candidates. In addition, the European Works Council may at any time, by majority vote, invite a representative from a trade union represented in an establishment of the SE to attend certain meetings in an advisory capacity. Furthermore, experts may be called in to clarify certain difficult questions and these experts can be drawn from the ranks of trade unions.

5. Powers of the European Works Council

The European Works Council is competent for all matters which concern the SE as a whole or several of its establishments. The Works Council is to be kept regularly informed on the general economic position of the SE and of its future development. It has to be consulted before important economic decisions affecting the employees are taken. Decisions concerning certain social matters may be made by the Board of Management only with the agreement of the European Works Council. If the European Works Council withholds its agreement, agreement may be given by a court of arbitration whose members are appointed by the European Works Council and by the Board of Management.

The European Works Council must give its agreement to decisions planned by the Board of Management concerning the establishment of a social plan in the event of closure of the SE or of parts thereof. Before making any decisions relating to the winding up of undertakings and mergers with other undertakings, the Board of Management must consult the European Works Council.

On the other hand, the competence of the European Works Council shall extend only to matters which do not involve the negotiation or conclusion of conventions or collective agreements concerning the working conditions of employees. Thus a demarcation line has been drawn between the powers of the European Works Council and of the trade unions.

The European Works Council is not to interfere with the role of trade unions nor with the duties of employee representatives organized at plant level under national arrangements. These representatives will continue to exercise their functions, unless otherwise provided in the Statute. Such provisions exist only in cases where a uniform representation of all employees affected by a decision of the Management Board is desirable both for the representation of employees' interests and the viability of the decision making process within the European Company. Nor is collective bargaining on working conditions a matter for the European Works Council. The draft of the amended proposal expressly prevents the European Works Council from engaging in such procedures, unless it is authorized to do so by the contracting parties within a European collective agreement. It is hereby intended to forestall any possible conflict with the functions of the trade unions.

Indeed, the proposed European Company Statute goes much further than that and gives the trade unions the new, additional opportunity to operate effectively in the specific environment of a company working at a transnational level. To these ends, it includes provisions enabling the European Company to conclude agreements with the trade unions represented in its different establishments on working conditions which are binding throughout the Community for all employees who are members of a trade union which is a party to such an agreement.

This reflects the feeling that the European Company will function better if the trade unions are sufficiently organized and possess specific rights at the transnational level on which the company works and are thus able to play an active role in the life of the undertaking.

"First World"
Relationships:
the Role of the OECD

MIRIAM CAMPS

Preface

The advanced, industrialized societies today confront a new era of global challenges and opportunities. These societies now face a recognized imperative to manage more effectively their increasingly interwoven economies. Simultaneously they face a formidable new array of forces—domestic and external—that will complicate their efforts and impair their capacity for effective management. Shifting, unsettled political and security relationships; increased sensitivity and anxiety among domestic interest groups to the consequences of economic interdependence; insecurity of supply and instability of prices of oil and other vital raw materials; louder and more credible demands—and pleas—from the economically disadvantaged nations: this is the environment of the "age of interdependence". Yet, as inhospitable as this environment may seem, the continued prosperity of the advanced industrialized societies, and the promise of prosperity for other peoples, depends importantly upon the political, technical and institutional ability of these countries to respond wisely and co-operatively to the new challenges.

How the advanced, market-based nations should manage their economic relations with one another and with other groups of countries under the impact of these new demands and pressures is the topic of Miriam Camps's present essay. Although she focusses primarily on the Organization for Economic Co-operation and Development (OECD) and the ways it might be made more responsive to these new needs, she is concerned as well with the interaction between co-operation in the OECD context and the evolution of the European Community, on the one hand, and the development of the necessary global management, on the other.

As she makes clear, the industrialized societies have developed unprecedentedly high degrees of co-operation and interdependence in the years since World War II. But their current level of co-operation is inadequate to the needs created by the inexorable growth in the intermeshing of their economic and social concerns. Their high level of interrelatedness in fact poses for them new problems, which, in turn, present dangers of political conflict as well as opportunities for developing innovative modes of international co-operation.

Complicating the choices of these governments has been the shift in global power structures and the diminished predominance of the industrialized economies in the international system. This shift has created new pressures for

211

confrontation among the advanced societies as well as between them and other societies. Mrs Camps explores these shifts and dangers in her short study. She also maps out those areas in which the industrialized nations might be able to co-ordinate policies to avoid risks both for themselves and for other societies. She distinguishes these issues from others which are beyond the capacity of the industrialized world itself to handle effectively and which, instead, require more global efforts. As Mrs Camps concludes, for the next few years, perhaps for the next decade, the OECD could play a unique role not only in assisting member countries to handle their relationships with one another but also in giving coherence to the global system, provided—and the proviso is of crucial importance—that the member governments are prepared to use the organization flexibly and in new ways.

Few are better qualified to conduct such an inquiry than Miriam Camps. As an official of the United States Department of State, she was deeply involved in the Marshall Plan and its European counterpart—the Organization for European Economic Co-operation (OEEC), the forerunner of the OECD. As an analyst and author she has contributed a stream of studies dealing with Western economic co-operation; among the most noteworthy have been *Britain and the European Community, 1955-1963* (Princeton: Princeton University Press, 1964); *What Kind of Europe? The Community Since De Gaulle's Veto* (London: Oxford University Press, 1965); and, *European Unification in the Sixties; From the Veto to the Crisis* (New York: Council on Foreign Relations, 1966). In 1974, the Council on Foreign Relations published her influential monograph, *The Management of Interdependence,* which sketched out in general terms her views of some of the central problems on the international agenda in the coming decades.

The Atlantic Institute for International Affairs, of Paris, and the Council on Foreign Relations, of New York, are proud to serve as co-sponsors of Miriam Camps's latest work. For the Atlantic Institute, her essay represents a particularly appropriate contribution to its series of Atlantic Papers which examine problems of the highly industrialized societies as well as their relations with the developing world. For the Council on Foreign Relations, her work is a stepping-stone in the Council's 1980s Project, a major attempt to put forward views of a desirable international environment, for the period of a decade or so from now, and proposals for how to achieve those desired conditions. As a Senior Research Fellow of the Council, Miriam Camps contributed to the planning of the 1980s Project and continues to help guide the work of the Project.

JOHN W. TUTHILL
Director-General
Atlantic Institute for International Affairs

RICHARD H. ULLMAN
Director, The 1980s Project
Council on Foreign Relations

212

Author's note

I wish to thank WILLIAM DIEBOLD and MICHAEL KUCZYNSKI for commenting on an early draft of this essay; both of them greatly helped me clarify my thoughts on a number of central issues. I should also like to thank LINCOLN GORDON and JOHN TUTHILL for many helpful comments on a later text and FABIO BASAGNI for preparing several interesting summaries of OECD activities.

So much has happened in the "OECD world" since I began writing this essay, that it seems prudent to record that the paper went to press in October, 1975.

Introduction

The question of how best to organize relationships among the advanced industrialized market-economy countries is once again on the international agenda. Pressures from the developing countries for a "new international economic order", the dislocations caused by the embargo and increases in the price of oil, and double-digit inflation coupled with high levels of unemployment have added impetus to the process of rethinking which was prompted by the breakdown of key elements in the Bretton Woods structure.

The search for the right relationship among the highly industrialized, market-economy countries has been a recurring quest ever since the US economic preponderance began to wane more than a decade ago, in the late 'fifties and early 'sixties. And, inevitably, proposals for institutionalizing or strengthening in other ways this central relationship have always tended to become entwined, on the one hand, with the narrower question of the organization of Europe and, on the other hand, with the wider question of the institutional management of the global economy.

In 1960-61 when the Organization for European Economic Co-operation, the European organization set up in the context of the Marshall plan, was transformed into an "advanced-country" organization, the OECD (the Organization for Economic Co-operation and Development), the dispute over the organization of Europe was particularly acute, and the most contentious issues in the negotiations leading to the formation of the new organization were rooted in the argument between the Six and the Seven. Those concerns are now a matter of history. But uncertainty and disagreements within the Six (now the Nine) about the nature of the union they were in the process of forming continued to bedevil the OECD. And arguments over roles and responsibilities still continue, although the preoccupations and the suspicions of the principal actors have shifted with the times. Some of the difficulties stem from the suspicion that is most often voiced by the French—but is not confined to the French—that the United States, despite its disclaimers, must, given the nature of power, have hegemonial aspirations and that the OECD must, almost inevitably, have its role in this design. But many of the difficulties are rooted in real uncertainty about where the boundaries between "European" action and "OECD" action should be drawn: what issues need to be discussed, what policies to be co-ordinated, which functions to be performed at each level? And how should the

214

inevitable areas of overlap be handled? The answers are not easy to find, for both economic and political considerations are involved, and sometimes they point in opposite directions. And in some cases the answer that corresponds with today's reality appears to complicate or to foreclose a hoped for future development.

The problem of defining the relationship—if any—that should be sought among the advanced industrialized countries and the institutional expression that should be given to this relationship also involves seeing how this central relationship is to be fitted into the broader pattern of global economic relationships. While the Bretton Woods machinery remained intact— or, if not "intact", was still thought to be easily reparable—there was an accepted framework which tended both to set certain limits to the scope for an "advanced-country" organization and to make the case for such an institution less persuasive. Now, with the floating of all the major currencies and the breakdown of much of the earlier system, the new-found wealth and power of the oil-producing countries, the mounting pressures from the developing countries for a "new international economic order", and the passage, at long last, of a trade act giving the US Government new authority to negotiate not only on tariffs but on other trade barriers, there is a new uncertainty about ground rules and other institutional arrangements. The main dangers in this new situation are obvious: a surge of neo-mercantilist policies; severe economic dislocation in some countries accompanied only too probably by political unrest, perhaps breakdown; increased polarization between the industrialized "North" and the developing "South". Countries undoubtedly feel freer to go down wrong roads when the old rules have eroded, or are felt to be no longer relevant. But there are some opportunities in the new fluidity if the dangers can be avoided. So much is now in the melting pot that a more ambitious restructuring of the array of international economic institutions than is normally contemplated could become politically feasible, if not today perhaps by the end of the decade, given the indispensable ingredient of far-sighted leadership.

This short paper cannot deal with the whole array of institutional questions that now needs to be rethought. Many of them were raised in a preliminary way in an earlier paper and will, it is anticipated, be explored further in later papers [1]. This paper focusses on what for lack of a more felicitous shorthand expression has come to be called the "advanced-country" relationship and, more specifically, on the kind of role the OECD should seek to play during the next few years and on the changes in structure, modes of operation and ways of thinking this would require on the part of the member governments and the secretariat [2]. Although for reasons given above this cannot be done without some discussion of intra-European and broader global relationships, neither one can of course be examined in any depth in this essay.

The Setting

The resurgence of interest in the OECD

After almost fifteen years of useful but for the most part rather low-key activity, the OECD has recently become the subject of headlines and leading articles. For the first time in its history an American Secretary of State—and a Secretary of State who does not lightly lend his prestige to international organizations—led the US delegation to the semi-annual OECD meeting in May, 1975. There have been two main reasons, or two main groups of reasons, for a resurgence of interest in what has come to be called "the advanced-country relationship". The first in point of time although not in terms of public attention was the growing awareness of how interlinked the economies of the highly developed, market-economy countries were becoming, how vulnerable each was to developments in the others, and how central the relationship among this group of countries was to the health of the global economic system. The shift in economic power—the decline in the preponderance of the US and the growth of new centers of economic power in Japan and Europe—began in the late 'fifties and early 'sixties, but many of the implications of the shift only became widely appreciated a decade later with the break-down in much of the Bretton Woods system (in large measure a consequence of the shift in power). The second main reason for the new attention being given to the advanced-country relationship in general and to the OECD in particular has come not from the recognition of the vulnerability of the members of the group to one another but from their vulnerability to the actions of third countries and, in particular, to the actions of the OPEC (the Organization of Petroleum Exporting Countries). And it has been as the umbrella organization which was to shelter both the new IEA (International Energy Authority) and the Financial Support Fund that the OECD made the headlines in 1974 and early 1975.

The oil producers, although no longer poor are for the most part "less-developed countries", and they have thus far maintained a remarkable solidarity with the other members of the "77". Moreover the dramatic effectiveness of one producers' cartel was bound to be infectious, and consuming countries were also bound to fear emulation even where it was unlikely. The oil crisis thus contributed to putting on the OECD's agenda not only commodity policy but, more generally, the response the advanced countries should now make to

216

the demands for a "new economic order" and to the specific pressures the ldc's can bring to bear to further their interests.

The actions of the oil-exporting countries in embargoing exports during the Yom Kippur war and in steeply pushing up prices, the consequential massive shift in real resources, and the continuing uncertainty about how the enormous credits being piled up by the oil producers would be used, by posing acute problems for most of the OECD countries have also, of course, strengthened the first set of reasons for renewed interest in the OECD—underlining the need for more consultation about, and probably more "management" of, the advanced countries own economic interdependence.

It is too soon to be sure how sustained this new interest in the OECD will prove to be: in the short term much will depend on how flexibly and efficiently the organization can respond to the new demands that are now being placed upon it. But in the somewhat longer term the answer will be determined by whether the key governments can agree on some rather fundamental ideas, or concepts, about the role and function of the organization. Are the advanced countries a "community" in any meaningful sense of the term? How should the functions of such an organization relate to the work of the European Community, on the one hand, and to the wider process of the institutional management of the global economy on the other? What kinds of role should an "advanced-nations" organization seek to play *vis-à-vis* other groups of countries? What postures and actions should it deliberately eschew? And so on.

Conceptual dilemmas

From its earliest days the OECD has been handicapped because it had no widely agreed *raison d'être,* no clear purpose from which its functions could be derived, few very precise commitments which governments were pledged to carry out, and no simple goals which commanded public understanding and support. The only shorthand label that has threatened to stick has been one no one wanted—that of a "rich man's club".

The formation of the Organization for Economic Cooperation and Development in 1960-61 was in part a response to the dispute over the organization of Europe and the American and French determination, following the break-down of the negotiations for an OEEC-wide free trade area, to deflect any fresh efforts at bridge-building between the Six and the Seven, a determination which owed much to the strongly held views of the Commission of the newly-formed Community of the Six [3]. But neither this somewhat negative motivation, nor its more positive counterpart—the desire to find a way to cool the temperature of the intra-European dispute and to contain the damage so that it did not spill over into the defense field—was all that lay behind the replacement of the OEEC by the OECD. The US had other, more forward-looking reasons for

217

taking the lead in urging the creation of a new organization in which it and Canada would participate as full members rather than as associates as they had done in the OEEC. Rightly, it felt the time had come to change the underlying premise of the US-European relationship: the OEEC had been the organizational expression of a donor-recipient relationship; implicit in the shift to the OECD was the recognition that this relationship had changed and that the era of US economic predominance was drawing to a close. There was, too, at this time a growing awareness of the need for a substantial and sustained transfer of resources to the developing countries [4], and the US, particularly in the light of its own trade deficit, felt the increasingly prosperous Europeans should help "share the burden". Finally, it was beginning to be recognized that, with the progress toward freer trade and payments and the new mobility made possible by the increase in the speed of transportation and communications, the US as well as the European countries could benefit from cooperation. Some forum was needed in which the major industrialized countries could discuss those aspects of their economic policy which directly affected one another and that could no longer be considered solely as matters of domestic concern. The fact that the word "European" was dropped from the title of the remodelled organization was not simply out of deference to its broader "Atlantic" character: the United States was already planning for the inclusion of Japan, although its views were not yet shared by many of the European Governments.

The addition of Japan and, later, Australia and New Zealand, ruled out one possible role for the organization, that of the institutional expression of an Atlantic partnership between the United States and Canada on the one hand and a unifying Europe on the other. But even had the geographic base not been broadened, General de Gaulle's veto on the enlargement of the European Community and his desire to decrease the US influence in Europe would have ruled out an evolution along these lines during his life-time.

For a time in the '60s the goal of a fifty per cent growth target for the decade from 1960-1970 for the area as a whole provided a framework for some of the work [5]. But a collective growth target for an area that has no economic or political structure was not very satisfactory, particularly when, as was then the case, one country—the United States—accounted for more than half of the total production of the OECD. In any event, by the end of the decade "growth" *tout court* had become a concept that was increasingly open to challenge.

Conceptual confusion is likely to be an enduring problem, for the rationale for the OECD will continue to be a multiple one, changing over time and not easily reducible to any formulation that would cover all its functions.

If the countries of the European Community were set on a clearly agreed, well-charted course to an economic and monetary union a case could be made for "trilateralism" and for reshaping the OECD as the institutional expression of a process of inter-bloc management between the three major centers of economic power—the US, the European Community and Japan. However, "trilateralism" (in any formal sense) as a long-term design raises a number of problems, some of which are discussed below [6]. In any case, for the next few years it would seem to be ruled out (again in any very structured sense) by the fact that the European Community is unlikely to be able to act as a unit on very many questions other than those covered by the customs union, and the commitment of the member governments of the Community to the eventual formation of a real economic and monetary union is likely to continue to be equivocal. Nonetheless, the European Community is already important as a center of economic power (and will become more so), and the dominance of the Community, the United States and Japan both in the subsystem of the advanced industrial countries and in the wider global system is the key to the significance of the OECD, despite the inadequacies of "trilateralism" as a guiding concept.

Another possible concept would be to view the "advanced countries" as themselves an economic and/or monetary union in embryo as the European Community may well yet prove to be. Apart from the difficulty that the present membership of the OECD includes some anomalies, it seems to me to be unreal—at least in any time period that is short enough to have an impact on today's decisions—to envisage the key countries in the group, and the United States in particular, accepting the political constraints inherent in the concept of an economic union.

However, although the advanced countries cannot be thought of as a group striving for common policies or even as a group of countries so far imbued with a sense of community that policies of the individual countries are normally tested against their compatibility with the "collective good", it would be misleading to go all the way to the other extreme and to regard relationships among these countries as totally devoid of political overtones. Some of the overtones are historical and an inheritance from the cold war, some are defensive in the face of the new difficulties posed by the oil producers, some reflect the sense that there *are* shared values and shared purposes among the advanced, democratic, market-oriented countries. The political overtones are mixed and each country would define them in somewhat different terms, but there is enough there to make the member countries feel they have some obligation to help one another, not simply an obligation to avoid putting spokes in one another's wheels. In short, there is a political motivation, however ill-defined, that goes a little beyond enlightened economic self-interest. But there is not a strong enough sense either of community or of threat so that there is any over-riding obligation to advance the common good of the group. Nor, of course, is there any commitment to the maximization of economic efficiency on an OECD-wide basis. The recent agreement setting up the Financial Support Fund is illustrative of a sense of common concern and a willingness to accept a measure of collective responsibility for the economic health of other members of the group even at some cost. But the underlying motive was partly a defensive one *vis-à-vis* the oil producers. And, as the agreement makes plain, the commitment is a strictly

219

limited one: it is not an open-ended pledge of mutual help, and it is strictly limited in time [7].

Since the OECD countries are not today—and there is little likelihood that they will strive to become—an economic unit, the process of pushing further their attempts to co-ordinate policies is bound to be a continuing experiment. And the willingness to co-operate closely with others in the group is bound to fluctuate with the general economic climate, waxing when a number of countries confront similar or interacting problems, waning when everything is going well. It may be argued that the advanced countries (or the OECD countries) are now so interdependent that they should deliberately undertake to negotiate the ground rules of a new relationship with one another, a relationship which, although it would fall short of the formation of an economic union, would nevertheless carry rather precise commitments about their common purposes and would imply commitments to the co-ordination of policy that go well beyond what is likely to emerge from a process of groping, experimenting, and trial and error. Or it may be argued that the external threat from the oil producers and the difficulty of arriving at agreements with the "77" in effect leave the OECD countries no option but to manage "the system" by themselves and primarily for themselves to the extent they are able to do so. The first is a stronger argument than the second, but it seems likely to be unwise and counterproductive to try now to negotiate a new relationship in general terms. As the ill-fated "Year of Europe" demonstrated, there is no concept of the advanced-country relationship that commands general support. But that is not to say that there cannot be much greater clarity about the nature of the rela-tionship—about the do's and don't's—than today exists. In a few areas—as discussed further below, trade policy is probably one—new commitments can be identified that the advanced countries should soon undertake; but in many areas it will not be a question of formally undertaking new intergovernmental commitments but of accepting the necessity and the legitimacy of intergovern-mental discussions at an earlier stage in the process of domestic policy forma-tion, of accepting the need to draw the line between matters of domestic concern and matters of common concern in new places (and to turn hard lines into broken lines) without trying to be too clear in advance just how far the process will go.

And beyond that, it should be possible to have a somewhat clearer view and one that commands a wider consensus about how the OECD (or the advanced-country relationship) relates to the development of the European Community and contributes to the evolution of a more efficient and more widely acceptable global economic system.

Roles and Functions

The reasons for various kinds of institutional arrangements among the advanced, industrialized, market-economy countries—or the tasks requiring collective action—can be grouped under three broad headings: (1) those that derive essentially from the high degree of interaction among the economies of these countries and the consequent inability of individual national governments to attain desired domestic objectives without close co-operation with other governments; (2) those that derive essentially from the desire of this group of countries to order its relationship or to co-ordinate its strategy *vis-à-vis* other groups of countries in order to increase bargaining power or to make more effective some aspect of the inter-group relationship; and (3) those that derive essentially from the need to give more coherence and greater effectiveness to the international system generally.

The lines between these broad categories are not firmly drawn: almost any specific activity—for example, discussions concerning the co-ordination of policies affecting the balance of payments—has aspects to it that would fit under each of the three headings. But the type of action that will be most appropriate depends in part on whether the function is one which is primarily of concern to the members of the group, or whether it is designed primarily to affect their relationships with third countries, or whether it is designed, more generally, to enable the great economic weight of this group of countries to be used to give stability to, or to promote change in, the international economic system. Accordingly the discussion below starts with those functions which are primarily of intra-group concern, then turns to the questions on which the "advanced countries" need to co-ordinate their policies *vis-à-vis* other countries —and the limits that should be set to such action—and, finally, concludes with some comments on what might be called the "system-tending" responsibilities of the group.

Co-ordination of monetary and macro-economic policy

It is not surprising that the discussions that have taken place in the Economic Policy Committee (EPC) and its three Working Parties (particularly WP-3 which is concerned with questions relating to the balance of payments) have been widely regarded as the most important aspects of the work of the OECD, for it is the cluster of inter-related, macro-economic policies coming within the purview of this set of committees that, today, most obviously requires some kind of collective "management" by the advanced countries in their own interest [8]. The questions for the future are not whether the advanced countries will need to improve their arrangements for consultation and co-operation on monetary and general economic policy but, rather, how far down into matters such as interest-rate policy and the appropriate magnitudes for budgetary deficits or surpluses, which traditionally have been regarded primarily as tools for managing the domestic economy, it will be necessary—and politically feasible—for the process of intergovernmental consultation to reach; what countries should be involved in the process; what operational content should be given to "consultations", i.e. whether the process should be pushed beyond an exchange of views to more formal acts of co-ordination; and how whatever is done among some group of advanced countries should be related to action on the European Community level, on the one hand, and to action on the broader global level, on the other.

A few years ago it would have seemed reasonable to predict that a reformed and strengthened IMF would be the focal point for the management of the international monetary system and that, within such a system, the countries of the European Community could be expected progressively to act as a unit. Had there been substantial progress toward economic and monetary union at the European level and a codification of new rules at the international level—rules which were expected, *inter alia,* to enable exchange rates to take more of the burden of adjustment under close IMF surveillance—and, of course, no dramatic development comparable to the steep increase in oil prices, the need for advanced-country action on monetary policy might have been a fairly limited one. The useful high-level but fairly low-key consultations within the OECD's EPC structure would doubtless have continued for a time, but they might within a relatively few years have been largely supplanted by bilateral discussions between the US authorities and the new European monetary authority, on the one hand, and between each of these and the Japanese. Now the prospects and the needs look rather different. Floating has become the order of the day. The work of the Committee of Twenty on the reform of the IMF has been put on ice and the Werner plan for a European Economic and Monetary Union has been effectively abandoned. A recent report by a group of experts (the Marjolin Committee, so called after the chairman of the group, Robert Marjolin, a former vice-president of the Commission) was brutally frank in stating that the political will needed to create anything that could reasonably be called a monetary union was not yet in evidence and that the Community had tended to move backwards rather than forwards in recent years [9]. The recent French decision to rejoin the "snake" may be a sign that an EMU is dormant rather than dead, but the political implications of a monetary union are much more widely appreciated today than they were when the unrealistically ambitious decisions of the Hague Summit were announced in 1969, and the next steps toward that goal, if they are in fact taken, seem likely to be taken against the background of far more intense and continuous consultations among the advanced countries than was the rule in the early 'seventies.

Although all the major currencies are now floating, none is doing so without a measure of intervention. And, contrary perhaps to the expectations of some of those who have advocated floating as a way to increase, or regain, autonomy, the need for fairly continuous consultation and a good bit of co-ordinated action among the key industrial countries in the management of floating rates has come to be widely recognized as necessary. Speaking to a meeting of the Atlantic Institute for International Affairs in November 1974, Robert Roosa envisaged the development of close co-operation among central banks "under the watchful eye of the International Monetary Fund". As he put it: "As the management of floating develops, each central bank will unavoidably be reflecting two judgements, which it must pair into one general view. First, it must have a view on the broad relationship of its own prices and availabilities for goods and services in trade, to those on average in other countries of importance for its own trade. Second, it must take a position of the likely, and appropriate, flows of capital (long and short) to be expected to move across its own exchanges. In working out acceptable zones for some intervention to help assure a degree of stability of the exchange rate between its currency and others, the central bank will form judgements as to whether the policies of the other countries are consistent with the approach to exchange rates that their central banks wish to take". And he went on to predict a "much more frequent, intimate, and thorough interest (and even involvement) of each leading country in the economic affairs of the others" [10]. Although Mr. Roosa was arguing—at this point—that the need to introduce some stability in exchange rate fluctuations would lead to this more intimate involvement of key countries in each other's domestic policies, he, like others, also reached the same conclusion starting from the other end and observing the inability—in an open system with huge amounts of highly mobile capital—of a country being able to accomplish its domestic goals using traditional implements of monetary policy unless those countries with whom it was most "interdependent" were pursuing compatible policies.

Today, many of those who in the past advocated floating rates and many of those who in the past advocated fixed rates are finding common ground not only on the inevitability of floating—for the near-term future at any rate—given the gross divergence in rates of inflation, levels of unemployment, etc., among the key countries and the huge amounts ef liquid capital, but also on the fact that the floating will and must be "managed" in some way. Floating has given governments more freedom to pursue incompatible domestic policies than they would have had in a fixed-rate system. But it has not "solved" the adjustment problem. In a world of Eurodollars, petrodollars and multinational enterprises there are too many transmission belts for governments to be able to pursue completely independent policies or to be willing to take all the adjustment on the exchange rate. Without more co-ordination of policy, fears of importing inflation, unemployment, or both, lead to self-punishing restrictions on trade and capital movements. And as Mr. Roosa implied in his remarks, the way floating is "managed" and how the necessary co-ordination of policy is achieved —where, by whom, according to what guidelines—seems likely to go far to set the pattern of international monetary co-operation for the next decade or so.

However, although there is a growing consensus that more "collective management" is needed, there is, as yet, no clear view on how or where this can best be done, or, indeed, on how far beyond technical management by Central Banks it is necessary or desirable to go. The signs point in several rather different directions. On the one hand, although the report of the Committee of Twenty which was charged with making proposals for the comprehensive reform of the IMF was shelved when the monetary system was overwhelmed with petrodollars and floating became almost universal, the idea of piecemeal reform of the IMF is still very much alive; and a new Committee of Twenty—the Interim Committee— has been established to provide for more frequent discussions among ministers and high officials from member governments between the annual meetings of the Governors. On the other hand, despite the formation of this new Committee of Twenty, the old Group of Ten (G-10)—which it was supposed to replace—has not, in fact, disappeared but seems to have a new lease on life. Its members are all advanced, industrialized, OECD countries; in contrast, the new Committee of Twenty represents the full IMF membership on a constituency basis roughly the same way as do the Executive Directors. Increased IMF activity has been matched by increased OECD activity: the negotiation of the Financial Support Fund—to be established in Paris and linked to the OECD; the setting up of an *ad hoc* committee within the EPC to keep under continuing review the financial impact on member countries of the changed energy situation and to monitor the market's ability to handle petrodollars; the formation of a group of economists of international standing to examine the constraints on growth. Not only have both the IMF and the OECD been given new committees and renewed attention during the last year or two, but there has also been considerable recourse during this period to what is being dubbed the G-5, that is the informal and sometimes very secretive meetings of the Finance Ministers, sometimes accompanied by the heads of the Central Banks, of the "Big Five"— the US, Japan, Germany, France and the United Kingdom. One must, of course, also add to the list of international meetings the monthly meetings of the European Central Bankers at the BIS (Bank for International Settlements) which are attended by a representative of the Federal Reserve Board; frequent meetings of the Monetary Committee of the European Community; and very close co-ordination among the members of the "snake" [11]. Finally, of course, there has been much direct consultation among key Central Banks and, one supposes, a good bit of agreed intervention in the foreign exchange markets.

What one thinks should come out of the current flux—how much intergovernmental agreement should be sought about rules for floating, how much co-ordination of policy is desirable, which institutions should be used for what purposes—depends to some extent on the time-scale in which one is thinking. For reasons I have discussed at some length elsewhere [12], it seems to me to be clear that in the not too distant future (i.e. the next decade or so) global institutional arrangements will need drastic reorganization to enable them to bear the "management" load that the emerging international economic system will soon require. But for the next few years—very likely for the next decade—it seems to me to be almost equally clear that governments are likely to be unwilling and unready to make the changes in assumptions about national policy and governmental structures that this would require. Some global institutions may well be somewhat improved—and the IMF seems more likely than most to be substantially strengthened—but the global institutions are not likely to be reformed radically enough to carry the entire management load. There will—almost certainly—be need for additional institutional arrangements to provide, *inter alia,* for the continuous consultation, surveillance, and co-ordination of monetary and other macro-economic policies the advanced countries must undertake because of their vulnerability to each other's policies of domestic economic management—their tendency to aggravate each other's problems by the way they handle inflation, recession, etc.—and their inability to deal separately with common problems, perhaps most conspicuously today large speculative capital movements. But it is important that advanced-country institutional arrangements in this field, as in others, be so designed that they help, not hinder, the necessary reform of global institutional arrangements: this is not always easy, but it should be a condition against which any special advanced-country arrangements are continuously tested.

For the next few years, in any case, the IMF, the OECD—and probably some limited group of advanced countries within that framework—the European Community, and the BIS all have important roles to play. For the present, none of the key countries is likely to be willing to bind itself to rules that are sufficiently precise and detailed so that actions designed to affect the exchange rate are taken more or less automatically. However, the primacy of the IMF as the rule-making body in the international management of exchange rates should be safeguarded. And as it becomes possible to give more standing and greater precision to the IMF guide-lines on floating, this should be done. The Central Banks and the BIS will clearly continue to play key roles in determining how to handle short-term disruptive fluctuations, and Central Bank intervention in the foreign exchange market will obviously be the main instrument used in the "management" of floating. But, as Robert Roosa pointed out in the speech already quoted, "a route will have to be found for co-operation not only between central banks across the exchanges, but also between Governments and policies that stand behind the central banks" [13].

When one departs from generalities and seeks to describe in more specific terms what the advanced countries should now be consulting together about and, even more, when one tries to push further and to define where they should commit themselves to some procedures, guide-lines, or codes of behavior, one runs into large difficulties. Perhaps the biggest difficulty arises from the fact that there is no good way to decide *in advance* how far into the realm of policies normally regarded as being mainly questions of domestic economic management it is now necessary for the process of international consultation among the advanced countries to reach. There is argument rather than agreement among the experts about many aspects of the way internal and external policies interact [14]. And, in normative terms, there is no "concept" or widely agreed goal from which principles can be derived.

As indicated above this absence of a guiding "concept" is not a trivial problem, but in terms of the OECD—or any other similar institution of advanced countries—it is likely to remain an insoluble one. The "advanced nations"—regardless of how in terms of specific countries that group is defined—are not an economic union in embryo. Nor are they an "optimum currency area" if that term is defined—as it must be—to mean not only the area for which it would be economically efficient but also politically feasible to have a single currency, with all the implications for central institutions and transfer of sovereignty that implies.

Sooner or later some basic political choices will have to be made. In the advanced industrial countries all economic policy is becoming a continuum, and where one draws the line between areas of policy that will be determined (mainly) autonomously and areas of policy for which the decisions will be reached (mainly) collectively—and with what group of countries— are essentially political decisions. Even on the European level the key countries are not yet prepared to make a choice—either one way or the other. It may be that the combined effect of a US reluctance to go very far toward genuine consultation on questions such as interest-rate policy and a renewed interest in action on the European level (the outcome of the British referendum and the French decision to rejoin the "snake" may be pointers) will mean that the monetary system evolves for a time, at least, around three blocs with considerable co-ordination of policy within each of the three blocs, the main burden of adjustment between the groups being taken on the exchange rate. Or it may be that the combined effects of the oil crisis, inflation, and recession will be to underline the interdependence of the advanced nations as a group and to cast a new kind of doubt on the European monetary option, i.e., adding to the existing doubts about the willingness of member governments to transfer powers to the European level uncertainty about whether that is the right place to try to draw a monetary perimeter.

For the present no one is ready to make final decisions; a period of groping for new relationships clearly lies ahead. It may be that after a time some of the kinds of discussion and consultation that are probably now best undertaken within the framework of the OECD should move to the global level (IMF), and it may become clear that some kinds of policy co-ordination are sensible among the European countries but not among the advanced countries as a whole. But for the next few years it would seem wise to experiment with new forms of closer consultation and not to try to force agreement too soon on a new international monetary system.

The kind of consultation that would seem to be called for is not dramatically different from what has taken place from time to time in the EPC and its Working Parties. During the last couple of years discussions in these OECD committees have ranged widely over most aspects of the demand-management and balance-of-payments policies of the member countries, and in particular of the seven countries that carry most economic weight in the OECD area—the US, Canada, Japan, Germany, France, the United Kingdom and Italy. All the key issues—inflation, recession, recycling, capital movements—have been analyzed by the secretariat and the member countries politely invited to consider modifying their policies when the interests of the group, or the good of a particular member country, seemed to point in that direction. What then has been lacking? [15] The main needs now are for a more forthcoming attitude toward the process of consultation on the part of the key governments and for more flexibility in the institutional arrangements. The key governments need to consult together more continuously, to be readier to discuss with one another problems they anticipate and their proposed ways of dealing with them, and to see intergovernmental consideration reach deeper into questions of domestic policy. Institutionally, arrangements are needed to make it easier to see and to deal with the inter-related aspects of questions that are now too often looked at and treated separately [16]. It is also important that a way be found so that this kind of more intensive, more continuous, more anticipatory discussion can normally take place on a more restricted basis than it has frequently been possible to do in the OECD. Specific suggestions about the adaptations in the OECD that now seem to be called for and the prospects for change are considered in a later section. The essential points to be made here are (1) that there is need for an intergovernmental mechanism that can facilitate close, continuing consultation among key governments on the full range of macro-economic policies, and (2) that the governments concerned should *not* seek to decide *in advance* what can legitimately be discussed or the nature of the obligations to modify policy that may result from the discussions. Willingness to *discuss* anything but no prior commitment to *do* anything are both important, for no one really knows where the stopping points, or breaks, lie on the continuum of policy measures. For a long time it was assumed that international surveillance of monetary policy could be linked to a country's recourse to the IMF, either for drawings on the Fund or for permission to make a change in par values. Now, despite general floating, it is clear that the need for international surveillance has not been reduced, for the economies of the advanced countries are so interlinked that measures taken in one context (e.g. changes in interest rate to affect domestic demand) have undesirable or unintended results (e.g. on capital movements). It is difficult to find rules that are acceptable to everyone for many reasons. But high on the list comes the fact that there are no longer

227

any well-defined and agreed lines to be drawn between policies of domestic concern and policies of broader common concern. Too sweeping a definition of what are matters of common concern inhibits governments too much; but too limited a definition ensures that intergovernmental action will be inadequate.

This difficulty of drawing lines comes through very clearly if one looks at the IMF's current guidelines on floating. Thus, in discussing the term "action to influence an exchange rate" it is stated that: "Monetary or interest rate policies adopted for demand management purposes or other policies adopted for purposes other than balance of payments purposes would not be regarded as action to influence the exchange rate" [17]. Perhaps a distinction of this kind must be made if one is trying to draft widely acceptable rules. But it is not a distinction that should be applied to discussions on monetary and general economic policy among that relatively small group of advanced countries which are strongly affected by changes in each other's interest rates and other measures of domestic demand management. The key advanced countries now need to be willing to discuss with one another virtually all aspects of their macro-economic policy; for, given the way their economies are interlinked, there is no clear place on the continuum of closely related policy measures at which to draw the line and to say that policies on one side of the line are always appropriate subjects for intergovernmental discussion while those on the other side of the line never are. Where the line should be drawn will be different at different times and it will be different for different countries. It may still be appropriate when drafting global rules to seek to distinguish between measures taken essentially for domestic purposes and those designed to affect the balance of payments. But in the more intimate, and less formalized, discussions among the advanced countries the test of what is appropriate for discussion must be the effect—anticipated as well as actual—of measures taken or not taken on other countries, not the intent behind the action, or inaction.

Multilateral surveillance in the OECD, as in other international organizations, has been one of the most useful techniques of the post-war world. But in several areas—macro-economic policy being perhaps the most important—the advanced countries now need to push beyond surveillance into the much more difficult area of prior consultation. The objective of consultation is not common policies, nor, in many cases parallel policies, but rather policies that are compatible and mutually reinforcing. And, given the great weight of this group of countries in the global system, they must be policies that meet the larger test of "global responsibility"—a point which is considered further below.

Trade policy and industrial policy

During the last few years there have been numerous suggestions, mainly emanating from American sources, that the advanced countries should adopt a goal of tariff-free trade in industrial products, extending the tariff reductions to the

228

less-developed countries without demanding a reciprocal lowering of the latter's tariffs. The US Government has not officially sponsored such a plan, however, and the reactions from other advanced countries, in particular France, have been cool. The usual argument that tariff-free trade among the advanced countries would eliminate the most solid cement of the common market has been a conspicuous reason for the European lack of response; but the goal of free trade in industrial products tended to attract less interest in the United States and elsewhere as governments became increasingly concerned with the deepening recession and as protectionist pressures became stronger almost everywhere. In the last year or two the central need has been to prevent backsliding; and, in the face of recession and the disruption caused by the steep increase in oil prices, the OECD scored an important success in negotiating and later renewing an undertaking that member countries would not seek to improve their own trade position at the expense of others by resort to import controls or export subsidies [18]. For the next year or so it seems probable that the major problem will continue to be to hold on to the gains that have been made since World War II in freeing trade. Perhaps some modest progress beyond that can be made in the context of the Multilateral Trade Negotiations (MTN) in Geneva, although it seeems unlikely that the latter will make much headway until after the 1976 elections in the United States.

Until such time as the advanced countries decide to go further among themselves than it is possible to do on a broader basis within the context of the GATT, is there need of or scope for institutional arrangements to promote discussions on trade questions among the advanced countries? It is desirable that countries in difficulty, notably today the UK, be encouraged to resist the temptation to use import controls or, if the temptation cannot in the end be resisted, that the use of import controls be under close multilateral surveillance. Probably the strongest pressure against a unilateral resort to import controls for members of the European Community is to be found in the Treaty of Rome. But, for so long as it is in effect, the recently negotiated Financial Support Fund provides a very strong incentive to resist their use or only to resort to them in a situation in which use has been explicitly sanctioned as a temporary measure as part of a package arrangement involving large scale recourse to the Support Fund. If a large drawing were to be made on the Fund and the temporary use of import controls sanctioned in that context, it would be reasonable to assume that these would come under surveillance by the Support Fund. But short of this situation, there are three kinds of role for the OECD: the first and most obvious is as a place for the concerting of the views of the advanced countries on trade policies *vis-à-vis* other groups, mainly the ldc's but perhaps also the Comecon countries. The scope for advanced-nation co-ordination prior to encounters with other groups of countries either within global organizations (GATT, UNCTAD) or otherwise is discussed in a later section, and that aspect of OECD action on trade policy will be considered in that context.

229

The second role is to promote rule-making in a few areas that are of major concern to the advanced countries but are not ripe for negotiation on a broader basis. Export controls would be a case in point, if effective rules canot be negotiated in the GATT [19].

The third role is of a different order and is probably better described as one concerned with industrial or structural policy. It is perhaps worth explaining what the term "industrial policy" as used here embraces, and why this approach is suggested [20]. Essentially the expression "industrial policy" is used to mean those governmental policies that directly affect patterns of production: who produces what, where. Thus it is a way of looking at the whole array of measures—tariffs, subsidies, and other non-tariff barriers (ntb's), environmental controls, special arrangements for particular sectors such as energy or agriculture, company law, regulatory instruments such as anti-trust laws, some aspects of foreign investment, some aspects of science and technology policy—that are designed to stimulate or suppress particular types of production, or that have important effects on the location of industry, whether or not they were designed with that purpose in mind.

The concept of indicative planning has long been a familiar one in some countries of the group, France in particular, and for such countries the concept of an industrial policy—a domestic industrial policy—is a commonplace. For other countries, such as the United States and Germany which have been doctrinally opposed to "planning" and have placed much greater reliance on the market, the need or desirability of even the sketchiest kind of planning remains much more controversial. Does the suggestion that there is a need for intergovernmental discussions on industrial policy require that the countries participating in such discussions have national plans at least in the French sense? If so, it is clear that one would be stirring up a hornets' nest [21]. The answer would seem to be a qualified "no", but the argument is a bit circular, for the reason for suggesting that it is useful to focus on industrial policy is precisely because various pressures are forcing governments to be clearer about their priorities and to have a better view of the pattern of production for which they are striving. For whether or not their starting point is something like the French indicative plan the kinds of decisions that the governments of the advanced countries increasingly confront are ones which will require them to have a view of what kinds of change in their industrial structures they are prepared to accept or to encourage. Technological change, environmental concerns and other constraints on growth, inflation and the drying-up of private sources of investment in some countries (e.g. the UK), high energy costs, and, perhaps, an upward trend in the prices of raw materials generally [22], the activities of the multinational enterprises and the reactions of host countries to those activities, the elimination of indigenous supplies of cheap labor and restrictions on immigration, and the desirable next steps in trade liberalization will all exert pressure in the same direction. So, too, will the increasingly organized pressures from the developing countries for improved access to markets. In short, for

230

many reasons the advanced countries confront a need to make structural changes in their patterns of production. Some of the needed change (e.g. much of that related to environmental concerns) involves a shift from the production of private to public goods and cannot therefore be left to the market; some of the change probably could in theory be left to the market (e.g. textiles, automobiles) but given the commitment of governments to social goals it is plain that even the most market-minded of the governments will in fact intervene to moderate the rate of change.

Clearly, given their high degree of interdependence and, in particular, the overwhelming importance of trade within the group, each country's decisions on measures that affect the pattern of production, whether or not the country has anything that can be legitimately called an industrial policy, are of concern to other members of the group. But there are obvious difficulties in drawing the boundaries for advanced-country action in this field. Some of the difficulties arise from the point made earlier, and which will recur throughout this paper, that the advanced countries are not, and should not be conceived of as becoming in the future, an economic unit. Therefore one should not be seeking to organize relationships in such a way as to maximise economic efficiency for the area as a whole with substantial costs both to national efficiency on the one hand and global efficiency on the other [23]. On the other hand, there is a common interest —although not one easily given operational significance—in each other's economic health: as indicated above, this is so not only because each member is affected by developments in the economies of the others but also because the group shares many common values and the key members of the group are linked by various security arrangements.

In considering the role for advanced country co-ordination in the general area of monetary and economic policy the chief tension or point of conflict is between action at that level and similar action within the European Community, that is, to some extent they are alternative "levels" intermediate between the nation and the global system, and extensive co-ordination of policy at the OECD level may weaken the impetus for co-ordination of policy at the European Community level—so long as the European Community is not clearly set on a course to full economic union. In the case of industrial policy there is some tension between these two levels. But there is likely to be much more risk in the case of industrial policy than in the case of monetary and economic policy that advanced-country co-ordination will not contribute to but create difficulties for the evolution of a more efficient global economy. Structural change is always painful, and the temptation will be great to strike internal bargains, to make concessions to one another at the expense of third countries. As commented on further below, this danger can be safeguarded against to some extent by giving greater transparency or visibility to OECD discussions. But it will be difficult to combine a process of more intensive advanced-country consultations on industrial policies of the kind that now seems desirable with an adequate system of safeguards, given the present disarray on the global level.

231

International consultations on industrial policy have in the past been mostly on a piecemeal or sectoral basis: textiles, steel, energy, agriculture. The last two sectors and perhaps some others will continue to need special attention, but what is being suggested here is rather different: it is really that just as with cyclical or macro-economic policy so with structural or micro-economic policy it is becoming increasingly difficult to draw the line between matters that are of purely national concern and matters that are of legitimate concern to other countries. This means that new kinds of intergovernmental action are now called for. An indication that the OECD countries are moving, albeit still rather tentatively, toward more concern with industrial structure was the decision at the ministerial meeting in May 1975, following a proposal made by Mr. Kissinger, to establish a special group of "distinguished economists" (some from within governments, some from outside) to develop longer-term growth strategies for the OECD countries. The motivation behind this suggestion is not altogether clear, but whether or not this was the intent it may prove to be a way of adding to the questions traditionally examined by the EPC in its Working Party 2 (growth policies) and Working Party 4 (price policies) some consideration of the longer-term structural problems which are here being called industrial policy.

In addition to identifying some of the structural changes that should now be accepted or encouraged—a task which needs to be undertaken whether or not it results from the work of this new group—the advanced countries should also now agree to some arrangements for continuing consultations on the broad lines of their industrial policies. As in the case of macro-economic policy, consultations should rest on acceptance of the fact that many of the measures taken essentially for reasons of domestic industrial policy—controls on or incentives to investment, subsidies, tax policies, etc.—may well be of legitimate concern to others. Some of these questions may be dealt with in the context of the GATT negotiations on non-tariff barriers (ntb's), but little is likely to be done about many questions, for they do not readily lend themselves to rule-making, until there is some political reality to the concept of a global economy. Again, as so often, one runs into the problem of concept when trying to define the purpose of advanced-country consultations. As indicated above, it cannot be to promote an efficient division of labor simply on an advanced-country basis, because the political base for such an approach is lacking and because it would distort further the global distribution of economic functions. But there is nevertheless a process to be started, both because the high degree of interaction among the members of the group legitimates a concern with one another's policies and plans and because more discussion of structure and of the mechanics of managing change is probably a necessary prelude to the shifts in global patterns of production that would seem to be needed if the ldc's are to be integrated into the global economy.

Looking to the somewhat longer term it seems probable that following the current multilateral trade negotiations under GATT auspices (the so-called

Tokyo Round) or, conceivably, in the context of those negotiations, the advanced countries should undertake among themselves new commitments on trade liberalization, a kind of super-code, which would supplement the more generally applicable but more limited commitments of the GATT [24]. If this were to be done, some institutional mechanism among the advanced countries subscribing to the new code would be needed, and the question would arise whether this was best done by having the new code negotiated and enforced within the OECD framework (as the code on liberalization of invisibles has been) or whether it should be done within the framework of the GATT. The right answer may be that any new super-code should be negotiated in the OECD but then transferred to the GATT, where it would be open to accession by any other GATT member and where the actions taken by the advanced countries among themselves could be subject to continuing scrutiny by the GATT secretariat. This would go some way to reassuring the non-participating countries that the actions taken were consistent with the broader obligations. The difficulty in this solution would come from the close interrelationship between the kind of discussions on industrial policy advocated above and the continuing surveillance of resort to safeguards and escape clauses that would be a necessary part of any new code. As is suggested throughout this paper, the OECD's role must be a flexible and supplementary one, filling gaps and experimenting with new kinds of international action. Once "rule-making" becomes possible and other countries are willing and able to subscribe to the rules, the function should normally be transferred to a broader forum with the OECD making the necessary adjustments in its own program.

Investment; multinational enterprises

Investment policy obviously cuts across the two large policy areas which have just been discussed: macro-economic policy and industrial policy. It is also a salient aspect of the problems of relationship with other groups of countries, today particularly the ldc's but increasingly the Comecon group as well. In the last year or two, the OECD has begun to devote more attention to various aspects of investment. One sensible proposal, that the Executive Committee in Special Session look at the trade-money-investment cluster of policies affecting the balance-of-payments as a cluster instead of separately in the traditional way, unfortunately foundered on the insistence of the US Treasury that monetary questions could only be discussed seriously in those committees which were the preserve of Treasury officials. Obviously if the kind of discussion on macro-economic policy suggested above were to be undertaken, today's tendency to treat closely related issues separately must yield to a more integrative approach.

Any real effort to discuss industrial policies along the lines suggested in the preceding section will involve a good deal more discussion of the conditions

233

affecting direct investment than has been considered necessary or even desirable by the advanced countries in the past, and will inevitably get into the vexed question of relationships between governments and multinational enterprises. Until fairly recently, much of the concern with multinational enterprises, at least within the advanced countries, has focused on the ways in which the MNEs global approach to production enabled them to escape national controls and to frustrate aspects of national policy: tariffs can be rendered meaningless by shifting production; capital controls can be evaded; "transfer-pricing" and other internal accounting devices can enable the large multinational company to profit from the differences in national systems of taxation. The OECD, like other international organizations, both governmental and non-governmental, has discussed ways of counteracting this undermining of national policies. And some promising work is underway on "rules of the game" on specific problems such as transfer-pricing and aspects of taxation [25].

In the last year or two, however, there has been a growing concern with a somewhat different aspect of the multinational enterprise/direct investment question, that is, with the nature of the bargains that are being made between host governments and foreign investors. Some observers predict that these bargains—the inducements offered to and the conditions imposed on foreign investors by host governments—will play much the same role in the future as tariffs did in the past, providing a rich source of international friction and distorting patterns of production [26].

The problem of the rules, if any, that should now govern the limitations placed on and the inducements offered to foreign investors is, of course, by no means limited to investment among the advanced countries. But there are good arguments for seeing whether in this area a substantial group of advanced countries can go rather further in agreeing on some "rules of the game", or, failing that, on procedures for consultation designed to defuse politically charged issues, than seems likely to be possible on a global, or near-global basis [27]. A high proportion of the world's investment takes place among the advanced countries, by far the largest number of multinational enterprises are domiciled in the advanced countries, the problems they encounter in their transactions with one another although troublesome are for the most part less emotionally and politically charged than those associated with advanced-country investment in the ldc's and, unlike the situation a decade ago, most of the key OECD countries now have both host and home country interests. Moreover, as indicated above, the conditions governing direct investment are central to any real attempt to grapple with problems of structural change and industrial policy.

Although it is a subject that falls logically in the next section of this paper rather than here, there may also be a case for the advanced countries seeking to agree among themselves on some ground rules to govern investment in the ldc's. In this area the advanced countries are competitors, but competitors that share a number of common problems. As discussed more fully in the next section, there is a danger here in intensifying polarization between North and

234

South. The line between agreeing on sensible common action to counter or discourage irrational and disruptive action and "ganging-up" and stimulating confrontation is a thin one and frequently not easy to draw. But there may well be a few rules of the game—there will not be many—that the advanced countries could and should first agree upon among themselves and then make it widely known that countries playing by these rules in their relationships with foreign investors will normally find it easier to attract investment than will those who flout them.

The kinds of discussion among the advanced countries on foreign investment that are now desirable illustrate four points that are common to all three large areas of policy that fall under the first heading: tasks that arise mainly from the advanced countries' interdependence with one another. First, here, as in many areas of economic policy, the advanced countries mainly need procedures for consultation and adjustment of policies rather than binding rules. Codes and rules can probably usefully be worked out to govern some specific aspects of a broad problem (e.g. taxation of MNEs, export credits) but much of what needs to be discussed and to be recognized by governments as legitimate for international discussion will not—in the near term—be reducible to codes. Second, many problems of economic policy which have tended to be dealt with narrowly as discrete trade, money or investment issues now need to be looked at, as well, as aspects of very broad, systemic problems (managing interdependence, promoting structural change). Third, whether matters are of domestic concern only or are of broader common concern depends on effect, not on intent. And fourth, in almost all cases where there is need for closer advanced-country consultation and perhaps some limited rule-making there is likely to be a need for a counterpart role on a broader basis, for example, the need for some although less intensive discussions of macroeconomic policy in the IMF and of industrial policy in the GATT and UNCTAD and for continuing UN discussions of mne's and other aspects of investment. In such cases the more intensive OECD action should not be at the expense of the global efforts but a supplement to, a stimulus to, and sometimes a testing ground for, action on a broader basis.

Relationships with other groups of countries

The DAC (the Development Assistance Committee of the OECD) or, more precisely, the DAG (Development Assistance Group) was established before the OECD itself came formally into existence. With European recovery from the war accomplished, attention was shifting to the needs of the developing countries. At that time (1960), apart from the United States, only the UK and France [28] had substantial foreign aid programs. The United States was becoming concerned with its balance of payments deficit and it was also coming to realize that, if significant assistance were to be given to developing countries, very substantial aid would be needed for many years. It therefore pushed for more European participation in the aid effort. The influential speech by Sir Oliver (now Lord) Franks already noted on the emerging importance of North-South problems pointed in the same direction. And it was fairly readily agreed that a development assistance group, which Japan would also be invited to join, should be set up without awaiting the outcome of the inevitably longer process of negotiating the details of the transformation of the OEEC into the OECD.

Thus, from the start the OECD has had as one of its central concerns the co-ordination and improvement—in both quantitative and qualitative terms—of the aid programs of the advanced industrial countries. But much has changed in the last fifteen years. The US bilateral aid program has shrunk both absolutely (in constant dollars) and in relation to those of other aid donors, so that whereas in the early 'sixties the US stood at or near the top of the list when aid was calculated in terms of a percentage of the donor's GNP, it now stands near the bottom; multilateral aid now accounts for a much larger proportion of the total DAC "official aid" some of the new oil-rich countries are becoming important donors; the World Bank is now playing a far more active role than it did in the early 'sixties and today provides much of the necessary research, co-ordination, setting of standards, goals, etc., that came mainly from the DAC a decade ago. Of more importance, the attitudes and to some extent the bargaining power of the ldc's themselves have changed. Today, direct resource transfers are only one of the ways, and, in the eyes of many ldc governments, the least of the ways, in which the redistribution of power, wealth, and opportunity to which they feel entitled should now occur. And it seems probable that if the OECD were being formed today, the DAC, that is a committee charged essentially with co-ordinating and improving bilateral aid programs, would not have a central role. This is not quite the same as saying that DAC has outlived its usefulness. It still has a role; although a less important one than it played during the 'sixties [29].

But, looking ahead, is the co-ordination of relationships with the less-developed countries, or with other identifiable groups of countries, an appropriate function for an advanced country organization, and if so what are the tasks that now require collective action?

Relationship with the OPEC
Recently the OECD has found itself in the limelight largely because the US Government decided it was a convenient umbrella organization for the International Energy Agency and the Financial Support Fund. Both of these arrangements have had a dual purpose: the first was to encourage the advanced countries to help one another overcome the difficulties and dislocations arising from the steep increase in oil prices and the sudden accumulation of very large and very liquid amounts of petrodollars, and to encourage the principal importing countries to take actions—conservation, standby sharing arrangements,

236

measures to stimulate production—designed to reduce their dependence on OPEC sources and to strengthen their ability to weather the consequences of any future interruption in supplies; the second purpose was to improve the bargaining position of the advanced countries *vis-à-vis* OPEC by altering the market situation and thus to make it more difficult for the OPEC to maintain the present high prices. Many of the measures taken—conservation, stimulation of new production, sharing arrangements, standby financial arrangements—obviously serve both purposes, providing mutual self-help and prudent insurance against future risks and strengthening the advanced countries' bargaining position by changing the market situation to the disadvantage of the cartel.

To some extent the aura of confrontation that attaches to these two agencies is inescapable. Neither would have been organized had the OPEC not created a new situation by the dramatic and concerted increase in oil prices. The kinds of measure the advanced countries needed to take to mitigate the effects of the new situation on their own economies, and to help one another, would inevitably have had the effect of weakening somewhat the bargaining position of the OPEC even had that not been a part—and a legitimate part—of the purpose. But much of the rhetoric that accompanied the early negotiations on the Energy Agency had stronger overtones of confrontation, of hitting back rather than searching for common ground, than was inevitable or wise. This was less true of the negotiations on the Fund, partly because they came later and passions had cooled somewhat (or reason had got the upper hand) but also because it was harder for the OPEC countries, or other critics, to see anything particularly "confrontational" in a stand-by arrangement the immediate purpose of which was to encourage the countries participating in the Fund arrangements to run unusually large trade deficits to cover their oil account, rather than imposing import restrictions or resorting to other measures which would have transferred the payments problem to other members of the group or to third countries. The French Government's decision to join the Fund despite the fact that it had refused to join the Agency was in part, although only in part, a reflection of this difference [30].

Accounts of the divergencies between the initial responses of the OECD governments to the embargo and the increase in oil prices and of the central issues in the negotiations leading to the formation of the two new agencies abound; and the texts of the conventions are readily available and need not be summarized here. What does concern us is whether there is likely to be a continuing role for an advanced-country organization concerned with energy, whether the kind of role the OECD-IEA played in this situation is a prototype for other situations, and the way the oil crisis has interacted with other pressures to lead to a new interest in using the OECD in a much more active way than heretofore as a place where advanced-country policy toward the ldc's is initiated and co-ordinated.

For as long as the threat of war remains high in the Middle East, and ideally for as long as their dependence on OPEC sources remains high, there is a clear need for the principal importing countries to keep the stand-by sharing arrangements that have been agreed in good repair, both to lessen the damage if there were a new embargo and to reduce the potency of the oil weapon. For a number of years, probably as long as a decade, there will also continue to be a problem of financial management. The money and capital markets may continue to be able to handle the huge flows of capital, but, at a minimum, their capacity to do so will require close surveillance by governments and a willingness to step in if necessary. There is also a shorter-term need to co-ordinate advanced-country bargaining with OPEC. Both the member countries and the staffs of the OECD-IEA have been sensitive to charges that the Agency was an instrument of confrontation and that organizing the consumers tended to harden the split between producers and consumers. And following the failure of the Paris conference in April 1975, which was supposed to prepare the ground for a full scale meeting between the main oil producing and oil consuming countries, there was a noticeable shift in emphasis. Stress was laid on the need for the consumers to organize themselves not simply for their own good but in order to create the conditions for a constructive dialogue with the OPEC.

The mutual interest of the OECD and the OPEC countries in avoiding confrontation is so obvious that serious negotiations seem probable before long [31]. In 1974 a total of 1,100 million tons of oil worth about $ 90 billion was exported from the OPEC countries to the OECD countries; this was about two-thirds of the OECD countries' total consumption of oil and about four-fifths of OPEC's production [32]. However, as the preparatory meeting in April amply demonstrated, the IEA—by itself—has too narrow a mandate to serve as the only or even as the main instrument for coordinating a dialogue with the producers, given the position of the OPEC countries that the price of oil must be related to the prices of their own imports and that the agenda must be broadened to include commodity policy and other ldc concerns. Moreover, even on the issues that are clearly within the scope of the IEA—prices, supplies—the interests and hence the views of the IEA member countries are so divergent that it is by no means clear that a fully co-ordinated US-European Community-Japan position can be found [33]. The ambitious hopes of the US negotiators that consumer co-operation in conservation and stimulation of alternative sources of production could be substantial enough soon enough to change in any very radical way the market situation seem likely to continue to be frustrated, not least by the unwillingness of the US Congress to take measures to compress consumption in the US. And the continuing sharp disagreements about the level and mechanics of the "safeguard price" which—under strong pressure from the United States—the IEA countries have agreed, in principle, to adopt to protect investors in new energy sources against a sharp decline in price and to ensure them of an adequate return on their investments, suggest that a rather transparent agreement to differ is more likely than is a common commitment strong enough to carry conviction [34]. In short, although there is an obvious need for the major consuming countries and in particular the US, Japan and Western

Europe to co-ordinate policies that affect their bargaining strength *vis-à-vis* OPEC, the IEA, as such, seems likely to have a rather more limited role to play than was originally seen for it in the probably prolonged process of bargaining that may soon begin.

Although it is a digression, it is perhaps worth looking briefly at the role of the IEA generally; for when it was launched early in 1975 it seemed to some people to be the prototype for a number of new functional agencies loosely linked to the OECD, a judgement that seemed to be reinforced by the subsequent decision to establish the "safety net" or Financial Support Fund, again loosely linked to the OECD. Not only does a proliferation of "IEAs" seem unlikely (and unwise) but it seems probable that the swings that seemed so obvious last January—away from Brussels and to Paris—and away from the OECD to semi-autonomous institutions like the IEA may be reversed, or at least arrested.

The IEA has four broad functions: working out the details of the sharing arrangements and putting them into effect if the need to do so arises; working with the oil companies to obtain better information and to provide greater transparency to the oil market; developing and implementing a long-term program to reduce dependence on imported oil supplies, including, on the one hand, measures to conserve energy and, on the other, measures to develop alternative sources of energy; and promotion of co-operative relations with the oil producers and other oil consuming countries. So far as the first two functions are concerned, it is obvious that for a time there is important work to be done and that it must be done by an agency that brings together the US, Japan and the European Community. It is also obvious that if there were another interruption in oil supplies the IEA would play a key role, and, depending on the nature of the crisis, the advanced countries might be impelled into a more far-reaching form of energy co-operation than today exists or, barring another crisis, seems probable.

So far as the third function is concerned—reduction of dependence, through conservation on the one hand and development of alternative sources on the other—some of the difficulties of working out an agreed program among the IEA countries have been commented on above. Undoubtedly the IEA will play a useful role both in encouraging conservation and in stimulating R and D. But the assertion that was fashionable in OECD circles that the establishment of the IEA sounded the death knell of any effective Community action may well have been premature. It is not a question of either/or. The European Commission has not thus far met with much success in its efforts to promote a common energy policy and the high hopes that attended the launching of Euratom were soon disappointed; but in the nuclear field many of the arguments for collective European action that lay behind the original proposal for Euratom are probably more valid today than they were when they were first put forward. And, despite the Community's lack of progress, it is rather easier to see the European countries pooling efforts and agreeing on a rational division of labor in the development of new sources of energy than it is to see "advanced-country" action that goes much beyond the pilot-project stage. Basic research will, of course, always escape institutional perimeters, and in the case of fusion it is sharing with the Soviet Union that may prove to be important. Finally, so far as the promotion of a dialogue is concerned, the IEA is, as indicated above, too narrowly focussed to play the co-ordinating role which has increasingly involved other parts of the OECD as well.

In short, contrary to some of the expectations that were current early in 1975, there would still seem to be scope for the development of a distinctive energy policy on the part of the Nine, if they choose to take that road. And the IEA, itself, seems likely to become progressively more closely integrated with the OECD, for many of the energy-related problems can be handled better by the broader organization. Thus the problems petro-dollars pose for capital and money markets can best be dealt with as part of the closer consultation on all aspects of monetary and macro-economic policy that is now desirable; the necessary surveillance of inward investment can be carried on as part of the more general concern with long-term capital flows and the elaboration of a code of conduct for investment; and the structural changes which are indicated by the need for greater economy in the use of energy and the need to channel vast sums to the development of new sources of energy, considered in the context of industrial policy together with other reasons for structural change [35].

Relationship with the ldc's

In most of the areas that have been commented on briefly in this paper there is a tension or a contradiction between what it is useful and sensible to do in the short to medium term and the direction in which it is preferable to try to move over the longer term. Perhaps nowhere is this more true than in relationships with the ldc's. It is quite clearly undesirable to contribute to a further polarization of relationships between North and South, developed and developing, rich and poor, however in precise terms these overlapping but not identical categories of countries are defined. Nor, as a rule, is it desirable to organize collective action among a limited group of countries if other countries are both strongly affected and can themselves become a part of the process without an appreciable sacrifice in terms of the purposes for which co-operative action is sought. There is undoubtedly something that smacks both of paternalism and of selfishness in an organization of rich countries promoting the co-ordination of policies *vis-à-vis* the poor countries: paternalism when it is said to be done mainly for the benefit of the poor; selfishness when it is said to be done in self-protection. All that being said, however, there would nevertheless seem to be a strong case today for advanced-country consultation, at a minimum, and beyond that for some co-ordination of policies, not simply on specific measures like investment, aid, and commodity policy, but on the broad question of the strategy to be followed in UN discussions on the "new international economic order".

240

It is an unhappy fact that the ldc's have themselves decided that pressure, confrontation, and the solidarity of the "77" are more likely to bring tangible results than is reliance on the conscience or the enlightened self-interest of the rich countries. If only the short term is considered, they may well have been right, for ldc demands stand a good bit higher on all international agenda than they did a few years ago. In any prolonged contest the developed countries would be far stronger than the ldc's, but neither rich nor poor would gain in the end from the distortions in the international economic system that would inevitably result from a prolonged period of confrontation. It may well be, however, that for a time there must be a period of greater cohesion among the ldc's, on the one hand, and of greater cohesion among the advanced countries on the other, and of hard bargaining between the groups. Very likely the ldc's like the advanced countries must experience for themselves the limits of "independence" before they can accept the obligations of "interdependence".

There is another, rather different reason for thinking that for several years, at least, the OECD should play an expanded role in co-ordinating policies *vis-à-vis* the ldc's. If no collective strategic thinking about the nature of relationships and no co-ordination of policies takes place among the advanced nations it seems almost inevitable that special arrangements of various kinds will grow up between groups of ldc's and particular advanced countries. In both the short term and the longer term, privileged arrangements of one kind and another seem less desirable—for the ldc's and in the interests of harmony among the advanced countries themselves—than arrangements that are more generally applicable. The old argument over the reverse preferences granted the European Community by the African associates is relevant here. The Lomé convention moves away from preferential trade arrangements and has instead sought to help most of the least-advantaged ldc associates through the so-called STABEX scheme for stabilising export earnings for countries heavily dependent on a single cash crop. As all statements on commodity policy always note in the first paragraph or two, the main raw materials or "commodities" have to be looked at separately, for conditions of production and marketing vary widely from commodity to commodity and no single prescription will suit many cases. But it is hard to believe that there will very often be a case where it makes sense for the European Community to follow one policy on a given commodity, say, rubber, the US a second, and Japan a third; nor will it very often make sense for some ldc's to have arrangements for their principal export product which other ldc's are denied. Both in the short term and in the long it is desirable that where there are to be new ways of dealing with particular commodities, or new trade rules, these should be agreed on as wide a basis as possible and be as general in their application as possible. In short, there are advantages both from a "world order" perspective and from the standpoint of the ldc's (as a group although not always from the standpoint of an individual ldc) in the OECD countries agreeing on the main lines of policy, rather than in adopting inconsistent and sometimes competitive policies.

241

The OECD Ministerial Council in May 1975 in response to prodding by the secretariat and the US Government (and, doubtless, a little useful collusion between the two) set in train much new work on the relationships with the ldc's in addition to adopting a Declaration on Relations with Developing Countries designed to demonstrate that the advanced countries were ready to discuss the issues that had proved to be stumbling blocks at the preparatory conference in April, and, more generally, to "pursue the dialogue with the developing countries, in all appropriate fora... in order to make real progress towards a more balanced and equitable structure of international economic relations" [36]. Two new high level committees were established, one to work specifically on commodity policy, the other to survey the "economic relations between Member countries and developing countries, with a view to identifying what new and other constructive approaches could be adopted on selected substantive issues, and to giving support and new impetus to negotiations in other bodies working on specific problems" [37].

The final paragraph of the communiqué made it plain that the ministers hoped these pledges of good faith and signs of increased activity would induce the oil producers to return to the conference table "for the resumption at an early date of the dialogue which was initiated in Paris last April". And the speeches of Henry Kissinger just before the ministerial meeting and statements by various American spokesmen since then have indicated clearly enough that these new activities in the OECD were intimately related to the US strategy on energy. Specifically, the IEA and the two new high-level committees in the OECD were to be the planning groups for the central aspects of the resumed attempt at negotiation and also the forerunners of the consumers' element in the continuing high-level commissions which, in the US view, might well be established following the conference.

The desirability of limiting to the minimum the amount of confrontation and polarization in the period ahead suggests that once the ldc's and the advanced countries are in a position seriously to try to reach agreement on specific issues it will usually be better for the negotiations to take place in organizations that are global in character rather than in negotiating conferences deliberately constructed on a group bargaining basis. This does not mean that all countries need participate in all negotiations. But to the extent possible—and there may well be cases when it is not possible save at too high a price in terms of efficiency— the negotiating framework should be a global one and the outcome to be sought whether it be a new set of principles or a new mechanism (e.g. buffer stock) or a new code of conduct should be an arrangement that is generally applicable to all those countries that have a legitimate interest in participating rather than being a deal or a bargain struck between blocs. Sometimes the GATT or the IMF will be the right umbrella organization for the negotiation, sometimes the UN. But if the latter is to play the role it should play and is not as now to contribute to a situation in which special deals become the rule rather than the exception, it is desirable that ways be adopted to make it possible for groups of countries willing and able to go ahead to do so without being impeded by others who refuse either to participate or to let others act without them [38].

In short, as was the case with the DAC when bilateral aid was central to the relationship between the advanced countries and the developing world, the OECD should play a planning and co-ordinating role, not an operational one. Many of the ldc assertions about the impact on their economies of existing trade and payments arrangements are exaggerated or plain wrong and many aspects of the new international economic order they claim to want would not produce the results they anticipate. Nevertheless, in concentrating on the international economic system they have, at least, seized the right stick. And the advanced countries have been curiously slow, as a group, to organize themselves to deal with the real problems that lie buried in the extravagant and sometimes abusive rhetoric [39].

Relationship with the Comecon countries

Although today it is the advanced countries' relations with the OPEC and the ldc's that call for more co-ordination, it is worth asking whether now or in the future the OECD should have a role either in expanding economic contacts with the command-economy countries or in encouraging more co-ordination of policy among the advanced countries *vis-à-vis* the Comecon group of countries on, for example, trade, credits, joint production arrangements. Partly because of the presence of the neutrals in the OECD, relations with the Soviet Union and the Eastern European countries have not been a natural subject for the OECD. Strategic trade controls have been handled in the COCOM, a subsidiary of the NATO, and any discussions having a security aspect should and doubtless will continue to be handled in that forum. For the rest, there may on occasion be subjects—credit conditions may be one—on which some exchange of views among the OECD countries is desirable, but, for the most part, it would seem desirable to leave East-West economic questions to the UN Economic Commission for Europe. As has been repeatedly emphasized throughout this paper, the concept behind the OECD should not be one of organizing a bloc of advanced market-economy countries to deal as a bloc with other groups, but rather to enable the advanced countries to perform more efficiently the management of their own interdependence, on the one hand, and to discharge more effectively the responsibility that inevitably rests on them given their preponderant weight in the international economic system. The need to co-ordinate policy *vis-à-vis* the OPEC countries arises mainly from the disruption OPEC policies have caused to the advanced countries' economies; if unexpected developments in Eastern Europe were to cause some comparable disturbance clearly a new situation would be created.

There may occasionally be particular subjects on which some exchange of views among the OECD countries is desirable. There may also be times, as economic exchanges expand, when it would be useful to co-opt one or more Eastern European countries to participate in a particular OECD activity. And, as discussed further below, in their capacity as "steerers of the system" the key advanced countries must be concerned with the better articulation between all the parts of the emerging global international economy. But short of some disruptive development comparable to the oil price increase, relationships with the Comecon countries as a group, should not, probably, be more central to the work of the OECD in the future than they have been in the past.

"System-tending", "steering", "leadership"

There is no good shorthand expression to describe the collection of tasks this heading is supposed to encompass. Expressions like "system-tending" and "steering" imply that there is more of an organized economic system than is, in fact, the case. And "steering" and "leadership" tend to suggest that the advanced countries enjoy some moral superiority or are striving for positions of hegemony or dominance. Yet despite the difficulties of definition there are four or five clusters of tasks, all more or less related to making the international system function better, now and in the future, on which the OECD could be useful.

It seems likely to be true that a *really* efficient international economic system requires either strong leadership by a single dominant country willing and able to underwrite the system, or strong "supranational" institutions endowed with real powers [40]. For two decades after the second world war the United States largely underwrote the economic system of what used to be called the "free world". That situation no longer exists, partly because the United States is no longer prepared to do the underwriting, partly because US dominance is no longer acceptable to the new centers of economic power—Western Europe, Japan, OPEC—and partly because any "leadership role", however benign in intent, is repudiated by many within the advanced countries and within the ldc's. Even were the attitudes of the OPEC and many of the ldc's less challenging it would be easy enough to demonstrate that it is unrealistic to suggest that a group of countries meeting intermittently in an intergovernmental organization like the OECD could perform the role of underwriter as, at times, a single power can do or as, perhaps, one day a stronger system of global institutions will do. Nevertheless, all that being said, given the present diffusion of economic power, the erosion of the rules that provided the "bones" of the post-war system and the widespread questioning of many of the assumptions underlying the rules, there would seem to be a number of ways in which the right kind of OECD could play a role of some importance in the troubled years that now seem to lie ahead.

There is a need for far-reaching reform of global institutions, but the kind of reform that is needed will not come quickly. There is too much rhetoric, too much passion, too little analysis, too little consensus. Deadlock would be a more probable outcome than agreement if any very substantial restructuring were

244

today attempted. And were agreement attainable it might well be worse than deadlock, for it seems probable that the kind of new arrangements that might be agreed upon today would tend to harden the lines between the four, or five, "worlds" into which the globe is divided. As suggested above, for a time there may well be resistance on the part of the ldc's to arrangements that reflect the fact of growing interdependence, and they may insist on what they may later discover to be an unacceptably costly form of "independence". This ldc insistence on an unreal form of national autonomy and sovereignty seems likely to be matched by a preoccupation with domestic problems in the advanced countries and a corresponding turning inwards.

All institutional reform cannot, however, await some ideal moment in the future. Too much interconnectedness exists. If no attempts are made to improve the functioning of the partial and imperfect system that already links economies there will be further deterioration. What is needed now is, therefore, a two-track approach: more analysis and more discussion in an attempt to reach a wider consensus on the essential principles of a reformed international system and also improvements in the way international economic problems are dealt with in the short to medium term, taking care that these short-term improvements do not set in concrete patterns of relationship and principles of conduct that seem likely to prove unworkable or unwise in the longer term.

The OECD could help move things along on both tracks. For example, more should be done through a process of analysis and discussion to achieve more consensus about the essential characteristics of the international system which should be the goal of policy. This is not a suggestion for an exercise in blue-printing the future or for sketching out "ideal-type" institutions. Rather the suggestion is that key policy-makers, assisted by the secretariat, should from time to time engage in free-ranging debate and discussions which were not tied to decisions on immediate policy options but were more concerned with the general direction of policy and with what Henry Kissinger would call "architecture". Such discussions would at a minimum be useful in revealing whether the separate national "visions of the desirable future" are in fact congruent or conflicting visions. Beyond that, they should encourage among the countries that still carry the greatest weight in the international system more thought about the essential principles of a reformed system. Simply to prepare to engage in discussions of this kind would force some governments that pride themselves on pragmatism and adeptness in responding to events to think in a longer time-span than they normally find congenial about key relationships among states, about which functions should be handled at what level—national, European, advanced-nation, global—about where the market is the right arbiter and the task is to make it perform better, and where it is not and something else is needed, and other fundamental questions.

The functions that fall along the second track are closer to the kind of work the OECD already does from time to time, that is actions that the OECD group of countries can take among themselves to help existing organizations perform better, and to plug gaps. The Rey Committee discussions on the next stages in trade policy and the discussions within the Group of Ten on SDR's are examples of how discussions among the advanced countries can give a new impulse or a new direction to global institutions. The "trade pledge" taken in the context of the oil crisis was an example of how action by the OECD can be critical in stopping erosion in the broader system. Some of the work of the DAC and some of the current work now underway on commodities and on surveying what is being done elsewhere to help the poorest countries comes under the heading of co-ordination and gap-filling. But more could be done among this group of countries to improve the functioning of the global institutions. Moreover if through the kind of discussions suggested above they are able to reach more of a consensus on some of the essentials of longer-term reform, stop-gap measures and short-term actions can become part of a purposeful process of piecemeal reform.

There is another related function that also comes under this general rubric of "system-tending", that is the task of spotting new problems and problems that have long lead-times, and of stimulating work on them before they become critical or unmanageable. Again, the OECD has had some success in this type of work. It was an early entrant into the environmental pollution field; it helped focus attention on the role of science policy in government; it helped separate myth from reality about the technological gap. But although it has played a useful role in identifying and stimulating work in new areas such as these, as an organization it has frequently tended to hang on for too long to whatever activity has been set in train. More effort should be spent on spotting problems and in activating work on questions which are not today urgent but must be acted on today if trouble in the future is to be avoided. But once work has been stimulated, the function should normally be floated off, sometimes to other intergovernmental organizations, sometimes to non-governmental international organizations. Sometimes governments or private organizations once alerted to a problem can simply be left to get on with the job.

Obviously this kind of activity should not be simply the prerogative of an advanced-country organization like the OECD; it must happen everywhere all the time. But the advanced countries have special concerns and special responsibilities in what might be called the frontier areas. Many problems of general concern tend to hit them first and only they are likely to have the resources— expertise as well as money—required to understand what needs to be done and to try to mobilize appropriate action.

Finally, there is a role to be played in crisis management. Both weaknesses in the existing organization and tactical considerations—whether sensible or otherwise need not be debated here—on the part of the US Government led it to seek to deal with the oil crisis in the first instance by organizing the principal consuming countries outside the framework of the OECD. It would not be hard to write a scenario for a better response to a sudden crisis: one element in such a response would be a more flexible institution, another would be a readiness on the part of the key advanced countries to put their common interests above their separate interests, a third would be their recognition of the wider responsibilities they inevitably bear as a consequence of their wealth and economic power for the health and orderly functioning of the wider system. It cannot be said too often that whether it be crisis management, short-term improvements in existing institutions, or planning for institutional reform the advanced countries have an obligation to look beyond their own welfare. They carry too much weight in the total system to shift the burden of responsibility or to yield to the temptation to write off the wider world as the easy way to respond to intemperate ldc demands.

A New Organization or an Improved OECD ?

The trilateral alternative

The obvious alternative to trying to improve the OECD to play the kind of role envisaged here is to build instead a closer relationship among the key centers of economic power: the US, Japan, and the European Community. If the European Community were in fact a European economic union the pressure to move in this direction would probably be irresistible, although it is at least arguable that even in those circumstances a formalization of the triangle would be a mistake. However the European Community is today so far from being an economic union that, somewhat paradoxically, trilateralism meets with resistance, both from those within the Community who do not want to be pushed faster than they are prepared to move toward union and see in any formal trilateralism an external pressure which they could not control, and from some "Europeans" who fear that an effective trilateral institution would undercut some of the political and economic pressures making for European unity, in much the same ways as Atlantic unity was seen to threaten European unity in the 'fifties.

Wholly apart from the resistance that arises from different expectations about the impact of "trilateralism" upon the evolution of European unity, there is the purely practical difficulty that would arise from the fact that the Community today acts sometimes as One sometimes as Nine and not infrequently gets stuck in immobility between the two modes. For this reason a variant of trilateralism that is heard in the United States (although seldom in Europe) is a closer relationship between the US, Germany and Japan. It is not surprising that this version has been propounded chiefly in the context of the management of international money, for clearly these are today the key countries in the monetary system [41]. But building trilateralism on Germany rather than on the European Community would fatally undercut the latter and tend to revive concern—in Eastern and Western Europe—about the German role. For these reasons it would have few if any responsible adherents in Western Europe and no US Administration would be likely to move, formally at least, in this direction.

Can the OECD adapt?

The OECD has been called a middle-aged institution and it has been characterized as an organization of civil servants talking to civil servants. Can it adapt to the kind of role that some advanced-country organization should now be seeking to fulfil, or would it be better to scrap it and create something new? Only governments can decide whether they are prepared to see the kinds of changes made that would enable the existing institution to respond to the needs of the future; if they are, self-regeneration should be possible. If they are not, it is unlikely that a new institution would prove to be much more of a success.

No one would, today, invent the OECD with precisely its present membership, its extensive array of "vertical" committees, its highly compartmentalized secretariat. There are good historical reasons why the institution is as it is; but no compelling reasons—other than the force of inertia—why the changes that now seem to be desirable cannot be made. If it can be accomplished, there are at least three interrelated reasons why adaptation would be better than starting anew. First, as constantly reiterated throughout this paper, it is desirable not to respond to the current irresponsible tactics and exaggerated claims of the ldc's by hardening lines. The formation of a new advanced-country organization would inevitably be seen as a step in this direction. Second, the category of "advanced countries" is changing. On the face of it, Brazil might well seem a more obvious candidate for membership in an advanced-country institution than Greece. Yet today the network of economic relationships and the attitudes of governments are such that, to put it at its lowest, neither the *presence* of Greece nor the *absence* of Brazil is much of a hindrance to effective advanced-country co-ordination of policy. This situation is changing, and it may well be that changes in membership at some time will become imperative. If that becomes the case, the arguments for a new organization would be appreciably stronger, for it is exceedingly difficult to make radical changes in the membership of an existing organization. But, for the present, the membership problem is probably best dealt with through more use of restricted committees and some co-option of countries for particular purposes. (This point is discussed further below.) Finally, looking to the longer term, it seems to me to be doubtful whether a separate advanced-country institution should be a part of the reorganized global institutional system that it is desirable to try to work towards over the next decade or two. Rather, it seems likely to be better to think of advanced-country tiers or chambers in a number of interrelated global functional organizations. In any case, the need now is not to move to arrangements that will approximate the kind of institutional arrangements that may characterize a reformed eventual global system, for views on that have yet to crystallize. Rather, the immediate need is for an adaptable, flexible instrument which can facilitate advanced-country co-ordination of policy, an organization which is willing to experiment with new techniques for fostering collective international action but one which will not stand in the way of the evolution, over time, of more effective global institutions.

In the self re-examination that has been occurring in the OECD during the last year or two, much attention has been given to two linked problems: how to improve the decision-taking power of the organization, and how to avoid work being unduly slowed down or paralyzed by the desire of all countries to participate in everything. The insistence of the United States government on setting up both the IEA and the Financial Support Fund *not* as subsidiary bodies of the OECD (although loosely linked to the OECD) was in large measure a reflection of the desire to have a stronger more operational form of organization than the OECD framework seemed likely to provide. Both the new organizations have limited memberships and both have weighted majority voting [42]. Although both new institutions will have operational functions in certain circumstances, neither may in fact play an operational role if there proves to be no need to invoke energy sharing arrangements or to mount a major financial support operation.

It is possible that in the years ahead there may be other areas where it is desirable for the OECD to acquire operational functions itself or to spawn an operational agency. But this seems likely to be an exceptional need. For the most part, as indicated in the discussion on functions, the OECD should now not be playing an operational role; indeed, it should usually be true that when any activity becomes operational it should be transferred from the OECD to some other institution, e.g., GATT, IMF, the UN, or floated off as a self-sufficient operation. The OECD should itself concentrate on four or five main tasks: it should (1) serve as a forum for more intensive and continuing consultation on those aspects of economic policy—mainly macro-economic policy but also, and probably increasingly, industrial policy—that although undertaken mainly for domestic purposes have repercussions throughout the international economy and in particular on the economies of the other advanced industrial countries; (2) largely growing out of the discussions envisaged under (1), attempt to see whether there are procedures that can be adopted or principles that could be codified: in most cases once rule-making becomes possible the function should be transferred to a global forum such as the IMF or GATT, although there may be cases in which the new code will remain for an appreciable time simply a compact among the OECD countries; (3) formulate a strategy in response to the pressures for a "new international economic order" and provide some co-ordination of policies among the advanced countries *vis-à-vis* the ldc's, being mindful of all the caveats to which attention has been drawn in the earlier discussion on this point; (4) promote collective strategic thinking about emerging problems and how they can best be handled, extending from crisis management, as in the case of oil, at one end of the spectrum to long-range planning for institutional reform at the other. And, finally, (5) as a consequence of, and a deliberate part of all the foregoing, it should seek to provide a measure of "steering" or leadership to the broader international economic system.

If these are the main things on which the organization should concentrate, voting is largely irrelevant, and much of the concern with improving the organization's capacity to take decisions is rather beside the point. The difficulties of membership remain however. Particularly, perhaps, in the sensitive discussions on the co-ordination of macro-economic policy it will frequently be desirable for the countries that have the major impact on the system as a whole to meet together by themselves. The smaller OECD countries must accept this situation or they will, in effect, ensure one of two other outcomes: either no discussions will take place or, more probably, discussions will take place outside the framework of the OECD, perhaps by the more or less formal constitution of the Group of Five which has met fairly often during the last year. It should be possible for the small countries to persuade themselves that neither of these outcomes is as much in their own interest as frank, free, and far-reaching discussions within the framework of the OECD, with the high probability that informally at least they will then be in close touch with, although not always present at, the discussions.

There are several ways in which restricted committees might be made more acceptable. In many cases it should not be difficult to arrange for the distribution of papers to those countries that have been "included out" of any particular committee or group. In some cases provision might be made for the occasional but not the regular participation of a country, in others for some form of group representation. Above all, if, as would be desirable on substantive grounds, there were fewer set patterns and more flexibility, fewer formally constituted committees and more coming together of different groups of countries for shorter periods of time, it should be easier to include all countries part of the time but very few countries all of the time. A deliberate decision to move to a new organizational pattern based on very few permanent committees and many more temporary working groups would not only help to break the current insistence on including all countries in all committees, it would also have the advantage of making it easier to co-opt non-OECD countries for membership in particular groups without further inflating the present membership of the OECD. Brazil, Mexico, Israel would be candidates for co-option for some purposes, Iran and Saudi Arabia for others, perhaps Poland and Czechoslovakia for others.

If the OECD is to play the role suggested in this essay there are other changes that should be made, in structure and in the roles and the responsibilities of the secretariat and of the representatives of member governments. In the first place, many now peripheral functions should be weeded out and work concentrated on a relatively few major issues. The OECD inherited from the OEEC a large array of committees which has become even larger over the years as new committees have been established to deal with new problems. There has been little sloughing-off of old work as new work has been added and little effort to streamline the organization. Although it would doubtless be possible for each of the more than forty committees to point to something useful it had done in the last year or two, "usefulness" should not be the only test for longevity: the activity should also be one that can be better done in the OECD than elsewhere and one that contributes directly to the achievement of the main tasks of the organization. In some fields—education, road research, tourism, fisheries are examples that come to mind, but there are others—it may well have been useful for the OECD initially to bring together experts from the member countries to compare experience and to discuss ways of solving common problems; but once this process of communication has started, there is no reason why many of the activities that are typical of the organization's work in these areas should not have been spun off [43].

In the second place, more should be done to integrate work done in separate but related areas. It is a commonplace that the interconnectedness between issues that have traditionally been handled separately is now posing new problems for management—national and international, public and private [44]. Action on one problem in one area produces ripples that create new problems in other areas; the solution to any particular problem frequently involves action on a half-dozen other fronts as well. The recent awareness of feedback, linkage and the other interactions which systems analysis has thrown into prominence is perhaps in some danger of fashionable inflation. Too great a concern with the interrelatedness of everything can lead to immobility. But the committee structure that has grown up in the OECD militates against focusing on interrelationships, makes it difficult to identify the trade-offs and to make linkages work for rather than against the desired outcome. This is a serious weakness, particularly if the institution is to try to encourage the kind of collective strategic thinking discussed above. The formation of the Executive Committee in Special Session was an attempt to overcome the tunnel vision that afflicts too much of the work and to try to look at clusters of interrelated issues. But far more needs to be done to break down the traditional, largely vertical committee structure, to regroup functions and to provide new horizontal cuts at sets of interrelated problems. Thus the kind of work on industrial policy that was considered briefly in an earlier section would not only be done inadequately but, probably, counter-productively, if it were entrusted to the existing Industry Committee and its special industry subcommittees. For the problem for the future is how to induce the right kind of change, and industry committees are conspicuously bad at recognizing obsolescence and the need for radical change in "their" industry. Nor could the Trade Committee as presently constituted do more than a small part of the job.

In the third place, and most importantly, there should be a presumption of change rather than today's presumption of continuity. No committee should be thought of as "permanent"; committees and the divisions of the secretariat that service them should have no prescriptive rights to certain subjects on which others encroach at their peril.

An OECD of the kind envisaged in this paper also needs a rather different kind of secretariat to perform a rather different kind of staff role than that required by functional intergovernmental organizations with clear mandates and well-defined activities. The professional staff must be more innovative, able and willing to do the kind of thinking that governments are not themselves normally inclined or very well equipped to do. It is not being suggested that the staff have executive powers delegated do it; the OECD is not, like the European Community, a group of countries which is seeking to create a new union on however limited a basis. Conceivably there may be particular operational functions which for convenience governments at particular times will wish to delegate, but for the most part the OECD and its subsidiary bodies should not have operational functions and the staff should have no executive power. What it does need is the acceptance by governments of its right, of its duty, to goad. This right is one that governments may accept in theory; but they will resist it in fact. No government likes to be pushed. The desirable relationship between international staff and governments is only conceivable if the staff is of exceptional intellectual quality—so good that its advice cannot be ignored—and if it is able to combine sensitivity for the legitimate preoccupations of governments with independence. Both staff and governments must conceive of the staff's role as one of helping governments overcome difficulties they all face, such as excessive compartment-alization, an inability to deal adequately with problems that have long lead-times, the reluctance to re-examine assumptions underlying ongoing policy. The way most international secretariats are organized does nothing to compensate for the divisions and the rigidities that are inherent in all government structures but, rather, tends to intensify them by setting up parallel structures: trade people talk only to trade people, money people talk only to money people, and so on. Clearly the OECD secretariat needs experts who can meet governmental experts on equal terms, but the secretariat need not be a slave to conventional ways of slicing problems. It could, for example, deliberately design its own internal organization to ensure that problems are looked at from a perspective which is different from that from which governments view them.

The OECD has built up an enviable reputation for quality in its statistical work and its economic analysis. Nothing said here should be read as suggesting that this work should be abandoned or that standards should be lowered. Excellent analytical work is just as essential to an organization which seeks to nudge governments into thinking about new problems and into new ways of looking at old problems as it is to an organization which has, rightly, prided itself on the excellence of the briefs prepared in response to government requests.

Perhaps the most difficult changes are those required of governments. The need for the small countries to accept more frequent recourse to restricted groups has already been mentioned. A bigger problem, particularly for the large countries, is the need for a change in attitude toward the process of intergovern-mental consultation, a willingness to see these consultations come earlier and bite more deeply into the process of domestic policy formation. A greatly improved process of intergovernmental consultation on all policies which have significant international implications within the framework of an effort at collective strategic thinking does not, perhaps, sound very dramatic. But if it could be achieved it would amount to a quantum jump—a major innovation in the process of organ-izing intergovernmental relationships.

In most cases it is more discussion among those responsible for policy formation in their own governments—not among government representatives specially briefed for the purpose, whether based in Paris or sent from Foreign

Offices—that is needed. The OECD already makes heavier demands for the direct participation of policy makers in its discussions than do many inter-governmental organizations. A shift towards even more intergovernmental con-sultation as a part of the domestic policy-formulation process would mean that ways would have to be found to enable the responsible officials to spend the necessary time in Paris, and it would also imply more of a house-keeping, less of a participatory, role for the permanent representatives accredited to the institution. Here a special problem arises for Japan and on a slightly less acute basis for Australia and New Zealand—less acute because there are more discussions they can opt out of. One possible way of easing their problems might be to hold some meetings in the United States; another might be to make use of the "revolution in communications" as a way of bringing Japanese in Tokyo into particular discussions in Paris.

Unlike many international organizations—the UN, the World Bank, FAO, and, in a differerent way, the European Community—the OECD has had no constituency, no outside groups that have looked upon the organization as in some way advancing their interests or in a more general way embodying ideals in which they believed. It has been an institution which civil servants trusted, economists found useful as a source of reliable statistics, and most other people knew nothing about. Rather curiously, there has been very little bridge-building between the OECD staff and serious outside research institutes such as the Brookings Institution in Washington or the National Institute in London, al-though some informal contacts are maintained between individuals. Partly as a way of loosening-up a slightly muscle-bound secretariat, partly as a way of strengthening its capacity for longer-term strategic thinking, it would be ad-vantageous to try to promote much more interchange of ideas, papers, and staff with research institutes of this kind [45]. The exchange with other centers of research would of course be easier if far more of the work of the OECD were of an unclassified character. A move toward greater openness would be desir-able for other reasons as well; for one thing it would tend to allay fears that the rich countries were ganging-up on the poor. There is obviously some tension between a desire to involve governments more closely with one another in the process of policy formulation and the desire to have the OECD operate with more openness and more transparency. But except in a few very sensitive areas more is frequently lost than is gained by the present close-to-the-chest approach and the instinctive assumption that all working documents must be confidential. The Commission of the European Community has, I should guess, gained in public understanding and support far more than it has lost from its quite differ-ent policy of positively courting the press and interested outsiders.

Finally, the OECD would do well to make a virtue of what has hitherto been regarded as a weakness, the fact that it has no clear overriding purpose, no constraining concept of its role, and an uncertain future. Governments are far readier to experiment with new modes of operation if they are not committing themselves irrevocably; other institutions look more benignly on temporary intrusions on what they consider to be "their territory" than they do on what appears to be a permanent encroachment. Rightly exploited, the chances are high that the OECD could draw added strength from the very fact of being "temporary"—a response to a current institutional need that gives no hostages to the future.

The OECD and the European Community

Perhaps nowhere would acceptance by all concerned that its future was not only uncertain but irrelevant to a decision to use it to meet a present need pay higher dividends than in the OECD's relationship with the European Community. Sterile rivalry has too often characterized the relationship between the OECD secretariat and the European Commission, and doctrinal arguments have not infrequently affected the decisions of governments about the handling of particular problems. There are real difficulties to be sorted out, however, for there are many areas in which the kind of action taken in one institution will affect the kind of action taken in the other; perhaps energy and money are today the most obvious. It is clear that the OECD should not be debarred from action in these overlapping areas or forced to await the evolution of common policies among the Nine; it is also clear that OECD action should not be designed to foreclose the development of common policies by the Nine. But although it is easy enough to lay down principles of this kind, they do not get at the heart of the problem. If it were clear that in, say, a decade the Nine would have a relationship with one another that could legitimately be described as an economic and monetary union, that is if they were irrevocably committed to a single currency (or arrangements tantamount to a single currency) and all that implies in terms of harmonization of economic policy, collective demand management, a common budget and a "supranational" monetary authority, the problem of fitting the Community into an institutional system with other advanced countries would not be, conceptually, significantly different from the problem of fitting the United States into such a system. There would, to be sure, be some special problems while the Community was in its transition phase, but, if the goal were a clear one, and one certain to be achieved within a period short enough to determine the character of ongoing policy, any more inclusive arrangements should, and could, be ones which assumed the participation of the Community as a unit.

This is not the situation today; nor does it today seem probable that the key countries of the Community—France, Germany, the United Kingdom—will within, say, the next two to three years—come to any very clear decisions about the extent to which their objective is to cross the very real divide between co-ordinating national policies and accepting common European policies. The economic situations in the major countries are too different to make common policies a sensible or feasible prescription. Conceivably the Federal Republic could,

255

in economic terms, underwrite an economic union; but the economic cost to the Germans and the political cost to the French and British in becoming German dependencies are too high to be contemplated by either side to the bargain. Even were economic trends within the Community closer together it is difficult today to see the political impetus needed for a quantum jump. The gains—more external bargaining power, more "independence" from the United States, less vulnerability to external factors of all kinds—do not today appear large enough to any of the governments, even the French, to be worth the cost: the transfer of substantial authority from the national to the "European" level with some loss in national freedom of action.

The probable outlook is for a continuation of the trend of the last decade; no abandonment of the eventual goal of an economic and monetary union; a gradual but steady increase in the amount and depth of consultation about domestic economic policies that have clear repercussions on other members of the Community; a growing habit of seeking to establish a Community position in negotiations with third countries. In addition one can reasonably anticipate some growth in the number and size of Community funds but not a substantial enough increase in the Community budget to give the Community institutions an important tool of economic management.

But beyond these reasonably safe predictions one begins to get in a gray area where what the Nine do *is* likely to be affected by what the advanced countries as a group do, in the OECD or elsewhere. One of the crucial questions would seem to be how the floating of the key currencies—the dollar, the yen, the deutschemark, the pound and the franc—is "managed" in the next year or two. Another is how any massive rescue operations, e.g. for the Italians or the British, are handled.

It would be nice if there were one "right" way forward, so obviously preferable that there could be little room for reasonable argument. But there are two broad alternatives and good arguments can be made for the likelihood and for the advantages of each. One way is for the Nine now to go a good bit further than the advanced countries as a group in co-ordinating their economic policies, to adopt common positions in any overlapping OECD discussions, and, in the event of a crisis for members of the Community to exhaust mutual aid from their partners before resorting to the Financial Support Fund. The alternative is for the essential co-ordination of macro-economic policy to occur among the key advanced countries, with the Nine doing little if anything more among themselves, and, in the event of a crisis, for the principal recourse to be to the Financial Support Fund. Which path is followed will depend partly on how willing the United States is really to embark on meaningful policy co-ordination and partly on the strength of the political support within the Nine Governments for Community action. Probably the most likely outcome, for the next few years at any rate, is a continuation of the present ambiguous weaving between these broad alternatives. A clear decision to follow the first path would accelerate the process of European unity—it would, in itself, be a reflection of a political decision to do so; a clear decision to follow the second path would slow progress down, but it would not be likely to be decisive for the future of European unity. The political and social constraints which pull against the economic arguments for integration are far stronger among the advanced countries as a group than among the Nine as a group. Moreover there is a resilience to the idea of "Europe" which is likely to find expression in other ways if parts of the economic route are, for a time, overtaken by action elsewhere. But there is also a reality behind the rhetoric of interdependence which suggests that even were the European countries to choose unambiguously to give priority to the development of the Community, "advanced-country" consultations and co-ordination of policies would still be needed and a reformed OECD would still have an important role to play.

Longer-term "visions"

All periods in history are, of course, transitional; and it is possible that in retrospect the decade of the 'seventies will look more settled in its main outlines than it does today. But looking at the international economic scene in the mid-'seventies one's dominant impression is of flux and uncertainty: there is much questioning of old assumptions about the governance of society at all levels from the local to the global, and there is a conspicuous absence of consensus on facts, on theory, and above all on goals or objectives. How much growth do we want, of what kinds, where? How much redistribution of wealth and of power do we want: within nations, between nations? Whose good are we seeking to maximize: that of the individual, of the state or of some other political unit, of the world?

It will be said, rightly, that there has never been consensus on questions such as these but that this did not prevent the development of a system, based on a framework of rules, which seemed to work reasonably well for a quarter century. Some will argue that this was so because the "world" for which the system "worked" was essentially a system run by and supported by the United States. Clearly the dominant position of the United States was part of the explanation, and the diffusion of power and the absence of new fixed points of responsibility are part of the reason for the present sense of confusion. But I suspect a more fundamental cause is that we are today caught in a process of transition between two modes of thinking about and of handling many economic problems, gradually and erratically moving from what might be called "international economics" to what might be called "world economics". Usually we think and operate in the first mode, but occasionally in the second. In the first, one is seeking a more or less frictionless interaction between external sectors of national economies, in the second, the efficient functioning of a closed global economy. Most of our attitudes, most of our assumptions, most of our

257

tools derive from the first mode, but many of our difficulties arise because in some respects— although by no means all—objective facts require a shift to the second mode. Compounding the difficulties arising from the growing lack of congruence between the span of political and social structures, on the one hand, and the scale of economic problems, on the other, is the fact that governments everywhere, but particularly in the advanced countries, are today required to satisfy a vast array of not easily reconcilable social wants [46]. And as one moves from focusing on the elimination of friction between nations to promoting the welfare of larger entities the lack of consensus on the kinds of question asked above about goals and objectives poses problems that are far harder to side-step than they have been in the past.

If, at least in part, changes such as these lie at the root of our present difficulties, it is obvious that we do not confront a situation in which we have only to study the world of today more intensively for a year or two and then to negotiate some new ground rules that will see us through the next quarter century or so. Nor are we in a situation in which we can expect that after a few years of upheaval the dust will settle, a new distribution of economic power will become apparent, and a new hierarchy will take over from the old and run the system. Instead it seems probable that we are in for a very long period of having to act in two different kinds of "world", handling some problems as "international economic" problems, others as "global economy" problems.

Reflections such as these suggest that institutional reform will be an evolutionary process, not a "new Bretton Woods". They also point to several general principles that should underlie the process. Perhaps the first principle and the one that it will be hardest to follow is that one must try to build into any new or reformed global institutions much more potential for evolution and for self-adaptation than has been usual. A second principle is that the global institutions must combine the discipline of common rules with the ability to tolerate differences: both the differences that arise from different values and the differences that arise from the fact that societies at different stages of development want and need different things. The third and fourth principles are that although primacy must be given to the global system, the global boat must not be overloaded.

Somewhat more concretely, these principles suggest that we should be working towards a capacity for global "steering", global ground rules for the main sectors of world economic activity, but a large measure of ancillary, decentralized, more intensive co-operative action—sometimes regional, sometimes functional—coupled with "global cognizance" of the decentralized parts of the system. For some functional areas, e.g., money, more can and must be done in the near-term on the global level than in other functional areas, e.g. industrial policy. But global rules wherever they exist should be over-riding and global cognizance a "right". This may mean that a desirable way to structure some global institutions will be in tiers or chambers so that countries desiring and able to go further among themselves in any area covered by global rules (e.g. trade liberalization) can do so, but that adequate machinery will exist for ensuring consistency between these actions and the global rules, and, more importantly, for making it possible for other countries to know what is happening and to have some recourse if affected. Thus it may be that eventually some of the functional tasks of the OECD (e.g. co-ordination of macro-economic policy) should be carried out by one tier or chamber in a reformed global institution and that the kind of "steering" role suggested above for the OECD in the near-term future should be done on a global level by a rather differently composed group of countries.

But speculations such as these take us well beyond the scope of this paper. For the next few years the question is whether the OECD can become the flexible, experimental, *unusual* institution the advanced countries now need to help them manage their own interdependence, and an institution which could help serve as well the wider purpose of giving coherence to the confused network of global economic relationships: or whether, after the brief period in the limelight it has recently enjoyed, it will slowly decline into irrelevance.

Notes

1. See Miriam Camps, *The Management of Interdependence,* Council on Foreign Relations, N.Y., 1974. Both the Council on Foreign Relations and the Atlantic Institute for International Affairs plan further studies in this general field.

2. The term "advanced countries" undoubtedly has pejorative overtones; but there is, as yet, no other commonly understood, shorthand phrase for the highly-developed, market-economy, for-the-most-part-industrialized countries, and therefore the phrase will be used despite its unfortunate overtones.

3. The Commission of the European Economic Community and many influential French officials felt that the cohesion of the Six would be undermined and the potential for evolution of the Community jeopardized if the trade advantages of the Common Market were to be secured either through an OEEC-wide free trade area or a free trade link between the Six and the Seven. The US Government, although it had taken no very clear line during the OEEC negotiations, came to share this view after the negotiations broke down at the end of 1958 and it became almost as anxious as the French and the Commission that no new attempts be made to find an OEEC solution to the trade dispute. During 1958 and 1959 the US was disturbed by its deteriorating balance of payments and this, too, led it to encourage the Six to meet the complaints of the Seven by adopting liberal global trade policies rather than by OEEC-wide schemes which would increase the discrimination against the United States. For details see Miriam Camps, *Britain and the European Community, 1955-1963,* London: O.U.P., 1964, Chapter VIII.

4. In the autumn of 1959, Lord Franks (then Sir Oliver) in a speech that attracted much comment had emphasized the key importance of what he, I think, was the first to dub the "North-South" problem: "If twelve years ago the balance of the world turned on the recovery of Western Europe, now it turns on a right relationship of the industrial North of the globe to the developing South." See Camps, cited, pp. 239-40.

5. The "collective target" for the twenty member countries of the OECD "taken together" was agreed upon at the first ministerial Council meeting of the OECD in November, 1961. Japan was not at that time a member of the OECD. For details see OECD, *Policies for Economic Growth,* Paris, 1962.

6. See p. 36.

7. The Fund's authority to make loans is limited to two years from the date of entry into force of the agreement. An applicant for a loan must have made "the fullest appropriate use of its reserves and... of other multilateral facilites." See Article V.

8. All the members of the OECD are represented on the Economic Policy Committee and on its Working Parties Two and Four, which are concerned, respectively, with growth policies and prices and incomes policies. Working Party Three is a restricted committee having as members the same countries as the Group of Ten which originally negotiated The General Agreements to Borrow with the IMF plus Sweden and Switzerland. There is no Working Party One. Although called Working Parties, WP's 2, 3, and 4 are formally constituted, standing committees.

9. Commission of the European Communities, *Report of the Study Group "Economic and Monetary Union 1980",* Brussels, March 8, 1975.

10. Atlantic Institute for International Affairs, *Spotlights on Inflation,* Paris, 1975, pp. 26-7.

11. The participants in the snake keep their exchange rates closely aligned with one another and float more or less as a group against other currencies. Although for a brief period all the countries of the European Community were participants in the snake, the UK, Ireland and Italy soon dropped out as, later, did France. Until the French rejoined the snake in the summer of 1975, only those countries whose currencies were closely tied to the D-mark were members, and the Bundesbank, in effect, "managed" the snake. The participants included Sweden and Norway although they were not members of the European Community.

12. See *The Management of Interdependence,* cited.

13. Cited, p. 27.

14. See, e.g., Denis Healey, the Chancellor of the Exchequer, in his Budget speech in April, 1975: "One of the disadvantages—or perhaps advantages—of being a finance

minister at the present time is the exceptionally wide diversity of views among professional economists... At present there are particularly fierce disputes about the causal relationships between the four components of a nation's economy which together... must add up to zero—the external balance, the financial balance of the public sector, and the balances of the corporate and personal sectors." *The Times* (London), April 16, 1975, p. 6.

15. The discussion throughout this paper focuses mainly on institutional questions, broadly defined. I have not sought to reach judgements on questions such as the accuracy or otherwise of the Secretariat's economic forecasting. For a critical view, see *The Economic Journal*, June 1975, note by D.J. Ash and J.C.K. Smyth, pp. 361-4.

16. One difficulty in organizing the kind of additional consultation among the governments of the advanced countries that now seems to be required arises from the fact that the way powers are shared between Central Banks and Finance Ministries differs from country to country. In the United States the Federal Reserve System is established by law and the Board reports directly to the Congress rather than the President. In the management of the domestic money supply the Federal Reserve System is formally completely independent of the Treasury although members of the Board are in close and continuous touch with their counterparts in the Treasury. But in the foreign exchange markets the New York Federal Reserve Bank (which does the intervention) acts as agent for the Treasury. The relationship between the Bank of England and the Treasury is rather similar, but both the Bundesbank and the Bank of Italy have a more dominant role, while the Bank of France probably has rather less independence *vis-à-vis* the Ministry of Finance.

17. *IMF Survey*, June 17, 1974, p. 183.

18. The OECD trade pledge was adopted for one year on 30th May, 1974, and renewed at the Ministerial meeting in May 1975. It affirms the determination of governments "to avoid recourse to new restrictions on trade and other current account transactions and the artificial stimulation of visible and current invisible exports". The government of Portugal was the only OECD government which did not renew the Declaration; however the British government emphasized the need for countries which were in a position to do so to pursue reflationary policies. (See *The Times* (London), May 30, 1975; the quote is from OECD Communiqué C(75)72(Final) June 3, 1975.)

19. It is also desirable that the OECD should improve and continue to enforce— if enforce is not too strong a word for the rather mild restraint it exercises—the Code on Liberalization of Invisibles.

20. In thinking about industrial policy I have been greatly helped by discussion with William Diebold of the Council on Foreign Relations.

21. See, for example, the sharp controversy that has been aroused in the United States by the proposals recently made by the Initiative Committee for National Economic Planning headed by Leonard Woodcock, president of the United Auto Workers, and Wassily Leontief of Harvard University.

22. Views about the long-term trend of commodity prices differ sharply.

23. Even where there are no special ties the impact on third countries cannot be disregarded, but there is a hierarchy of interests which, rightly or wrongly, is generally accepted, i.e. one which puts national interests top, global interests bottom, and the interests of allied countries somewhere in between.

24. A detailed plan for such a super-code has recently been drawn up by a group chaired by John Leddy and meeting under the auspices of the Atlantic Council. See *GATT Plus: A Proposal for Trade Reform*, The Atlantic Council of the United States, Washington, D.C., 1975.

25. There have been six OECD subcommittees working on various aspects of the MNE (multinational enterprise) problem, as has the Business and Industry Advisory Committee (BIAC) of the OECD. Early in 1975 the OECD established a Committee on International Investment and Multinational Enterprise to pull together this detailed work on rules or norms for MNEs. It will, presumably, look at some aspects, at least, of the trade-industrial policy-investment nexus.

26. See, for example, C. Fred Bergsten, "Coming Investment Wars?" in *Foreign Affairs*, October, 1974, pp. 135-142.

27. It is probably too much to hope for even OECD-wide agreement on rules, although it might be possible to agree on procedures. Both Canada and Australia have shown great reluctance to participate in the discussion of rules limiting government action on direct investment and neither participates in the OECD work on MNEs.

28. In terms of percentage of GNP, Portugal also ranked high as an aid donor, but all of its aid went to its African colonies. British and French aid was also concentrated on their former possessions but, particularly in the case of the UK, this was not much of a distortion. Recently, Portugal has resigned from the DAC and Finland has joined.

29. As a sign of the times, it is worth noting that the work the DAC had been doing in encouraging the stimulation of food production in the ldc's has now been transferred to the new Consultative Group on Food Production and Investment which is linked to the World Bank.

30. At various times in the negotiations that led up to the formation of the IEA both the US Government and the French Government took inflexible positions, sometimes on trivial matters such as the site of meetings. The French decision not to join the IEA was compounded of several factors: pique, concern at what it felt was an unduly confrontational posture on the part of the United States, desire not to affront the Arabs, belief that there should be a distinctive "European" policy, all played a part.

31. As this paper went to press (October, 1975) representatives from some of the oil producing countries and oil consuming countries were meeting again in Paris in a fresh attempt to prepare for a full-dress conference at the end of the year.

32. The figures are from the Torrens paper prepared for the European study group of the Atlantic Institute.

33. The fact that the French have not joined the IEA is, of course, another source of weakness in the IEA as a bargaining instrument.

34. For a statement of the US position on how best to insure against the downside risk see Thomas O. Enders, " OPEC and the Industrial Countries: the Next Ten Years", *Foreign Affairs*, July 1975, p. 632. This article also gives, more briefly, the views of the countries which find difficulty with this approach.

35. "Estimates of financing required over the next decade for energy development in the industrial countries center in the trillion dollar range (in 1974 dollars), equivalent to a fifth or a fourth of expected total capital formation." See Thomas O. Enders, "OPEC and the Industrial Countries: the Next Ten Years", cited.

36. The quotations are from the Declaration published as an annex to the OECD Communiqué following the Ministerial meeting on 29th May, 1975, C(75)72.

37. The quotations are from the communiqué cited above.

38. There have been various suggestions put forward about how this might be done. Lincoln Bloomfield has suggested an arrangement for what he calls "coalitions of the willing", Harlan Cleveland for "consensus decision making". Recently the Group of Experts on the Structure of the United Nations System put forward a somewhat similar idea for limited negotiating groups. See *A New United Nations Structure for Global Economic Co-operation* (E/AC, 62/9), May 28, 1975, p. 31.

39. For a particularly useful short article separating the wheat from the chaff, see Lincoln Gordon, "Third World's Rights, and Ours", *The Washington Post*, July 27, 1975.

40. Professor Charles P. Kindleberger takes this position in a number of his writings. I should put a higher probability than he does on being able to find ways to "manage the system" in a *reasonably* efficient way in the absence of either condition.

41. See, for example, C. Fred Bergsten, "The United States and Germany: The Imperative of Economic Bigemony", in *Toward a New International Economic Order: Selected Papers of C. Fred Bergsten; 1972-1974*, Lexington, Mass.: D.C. Heath and Co., 1975; and Ronald I. MacKinnon, *A New Tripartite Monetary Agreement or a Limping Dollar Standard*, Princeton Essay in International Finance, No. 106, October, 1974, Princeton, N.J.

42. In both cases the membership is rather more extensive than was originally envisaged. It is significant that the United States does not have a blocking vote in either organization.

43. It may be argued that many of these committees are reasonably self-contained, do not involve the same people as the priority tasks, and are supported by Part II of the budget; that is, only those countries that join in a particular activity pay for it. Nevertheless, servicing the committees dissipates the energies of secretariat, permanent representatives and those elements of the member governments that service the OECD at some cost to other activities.

44. It is of course not only the "interconnectedness of things" that is increasing, but also the *awareness* of interconnectedness that is growing.

45. In May 1975, the Japanese Government proposed that the OECD should undertake a long-term research project on "The Future Development of Advanced Industrial Societies in Harmony with that of Less Developed Countries" and offered to make a special grant of about one million dollars for the purpose. Although reactions to the Japanese proposal have been rather mixed, it seems probable that some other countries will agree to fund a three-year research project dealing with this general subject and trying to look much further into the future (c. 20 years) than has been customary. If such a project is undertaken, the secretariat plans not only to bring in additional outside experts but to establish contacts with outside institutes engaged in "futures" studies. Contact with outside institutes will obviously be important if some version of the Japanese project is undertaken. But interchanges—of both staff and ideas—with independent research centers should be an ongoing process and not limited to large, discrete projects such as this one.

46. The problems posed by the lack of congruence between economic scale and political structures arise not simply from the fact that for some purposes one must think of the global economy. Some economic problems require regional solutions, some a solution among the particular group of countries that share certain characteristics, e.g., a major position in the money market.

ABOUT THE AUTHORS

BENJAMIN C. ROBERTS is head of the Industrial Relations Department at the London School of Economics. He is also the founder and former President of the International Industrial Relations Association.

GUNTER GEISSELER is the former Chief Legal Adviser, Mannesmann AG.

RUDOLF J. VOLLMER is the Labour Attaché of the German Embassy, London.

FRANCOIS LAGRANGE is a member of the French Conseil d'Etat. He is also the Rapporteur Géneral of the Sudreau Committee.

FINN GUNDELACH is the European Commissioner for the Internal Market and the former Ambassador to the EEC.

LOUIS CAMU is honorary Chairman, Banque Bruxelles-Lambert. He is also the Chairman of the Economic Committee of the Atlantic Institute for International Affairs.

WOLFGANG HAGER is Senior Research Fellow at the German Council on Foreign Relations, Bonn.

MIRIAM CAMPS is the author of the Management of Interdependence and other works. She is also the consultant on Foreign Relations, New York.

JOHN S. MARSH has his M.A. (Oxford) and a post-graduate diploma in agricultural economics. He is a reader in the Department of Agricultural Economics and Management at the University of Reading and author of works on the Common Agricultural Policy and the impact of the enlargement of the EEC.

DENIS BERGMANN, Ingénieur Agronome. He received his Master of Science from Cornell University. He is Research Director, Institut National de la Recherche Agronomique, Paris, Chargé d'Enseignement, Paris I, and a member of the Vedel Commission on agricultural policy.

LORD KALDOR is a professor at Cambridge University and Advisor to various British Governments.

H-B. KROHN is the former Deputy Director General of Agriculture, and is presently the Director General of Development and Cooperation with the Commission of European Communities, Brussels.

M. ROSSI-DORIA is a professor at the University of Naples and President of the Agricultural Committee of the Senate of the Italian Republic.

J.A. SCHNITTKER is the former under-Secretary of Agriculture, and is presently an economic consultant in Washington D.C.

C. THOMSEN is a member of the Royal Veterinary and Agricultural University, Copenhagen.

P. URI is the counsellor for Studies with the Atlantic Institute for International Affairs. He is a professor with the University of Paris (Professor Paris I), and a member of the French Economic and Social Council.

H. WILBRANDT is the director of the Institute für ausländische Landwirtschaft an der Georg-August Universität, Göttingen.

ABOUT THE ATLANTIC INSTITUTE
FOR INTERNATIONAL AFFAIRS

The Atlantic Institute for International Affairs is an independent international organization based in Paris. Its purpose is to assist in solving problems which are common to the Atlantic countries and, to an increasing degree, countries with similar political structures and levels of development, such as Japan, Australia, and New Zealand. Through basic research and regular programs of conferences, the Institute deals with three types of issues: the relations of its member-countries among themselves; their relations with developing countries; and their relations with communist countries.

The Board of Governors of the Institute, under the chairmanship of John H. Loudon, is composed of 70 eminent men and women from 21 nations. Under the guidance of the newly formed Research Advisory Council, consisting of 11 leading international scholars, the Institute's work has been increasingly oriented toward today's major international economic problems and their political implications. Whether it be in the form of books, periodical reports, or informal recommendations to governments and international organizations, the emphasis of all the Institute's activities is toward policy-orientation and action.

The Institute and its international staff are directed by Martin Hillenbrand, who is also the editor of the Atlantic Papers, a series of papers reflecting the Institute's areas of interest.

Published for the Atlantic Institute for International Affairs

*DEVELOPMENT WITHOUT DEPENDENCE
                    Pierre Uri
                    foreword by
                    William P. Bundy

DILEMMAS OF THE ATLANTIC ALLIANCE:
Two Germanys, Scandinavia, Canada, NATO, and the
EEC (Atlantic Institute Studies—I)
                    Peter Christian Ludz,
                    M. Peter Dreyer,
                    Charles Pentland,
                    Lothar Rühl

ENERGY, INFLATION, AND INTERNATIONAL ECONOMIC
RELATIONS (Atlantic Institute Studies—II)
                    Curt Gasteyger,
                    Louis Camu
                    Jack N. Behrman

Published for the Atlantic Council of the United States

THE FATE OF THE ATLANTIC COMMUNITY
                    Elliott R. Goodman

U.S. AGRICULTURE IN A WORLD CONTEXT:
Policies and Approaches for the Next Decade
                    edited by
                    D. Gale Johnson and
                    John A. Schnitkker

*Also available in paperback as a PSS Student Edition